Monogamy

MONOGAMY:

ITS SONGS AND POEMS

Robert von Hallberg

To Jennifer,
gracious advocate
of Pound's achievements.
With much gratitude.
Bob

Hadley 4/16/23

DALKEY ARCHIVE PRESS
Dallas / Dublin

First Dalkey Archive edition, 2023

Library of Congress Cataloging-in-Publication data: Available.

ISBN Paperback: 978-1-628974-00-3
ISBN Ebook: 978-1-628974-26-3

Interior design by Anuj Mathur
Cover design by Kit Schulter

www.dalkeyarchive.com
Dallas / Dublin

Printed on permanent/durable acid-free paper.

They say that love's a word,
A word we've only heard,
But can't begin to know
The meaning of.

—Sylvia Dee, "Too Young" (1951)

Contents

Introduction

For some poets, any subject will do: Elizabeth Bishop, the items on her desk; Frank Bidart, anorexia; Robert Pinsky, the invention of the saxophone. But love poems return one to a closed set of topics. They constitute a strong version of literary tradition centered on the concept of monogamy. And they have a ready readership, especially in the US, where paradoxically one reads repeatedly of the death of poetry. Americans have seen an extraordinary century and a half of poetic achievement. Everyone recognizes the distinction of Whitman and Dickinson, of Frost, Stevens, Pound, Eliot, Williams, and Moore. But few critics reckon with the younger writers, born after Marianne Moore and before Gary Snyder, who remade the popular song: Irving Berlin (b. 1888), Cole Porter (b. 1891), Lorenz Hart (b. 1895), Oscar Hammerstein II (b. 1895), Yip Harburg (b. 1896), Ira Gershwin (b. 1896), Mitchell Parrish (b. 1900), Dorothy Fields (b. 1905), Johnny Mercer (b. 1909), Frank Loesser (b. 1910), Sammy Cahn (b. 1913), Betty Comden (b. 1917), Marilyn (b. 1929), Alan Bergman (b. 1926), and others.[1] The lyrics known as the Great American Songbook constitute an indisputably potent achievement.[2] When teaching poetry, one speaks of the authority of the canon. *The Norton Anthology of Poetry* gathers poems selected by critics, scholars, and teachers. Students are instructed about the art and meaning of these poems. But the Great American Songbook is an anthology held in the memories of millions of listeners all over the world, and generation after generation of vocalists renew this musical canon with fresh renditions.

The popular song stands up well to comparison with the poems in the *Norton*. Canonical poems, popular songs, and light verse were parts of a single literary tradition. This is to say not that poems and songs are identical, only that they are often very close, and that many excellent songs directly invoke familiar lyric poetry.[3] We have much to learn about ourselves by examining this rich version of verse culture, the mix of "high and low," call it. In particular, one sees ideas and beliefs engaged by different audiences, some small, others not. Scholars of medieval literature have shown that the poets of southern France and Tuscany presented the West with a religion of love.[4] In the following pages, I sketch out an ideology of romance that dominates contemporary imaginative life. It derives from canonical poems and popular songs, and those songs also rest on light verse models.[5] I move back and forth between canonical poems and popular songs because they are congruous parts of one artistic effort: a rich, subtle Book of Love. If the seams in my exposition are governable, I am probably right about the coherence of a single verse culture; if not, not.

Love songs are expressive, but normative too: "Hello, young lovers, wherever you are . . . be kind, be faithful and true." Love stories and films reveal the peculiarities of loves. But songs, short, get at the norms. They embed ways of feeling in memory. When actual adversity arrives, songs sound painfully prophetic—the sweet pain of melancholy. One memorizes them, effortlessly, and then appears to *remember* how to feel.

In time these forms of feeling seem love itself. I am simplifying the process, and the songs are thankfully less simple than they appear. They engage a wide range of recognizable feelings and situations, but their implicit instruction is impressively definite, given the difficulty of the topic. In the chapters that follow, I analyze what songs and poems say about love, especially what they say in relation to what they acknowledge as *already said* about love. Yeats famously wrote: "I strove / To love you in the old high way of love." The Monotones then asked in 1957: "Who wrote the Book of Love?" Yeats and these doo-wop musicians understood the code-effects of song, and they had good artistic reasons to treasure the code.

A code is a brief for a governed life, for restraint. The troubadours encouraged noble behavior within a wanton social class. Love songs preserve doctrines of love's ways, because even the concept of love erodes. A singer or jongleur demonstrates how concepts may be felt in the mouth and throat and kept in memory. "I stand before you," a singer seems to say, "to avow this manner of loving, this image of the lover."[6] The presence of a performer demonstrates that the songs' ideals can be avowed with courage and beauty, and many performers—think of Frank Sinatra and Joni Mitchell—claim to have *lived* the lyrics. Songs express a need to live, even in private, so attractively and memorably that art may be made of one's acts. The lovers' private sphere, noble and recognizable because of the code. Their storied lives, despite confusion and pain, make a sense one hears as shared and enduring. Each performance invokes a poetics of presence validated by the song's musicality.[7] The poems and songs I discuss solicit pathos, but very few are simple or shallow. Modernist poets showed that meaning flowers in the spaces between words; what is *not* said, plump with significance.

The objective of a love song is to express affection and report change. How to do that freshly and convincingly is a challenge. Songwriters seek a feeling of conviction. Johnny Mercer sought a "really simple way of saying 'I love you' . . . the way a guy in a saloon would feel it."[8] Some lyricists admit to laboring patiently over a song, as Oscar Hammerstein II and Ira Gershwin routinely did.[9] More often, though, lyricists speak proudly of a speedy delivery. When Dorothy Fields praised her composer-partner Jimmy McHugh, she used a word rarely used to characterize a poet: "very facile."[10] That adjective means both easy and simple. One refers to a graceful style in terms of ease, but simplicity is a controversial feature of love songs. Elizabeth K. Helsinger analyzes concepts of song that moved nineteenth- and twentieth-century British poets. In particular, she addresses idealistic accounts of the relations between poetry and song. Poems imitate an associative process whose motive power derives from sound patterning, the leaping "backward and forward across the sequential unfolding of a line on a page, the syntax of a sentence, and utterance in time, or the logic of deliberative reasoning, discovering novel semantic relationships that sound patterns suggest."[11] This is the objective of Mallarmé, Eliot, Stevens, and Pound, and of their successors: that the sonic resources of poetry take minds to unfamiliar destinations. The work of these poets is obviously difficult, discontinuous, obscure. Their critics and interpreters seek patterns of coherence on the other side of those complications.

With love poetry and song, a critic has the opposite task: to see beyond apparent simplicity. Bob Dylan dismissed love lyrics, "I love you and you love me, ooka dooka dicka dee." One already knows what such poems and songs say, because they rest on commonplaces, often complacently. Broadway musical theater supported the work of the most talented songwriters the country has seen, but critics have not looked to its songs for enlightenment. D. A. Miller begins his book on the musical with the notion that this genre was spared from becoming "an object of serious thought."[12] Few critics regard these songs as intellectual efforts. My job is to identify and interpret love poems and songs that revise commonplaces and take minds where they might not otherwise go. Not an easy job, because love songs generally appear to speak satisfyingly for themselves.[13] But many love songs are not simple, and other forms of love poetry are discursive, analytical, speculative. Yet the idea of a love song as joyful, brief, and simple is always a part of one's understanding of even the most intellectual love poetry. One measures love poetry against this concept of song. Why is it misleading to consider Marvell's "To His Coy Mistress" a love song? Why should joy, change, and simplicity be difficult of access? To the extent that such access is rightly difficult, many love songs are considered minor, slight.

The following chapters track the circulation of ideas and beliefs through poems and popular songs. The songs I cite display memories of what is traditionally understood as poetry, because some of these songwriters were lifelong readers of poetry, but more commonly because songwriters remember the poems and verse that moved them in their youth. Yip Harburg recalled:

> In high school I worked on the newspaper. Began writing things with more sophistication—light verse . . . When I got to City College, I began to send in stuff I'd written to Conning Tower, a column Franklin P. Adams ran in the old *World*, a hell of a good paper. Verses. You see, at that time [c. 1912-15] everyone

> was writing light verse—sonnets, acrostics, things like
> that. Dorothy Parker, Deems Taylor, Edna St. Vincent
> Millay, George Kaufman, Marc Connelly, you name
> them . . . My classmate at college was Ira Gershwin
> . . . We began collaborating on a column for the City
> College newspaper. Yip and Gersh. He was always
> interested in light verse, too. He introduced me to a
> lot of things that I'd not had access to. That was the
> first time I heard W. S. Gilbert's lyrics set to Sullivan's
> music. Up to that time I thought he was simply a
> poet![14]

To describe song lyrics as descended from light-verse may confirm one's conviction that poems and song lyrics are significantly distinct. Poets often title short poems "Song" to indicate not only that the poem is driven by lyrical diction and prosody, but further that it is acknowledged to be short and simple in its statement. When one distinguishes songs from poems, modesty seems pertinent, as in "this is just a song that came to me," or one that is a pleasure to sing and hear. It suggests lightness with regard to originality of subject, satisfaction with what is familiar. The poems and songs I discuss maintain close proximity to commonplaces, but they often revise familiar notions. Many songwriters seek simplicity, some only seem to do so; some are frankly skeptical of the intellectual aspirations of poets. Joni Mitchell regarded T. S. Eliot's *Four Quartets* as pretentious, not profound.[15] Many readers and songwriters regard songlike verse as an alternative to intellectuality.

To sing is nonetheless a traditional term for making poems. "Who would not sing for Lycidas?" Milton asked at twenty-eight. Samuel Johnson famously insisted that this elegy is not heartfelt, that pride—not grief—moved Milton to eloquence.

Johnson heard a *will* to song, a dissonance between heart-song and art-song. Love songs are ostensible expressions of feeling, but performances too. There is no separating ambition from lyric poetry. The fit of words to sounds indicates a plausible physicality. When a fit is found, without instrumentation, the grandest poetic ambition seems fulfilled, because signs are wed to personhood. A deep charm, because finally inexplicable, its effects, of unknown origin. The expression "the ring of truth" suggests that sonorous formulations conform to truth. Without music, Nietzsche wrote, life would be an error.[16] But Johnson was a great skeptic and required truth of feeling in even highly conventional language. With speech, one works through stores and courts, chiseling, guarding one's valuables. A singer puts that away by arranging syllables so that the meaning of a few words, uttered by an actual voice and timed to a sustained beat, seems heartfelt. Song asserts immunity from social restrictions recognized in ordinary language. The roots of the word "song" are Teutonic; no related forms are found in other language groups. Poets seek in song simplicity and strength; they mean to sound deeply *native*. Even up-tempo virtuosos like Jon Hendricks and Bobby McFerrin display the far reaches of what a human voice can do—its nature stretched out.[17] Singers dwell in their lyrics; sincerity, for the moment, obvious.

Why are words set to music more widely pleasing than words fitted to syntactic or rhythmic structures (which literary critics call "musical")? It is the instrumental music, one reasonably says, but vocal versions outsell instrumental versions of the same tune. Or maybe it's that the American popular song has attracted extraordinary literary talent. But the verbal resources of most of those writers from the 1920s through the 1960s were familiar, to put the matter gently. They recirculated literary conventions that were no longer timely to readers of poetry: "Heaven, I'm in heaven . . ." Practical critics repeatedly attribute the success of particular poems to their resistance to conventions of expression. Yet here is abundant evidence that even dusty conventions interfere not at all with the power of art. Frankly conventional language has great power when set to music. Songwriters, generation after generation, modify the poems of school anthologies into lines that can sing to the young. John Donne in "Holy Sonnet 1" wrote: "And all my pleasures are like yesterday," which is revived by inversion in Lennon and McCartney's "Yesterday": "All my troubles seem so far away." The elements of Donne's line survive by reversal: pleasure→troubles; yesterday→far away; time→space. Not his assertion but its structure endures.

Students of literature are told routinely that originality is a post-Enlightenment concern, that classical rhetoric accounted for art in terms of conventional turns of expression (tropes) elaborating on familiar subjects (or topoi). Johnson recognized "Lycidas" as an instance of pastoral elegy, but nonetheless demanded sincerity. His esteem for authenticity was not new: in 1582 Sydney had advised poets: "Look into your heart and write." And that, surprisingly, put love poets at a disadvantage, for their subject is unavoidably traditional. The most influential European love poet had no experience of his beloved; of the mother of his children, he wrote nothing. Three centuries before Sydney, the Provençal poet Gui d'Ussel expressed the difficulty:

> I should make songs more frequently, but it bores me
> to say each day that I sorrow and die for love, for all
> know how to say as much. That is why I must find new
> words set to a pleasant melody; but I can find nothing
> that has not already been said and sung.[18]

And Billie Holiday in 1940 sang of

> The same old story
> It's as old as the stars above
> The same old story
> Of a boy and a girl in love.
> The scenes say more moonlight
> The times say more June night.
> Romance's the thing
> Two hearts away deep in a dream
> The same old story,
> It's been told much too much before.
> The same old story,
> But it's worth telling just once more.
> It's all fun and laughter
> They lived ever after in ecstasy.
> The same old story, but it's new to me.[19]

Songs and poems have led one to expect these words. The fit is nonetheless sweet. Lady Day pushes right past the conventionality that bothered Gui d'Ussel, confident that popular songs gracefully bear altogether familiar language. The experience itself—or the "scenes" and "times"—she says, invokes the corniest rhyme of all: June/moon. Conventions comfort, a serious good, as a novice gives the heart away. The objective of a songwriter is to render a traditional subject in a manner that meets Johnson's sense of authenticity: the feel of an actual person whose voice finds power even in clichés. Proverbial expressions summon the fire and assure those burning that many have survived the flames. We're in this together.

Some poets decline to report symptoms and seek, as Marvell did, a general account of love. What could be more useful than an improved definition of this abused term? Pierre Hadot refers to a rhetorical theory of writing that appealed to engaged intellectuals of the early twentieth century. Commonplaces, he says, are

> formulas, images, and metaphors adopted by philoso-
> phers and writers like prefabricated models, which they
> think they use freely, but which nevertheless have an
> influence on their thought. They hold sway for centu-
> ries over successive generations like a kind of program
> to be realized, a task to be accomplished or an attitude
> to be assumed, even if, throughout the ages, the mean-
> ing given to these sentences, images, and metaphors
> can be profoundly modified.[20]

The objective of poetry, then, is to preserve and prosely-
tize by renewing particular forms of expression and thereby
understanding. Exactly because listeners recognize set subjects—"I only have eyes for you," "my baby's gone," "I'm in
love again"—they notice even slight variations of familiar thematic structures. Eliot spoke famously of poets who purify
the dialect of the tribe. Pound understood this "program to
be realized" as philology *engagé*. "The individual cannot think
and communicate his thought, the governor and legislator
cannot act effectively or frame his laws, without words, and the
solidity and validity of these words is in the care of the damned
and despised *litterati*."[21] Hadot similarly notes that commonplaces inspire "the practice of life itself." Michael Riffaterre
rightly reminds one that the philological work of poets is rarely
explicit. The terms under scrutiny are (always, on his account;
often, on mine) not uttered. One may doubt that the lexical
refinements of poets since 1900 have circulated sufficiently

widely to fulfill Pound and Eliot's visions of art's civic consequences, but popular songs could hardly have circulated more widely. Effective lyricists bring poems to the masses. Their songs derive partly from their dialogue with poems; for listeners, the songs constitute an indirect engagement with the thematic concerns of canonical poems.

Kenneth Burke held that "each work of art is the addition of a word to an informal dictionary."[22] That ambition is often audible at the level of the line as well. Emily Dickinson was a master lexicographer: "Remorse is memory awake." Pound later attempted this project in Canto 45 in the line "With usura hath no man a house of good stone."[23] One recalls many definition songs: "Love is wonderful the second time around." Poets revise established terms. One knows something of remorse, usury, and second loves before engaging these poems. Some poems generate critical philological instruction, however unhandsome it is to say so. What of poems that define something too elusive for a single term (Burke's point)? They define something of general significance, even when no one name is called out. Riffaterre in 1978 revived the theory that poems derive not from strong feeling, as Sydney suggests, but from an intertext, or *matrix*, that a poet transforms. Riffaterre alerts one to the *implicit* philological work of poems. The dominant terms under scrutiny are not uttered. His never-named *hypogram* is a thematic reduction of a poem; its existence is hypothetical, known to readers as an absence or even taboo.[24] The repressed hypogram recurs as a neurotic symptom, an implicit sum of its displacements, but it unifies a text by adding a "poetic quality" that the words alone lack.[25] A poem, then, is a periphrasis, a "word game."[26] A traditional but disappointing conclusion. One needs both accounts of rhetoric, Hadot's and

Riffaterre's, because many poets are silent about the terms they scrutinize. Their concern is not an effect on social practice. But there is too the aspiration of writers to improve or extend the inherited medium. Signposting makes practical sense for them.

Critics of poetry focus overwhelmingly on the sense of words, even though the term "lyric" refers to musical accompaniment. Riffaterre, for example, begins *Semiotics of Poetry* with this claim: "I . . . submit that the difference we perceive empirically between poetry and nonpoetry is fully explained by the way a poetic text carries meaning."[27] The matter of poetry is meaning, in his account, and a poet's objective, to convey meaning. The distinctiveness of poetic language is "fully explained" by reference to the instrumentality of formal devices. This is bluntly stated but it characterizes general practice, even among critics of poetry. Were this view adequate, one could expect more poets to forage greedily (as Pound, Moore, and Olson did) among the intellectual disciplines devoted entirely to the pursuit of knowledge and the construction of meaning. Unfamiliar explanations of the physical, natural, and human orders abound in academic annals. Poets might affix their devices to these expositions and convey fresh meaning, as Riffaterre says. With such splendid resources on offer, poets would not reasonably return to the themes of desire and death, because those areas of meaning entail inevitable competition with the illustrious dead. Yet love poets—more even than elegists—return to thoroughly traditional topoi. This is as true for strenuous poets with modest audiences as for popular songwriters. Wilfred Sheed, writing about the limits of Irving Berlin's education, remarked: "Most lyrics are simply verbal clichés about emotional clichés, so . . . maybe the less you know the better."[28]

The chapters of this book rest on commonplaces.

Chapter 1: Desire is monogamous.

Chapter 2: Romance is mush.

Chapter 3: No Love, no life.

Chapter 4: Love rushes.

Chapter 5: Love is joyful.

Chapter 6: Hearts are fickle.

Chapter 7: Money can't buy love.

Chapter 8: Love abides.

My analysis of each topic pursues *the unapparent*, what Riffaterre called hypogram—a twisted, repressed version of a commonplace. Artistic distinction often comes from the making strange of what only seems familiar, known. Yip Harburg said, "The task is never to say the thing directly, and yet to say it—to think in a curve, so to speak."[29] Where I have chosen my texts well, this has been easy: a matter of looking not beyond general topics, but *within* their distinctive contours. My focus: poems and songs that, implicitly, reveal the strangeness of commonplaces. These texts constitute a mini-anthology: each one, an instance of excellence, and of the vigor of shared desire. An advantage of adhering to commonplaces is that readers know what is at stake. If a poem seems mediocre or irrelevant to the commonplace, I have failed my task as anthologist or advocate. May such lapses seem to you few.

Love songs require words, yet reach beyond speech. Words set to music deliver immediately accessible formal pleasure. For comparable pleasure in a poem, one must not just recognize but really *hear* or otherwise feel prosodic schemes, syntactic structures, and vowel tones. Lawrence Kramer observes that, to understand song generally, one needs "to take account of how and why meaning is so regularly cast off."[30] Musicality stands for something inexplicable. Songs speak of love as of an enigma beyond grammatical explanation; musical orders are explicable, but not their power. This is only less obviously true of poems; songs and poems alike derive from an aspiration to communicate deeply. Pound says that a poet wishes to present "an idea and its concomitant emotions, or an emotion with its concomitant ideas, or a sensation and its derivative emotions, or an impression that is emotive, etc., etc., etc." That wish may produce a howl, but then, with art a dance or music. In time an artist develops that into "music with words," then "words with music, and finally into words with a vague adumbration of music, words suggestive of music, words measured, or words in a rhythm that preserves some accurate trait of the emotive impression."[31] The conjunction of sound and sense, resonance and semantics may seem wondrous.[32] A shapely meeting of rival orders warrants the sense of what songs and poems say, and implies that this composite order goes further than can be explained. Musicality arrests skepticism, at least temporarily.

Wordsworth wrote memorably of the effect of song in "The Solitary Reaper" (1807). He comes upon a Scottish peasant singing while laboring in a field and is struck, as the title indicates, by her isolation: she is "single" in the first line, "solitary" in the second, "by herself" in the third, "Alone" in the fifth, and then inevitably "melancholy" in the sixth. With utterly conventional figures he speculates in the second octet about the character of her song. In exasperation at his own effort, he begins the poem again in the third octet: "Will no one tell me what she sings?" To understand a song in a foreign tongue is cognate here with understanding a single woman. Both are unknowable. He seems certain that she sings of loss, as if only that would move a young woman to song.[33] The final octet is in the past tense, marked as reflection on the scene presented in the first three stanzas. The topic of loss leads reasonably to that of compensation.

Whate'er the theme, the Maiden sang   25
As if her song could have no ending.
I saw her singing at her work,
And o'er the sickle bending—
I listened motionless and still;
And, as I mounted up the hill,   30
The music in my heart I bore,
Long after it was heard no more.

Memory is obviously an archive of feeling as well as information. The effect of inscrutable song should be slight, from Riffaterre's point of view, but on the contrary: what is imperfectly understood has enormous staying power. The meaning that eludes us is essential, because it summons understanding. Kramer argues that "songfulness makes meaning extraneous," but Wordsworth and his heirs show that elusive song stimulates curiosity.[34] Mystery calls and one goes searching. His poem is framed as a lesson on the nature of music and song. It is not the theme, what one imagines her sense to be—traditional or contemporary—that renders the song memorable. Its meaning is less in language than in a sympathetic feeling for the vigor and persistence of another aspiring individual. The strange thing is that this poem about powerful song itself resists songfulness. It is wrought in iambic tetrameter lines, though the fourth line of each of its four eight-line stanzas is clipped to a trimeter. The rhyme scheme is alternating in the first four lines and couplets in the last four of each stanza. But the first line of the poem registers resistance: the rhyme with line three is largely suppressed—"field"/"herself."

Behold her, single in the field,
Yon solitary Highland Lass!
Reaping and singing by herself;

That starts the poem off on a nonconformist note, though there is a crypto-rhyme in the f ē l / ě l f pattern. In the last stanza, that initial nonconformity is recalled by the thorough lack of rhyme between lines twenty-five and twenty-seven: "sang"/ "work." Work apparently does not belong in this context; that is not the lass's function here, nor the poet's concern. I take these crafty irregularities as whispers of his own distance from songlike poetry.[35] The second stanza would be excised entirely if he felt committed to the brevity of song. It's a lapse, mere versification.

Lyricists, like poets, gladly follow the song that got away. In Hoagy Carmichael and Mitchell Parrish's "Star Dust" (1927-29) a forsaken lover only half-complains:

> You wandered down the lane and far away,
> Leaving me a song that will not die.
> Love is now the star dust of yesterday,
> The music of the years gone by.[36]

Parrish pulls into popular song some conventional props of romantic poetry, and with great success. Wallace Stevens too returned to Wordsworth's poem in "The Idea of Order at Key West" (1935). He made the maiden's song grander by likening it to the surf, sea-sound song, but "more than" what he considered "the meaningless plungings of water and the wind" (ll. 28-30). Five years later, Rodgers and Hart published "It Never Entered My Mind," which also recalls Wordsworth:

> Once you warned me
> that if you scorned me
> I'd sing the maiden's prayer again
> And wish that you were there again

To get into my hair again.
It never entered my mind.

From song to prayer, presumably for a lover or husband; Wordsworth's poem circulates, altered, through anthologies, textbooks, classrooms, Broadway musicals, and then jazz clubs. What survives is not its paraphrasable sense, but a concept of indefinite and abiding song. Enduring affect, deliciously vague, is a measure of song's vigor.

The topics of love-songs go back to the vernacular love poetry of southern France, though even earlier poems shape the love songs of the living.[37] Sappho showed that a love poet speaks of intense physical adversity.

> . . . my tongue breaks down, and then all at once a
> subtle fire races inside my skin, my
> eyes can't see a thing and a whirring whistle
> thrums at my hearing[38]

Not the beloved's beautiful but the lover's heated body is her subject. The love poem as complaint is evident too in Archilochus. Much later, the Roman poets Catullus and Propertius developed the triangular topos of obsessive lover, rival, and promiscuous beloved. Troubadours eliminated promiscuity and devised a system of fine love that haunted later lyrics. Their innovation seems, at its inception, unconnected to any other changes in the "economic, political, or social life of the Middle Ages." Maurice Valency finds no sign "that anything of unusual character was going on with regard to the relations of men and women during the period when the amatory poetry of the troubadours was taking shape [1050-1100]."[39] Mid-twelfth-century France was a different matter, according to L. T. Topsfield:

> Abduction, seduction and sexual license were rife
> among the noble class for whom marriage was often
> a business contract for the strengthening of territory
> or an alliance, or for the provision of heirs. Spiritual
> lethargy possessed the Church in the South, and heresy
> was on the increase. In this state of social and moral
> confusion the nobility needed a new and distinctive
> code of behaviour by which it could affirm its identity
> and role in society.[40]

Love lyrics proposed corrections to the mores of a ruling
class. The code of fine love (*fin 'amor*) had a harsh setting.[41]
The shift of attention in the courts from fighting to seducing is extraordinary, and scholars have reached little consensus about its cause.[42] The value most trumpeted in Provençal
poetry was *mesura*, or just proportion.[43] In thirteenth-century
Tuscany, the most famous heir of the poets of Occitan devoted
his first sonnet in *La Vita Nuova* to the willful cruelty of the
god of love—as if to indicate that the new life begins with a
toll demanded of those who serve love, not reasonably but
ravenously.[44] Behind admiration and pledges of devotion in
Provençal poems is the bellicosity of fighters. Figures of con-
tention, abjection, and loyalty remain central to love poetry.
Take the topic of love from afar, an obvious concern of warriors displaced from families and friends. Soldiers must maintain commitment to their objectives and their patrons, especially when adherence to their cause entails adversity and dim
prospects. That is when a warrior proves his mettle. A monogamous lover's challenge is not dissimilar. The troubadour lover
is constantly claiming loyalty to a cause that appears unlikely

to succeed. Love is presented as a test for these poets, as battle is for warriors. The poets made art of their commitment in adverse circumstances. That topos spread first to Italy and then well beyond. Now one can hardly measure romance's debt to a milieu of enforcers.

The troubadours did not invent new emotions; they founded a genre of love song that made certain feelings and values fashionable, as Maurice Valency says.[45] Their poetry was written in a learned dialect, or poetic diction, not in the idioms of southern France at the time.[46] Just as knights came from different social classes, so too did itinerant songsters who addressed court audiences.[47] Alongside skillful fighters and songwriters were jongleurs—professional performers—who brought to the courts an ability to conform their behavior to scripts written by others; they were paragons of adaptation whose success at court indicated to audiences the constant possibility of change. These ironists of love poetry established distance from the literal sense of their material, and from immediate audiences. They complicated sincerity with a third voice: that of neither the lover nor the beloved. (Aphrodite had spoken as the ironic third, in Sappho's hymn to her, long before this, of course.) In about the year 1200 Raimon de Miraval wrote in verse that a jongleur mixes "acts of wisdom with acts of folly, for a man who is too wise has little worth among men of high reputation."[48] These performers were rowdy and resistant. Like an Elizabethan jester, a jongleur employed a protected persona: of a court, but outside it too. He surprised audiences, reversed their moods.[49] The cleavage between expression and performance that Johnson heard centuries later was prominent in these songs, and survived. Sinatra and Sarah Vaughan sang what others wrote; they were paid to pretend that the words were their own. In sounding particular words through their throats, jongleurs displayed a method of physical adoption that might be imitated by any listener. Song sets even ardent words free from their most literal sense. The recovery of the troubadour figure in US popular song in the 1960s was meant to heal that rift between expression and performance. Out with the jongleurs! Joni Mitchell, Bob Dylan, and Carole King performed a return to native sincerity, as Sinatra two decades earlier had seemed to do effectively.[50]

Provençal poetry moved rapidly through Europe and brought with it strenuous and still familiar ideas of intimacy. By 1170 "the poetry of love was already firmly established," Valency observes, "in Alsace, in Switzerland, in Germany, in Austria, Italy, and Spain."[51] Troubadours traveled around the Italian countryside, writing songs of praise for wealthy court people, and brawling in taverns. Their prosodic forms and topics were gradually absorbed into Italian poetry during the thirteenth century. The sonnet originated in the 1230s at the court in Palermo.[52] In Florence, in the latter half of the thirteenth century, Cavalcanti, Dante, and then Petrarch, imitating Provencal models, grounded lyric poetry in pious devotion to a beloved and to Love itself. Here is Dante Gabriel Rossetti's translation of Dante's first sonnet (written between 1292 and 1295):

> To every heart which the sweet pain doth move,
> And unto which these words may now be brought
> For true interpretation and kind thought,
> Be greeting in our Lord's name, which is Love.
> Of those long hours wherein the stars, above,   5
> Wake and keep watch, the third was almost nought,
> When Love was shown me with such terrors fraught
> As may not carelessly be spoken of.

He seemed like one who is full of joy, and had
My heart within his hand, and on his arm   10
My lady, with a mantle round her, slept,
Whom (having wakened her) anon he made
To eat that heart; she ate, as fearing harm.
Then he went out; and as he went, he wept.[53]

This poem is a warning of the monstrosities of romance, not a hymn to love. The naming itself of Love is so significant that it closes the syntax of the first quatrain; the abstraction of Love from experience is essential to the establishment of an intellectual cult (l. 4). Rossetti's style is scrupulous, fearful of speaking wrongly or "carelessly" (l. 8). Both quatrains close with advisories about proper speech. The authority of Love and submission itself are shown to be terrible. One knows that eros fuels a desire to dominate the beloved. The poem presents domination and submission as dynamics of the concept of Love itself, not as drives of one or another lover. That is the poem's metaphysical work. Domination is commonly described as an ugly male drive, and submission as an alluring female characteristic. Jessica Benjamin argues that domination and submission are complementary; that each is known in relation to the other. Men and women in love share this dynamic.[54]

Dante's point is that the dynamic itself resides in neither lover nor beloved but in the idea of Love itself. No one party is to blame for the injuries of romantic domination. The speaker's inhibition in face of this terrifying dynamic can be heard in the inverted syntax and rhythm of several lines. Caesurae are repeatedly placed just before or within the last foot to indicate trepidation about closure (ll. 5, 9,11, and 14). The strangeness of Dante's narrative led me to consider the poem a Blakean inversion of Christian doctrine, but it is instead an earnest analysis of what is entailed by the scripture "God is love" (1 John 4:8, 16). The abstraction that this notion entails is demanding of the human spirit, because it urges one to rise well above one's own loves, to subordinate them to a metaphysical concept of love as Lord or plenipotentate of all. Submission to this faith is not comforting, for it requires estrangement from the loves that derive from experience. What Dante predicates of Love exists in *thought* or faith. Love is not the Prince of Peace but a paradoxical figure, apparently joyful (l. 9) but an instigator of atrocity (ll. 12-13). That love is called the "sweet pain" in the first line is unsurprising, but the subsequent characterization of Love as one who rues his own efficacy (l. 14)—that is surprising, though Love is only performing his announced paradox. Love himself suffers in submission to his regime. Poets continue to translate this poem because its view of devotion is recognized as deranged, yet true.

Provençal poets invented a romance of severe discrimination. Its first feature is its locus in one woman, not in many or all; the mobility of eros, desire of many women, is a fact acknowledged only by insistence to the contrary. What Alain Badiou speaks of as the chanciness of erotic desire is suppressed.[55] The one woman has angelic beauty, superlative features. The *blazon* (her lips, her neck, and so on), an inventory, as if this love were *warranted* by qualities of existence, not imagined by a lovestruck admirer. The approach to her is perilous, because she is married to a powerful lord, or of a higher social class, or simply unacquainted with the poet. She had to be of such exalted stature that, as Valency says, "the very thought of proposing an intimacy" would make the poet tremble.[56] Provencal poets used *singhals* or veiled names to refer to the "immensely remote" ladies who could not be named straightforwardly. The extraordinariness of the poet's love had to be understood as a danger to social order.[57] But the pursuit of *blocked* romance needs another explanation. Why promote romances that cannot lead to fruition, to contentment? Pound argues that the courts where these songs flourished were full of contentment, even boredom. Blocked love bred intrigue, or the mere thought of it, an imagination of change.

Love poetry was then and is still an artful distraction, more entertainment than chronicle. Paolo Cherchi argues that marriage and social class were topoi motivated by romance narratives: adultery "may not have any historical foundation, but what matters here is the degree of difficulty it creates for the fulfillment of love."[58] "A passion—real or fictitious, adulterous or not—gives rise in the case of the troubadours to a discourse that is offered as an end in itself," Paul Zumthor says, "independent of the real-life origin. The question of 'sincerity' is not worth asking."[59] The poets survived by adhering not to experience but to conventions recirculated through poem after poem, as Elisabeth Schulze-Busacker observes.[60]

Provençal poems express worry. In romance a warrior must not exert force, though he proudly absorbs it. Fine love features beautiful women in a state of rest, their poet-lovers threatened by indifference or rejection, jealous husbands, or gossiping observers. The lover is under siege, drained of confidence, boastful of all he is ready to endure on behalf of his love—as a soldier boasts of the adversity he stands ready to endure. Admirable lovers still sing of a willingness to withstand difficulty: "I'll cry for you, die for you . . ." Like a soldier alone in a trench. Fourteenth-century Italian poetry installed ideals to emulate, but also to overcome. Late sixteenth-century English translations of Petrarch established the lover-as-beset. A Petrarchan lover suffers long and hard, as a test of ardor. At times he conceives of his beloved as a cruel enemy; other moments, the enemy is Love itself. Constantly he is locked in combat, and outmatched. Fealty is a soldierly virtue at the heart of monogamy. When seventeenth-century poets frankly assert the pursuit of pleasure and liberty, they honorably put behind them this romance of militant and pathetic endurance.

Johnson thought an elegist should name the mourned one, as he does Robert Levet; praise should be specific. Modern philosophers propose love as a discipline of the spirit that teaches one the value of differences among people. But the romance depiction of women is abstract. The Provençal women had some flesh, but the Tuscan women were insubstantial: "We have no idea of where they come from or where they go," Valency observes; "their very nature is in doubt, whether human or divine. We have no precise idea of how they seemed, tall or short, blonde or dark, nor what it was, precisely, that the poet wanted of them."[61] It matters that Dante and Petrarch wrote devotedly of their deceased beloveds. Love braves time; carnality cannot. The task of a beauty is to gather admiration, and then to depart. The Trojan elders want rid of Helen: "Let her go back to the ships, / Back among Grecian faces . . ." (as Pound puts it in Canto 2). The physical presence of a beautiful woman is a hazard. The death of a beautiful woman, Poe much later said, is the most poetic subject. The Italian poets were concerned with an intellectual love more than the enduring physical presence of women. Ever after lovers boast of devotion to ideas. Pound's question in Canto 47, "Hast thou found a nest softer than cunnus . . . ?" is heterodox. Few songs refer to a beloved's breasts or genitalia. Many speak instead of her eyes, windows to the soul.

The great love poetry of the English Renaissance is certainly carnal, but spectacularly intellectual too, even bookish, after Tuscan models. Provençal-, Italian-, and English-language love

poets refused to set mind against heart, and instead discrimi-
nated cause from effect, and imported analytical distinctions
from law, science, and philosophy. The terms of Marvell's "The
Definition of Love" (1649-51) register the fact that his interest
is not particular. Here love engages logic at the level of diction,
with categorical modifiers and predictive syntax: "alone" (l.
5), "could ne'er . . ." (l. 7), "always" (l. 12), "therefore" (l. 17),
"all" (l. 23), "every" (l. 26), "never" (l. 28), "Therefore" (l. 29).
English poets typically insist on the compatibility of mind and
lust. Marvell's title asserts a most general explanatory scope.
Within eight vigorous quatrains of strictly regular and firmly
rhymed iambic tetrameter that might well be sung—if a particularly philosophical jongleur could be found—he entertains
questions about the source, kinds, and practical effects of love.

I

My Love is of a birth as rare
As 'tis for object strange and high:
It was begotten by Despair
Upon Impossibility.

II

Magnanimous Despair alone   5
Could show me so divine a thing,
Where feeble Hope could ne'er have flown
But vainly flapped its tinsel wing.

Marvell's abstractness is essential to the poem's effect: a firm
will to say only what he wishes to say, nothing more, and very

little of what is expected of a love poem. He invests nothing
in pretty figures. All but one word of the first two lines are
monosyllables; with line three he shifts to another idiom. Lines
three and four arrive at a pithy, strange adage. This opening
stanza demonstrates the objective of the entire poem: stun-
ningly definite formulation and intellectual surprise. Lines
seven and eight dismiss hope as weak, and that had been what
any number of earlier love poets had said was their reason for
continuing to live. This toughly phrased praise derives from
still vital Tuscan rhetoric of fire and ice. With line one, one
thinks of Spenser's Amoretti 81: "Fayre is my loue, when her
fayre golden heares, / with the loose wynd ye wauing chance
to see." Or Shakespeare's Sonnet 130: "And yet, by heaven, I
think my love as rare / As any she belied with false compare."
(Or even the opening of Bob Dylan's "Love Minus Zero/No
Limit": "My love she speaks like silence, / Without ideals or
violence, / She doesn't have to say she's faithful, / Yet she's true,
like ice, like fire.") Marvell is austere, chilly by comparison.
His first two words are deliberately misleading. One expects
"My love" to refer to one beloved, but he speaks instead of his
own ability to love as a concept. This is why "'tis" appears in
line two, where "she" might be expected, and where the syntax
refuses the symmetry expected for the comparison. "My love"
is an "it"! There is a long tradition of enigmatic reference to
a beloved. But Marvell goes very far to avoid identifying any
beloved. The poem has three feminine pronouns, but they refer
to Fate. With each iteration he insists on what is withheld. His
is an intellectually superior subject. A reader should see that
at the outset.

The first two feet are rhymed (love/of), song-like, but the
poem is rooted in schoolish idioms of abstract analysis rather
than in a plausible natural speech. This becomes increasingly

clear as the figures unfold in the last three stanzas, but it is already evident in the distinction between origin and object (l. 2). Where does love come from, he asks, and what does it seek—questions derived from Aristotelian categories of causation. "The poem is an exercise," Nigel Smith observes, "in different kinds of explanation, logic, and logic's subversion by paradox and oxymoron. Geometry, through Euclidean rules, is a structure for the poem."[62] The intellectual flights of Donne display vivacity of mind and the pleasures of invention. That playfulness is not Marvell's here; instead he demonstrates vigorous and disciplined disputation. The beloved's appearance is irrelevant, as is the quality of feeling experienced by the lover. Correct explanation is the poet's concern. In lines one and two he is far from the immediate objective of seduction. However, lines three and four are lusty, and marked by a shift to polysyllables: below the surface of this abstract diction is a reference to carnal coupling. "To beget upon" is a predicate, like "sire on," used for animals as well as people. That a beloved is praised by this explanation is true, but only oddly, and to no practical end. This is a retrospective love poem insofar as it is particular at all.

Marvell elaborates a stunning account of love-beset, but not a representation of experience. Other lovers are said to approach despair as their advances are ignored or rejected, but despair is here the origin of a distinctively rare love. The second quatrain indicates that he gives his spirit more to the dark than to the light, but actually the language is so general that one only reluctantly infers this familiar but personal admission. "Magnanimous Despair," he says paradoxically, since largeness of spirit is the last thing one ordinarily attributes to a state of hopelessness. This quatrain (especially lines five and six) is such a mouthful that one is wickedly enticed by the extensive power of hopelessness. Aristotle relates the virtue of magnanimity to generosity (*Nicomachean Ethics*, 1123B-1125A), whereas Marvell connects dejection and generosity of imagination. Hope is more constrained than despair by a faint sense of what is attainable (ll. 7-8); to the desperate, the worst seems all too easily attainable. The object of this lover's affection is so high that he could not have hoped to have him or her. Lack of all hope left his imagination open to a further reach of spirit.

The spirit of his beloved magically corresponds to his own. The beloved's volition is evidently so settled that it requires no discussion. He suffers no doubt of his welcome by the beloved (ll. 9-10). "High" (l. 2) customarily refers to station, but that is not a necessary inference here. The poet insists on a hierarchy that removes his beloved from his grasp, no matter, in mere fact, whether the hierarchy is social or metaphysical, unless a breach is envisaged. (The verb "crowds" [l. 12] insinuates a common noun for anonymous social groups: a slight indication that the constraints on the lovers may be social, and the only such suggestion; the poet's attention is rather on the cosmic underpinning of social structure, the grandest warrants of what is called "Fate." Fate holds sectors apart, hierarchies and structures in place (ll. 15-20). Geometry and astronomy are permanent, fixed. Social change or even just the negotiation of social difference is of no relevance. Nor is any suggestion made that the world might be improved by a liberty that would allow these star-crossed lovers erotic fulfillment—or, as the poem says, to "close" (ll. 23-24).

III

And yet I quickly might arrive
Where my extended soul is fixed,   10

But Fate does iron wedges drive,
And always crowds itself betwixt.

IV

For Fate with jealous eye does see
Two perfect loves, nor lets them close:
Their union would her ruin be,   15
And her tyrannic power depose.

Fate's oppressive force, a familiar complaint (but without
any suggestion that he suffers more than others) is a general
condition of life itself. The commonplace of star-crossed lovers
is a figurative representation of this situation. No history is to
be written of Fate, nor any end to her reign plausibly foreseen.
This is the point of naming the block on his love "Fate." The
allure of fine love is such that, despite a beloved's high station, a
lover might well expect to arrive unimpeded at his object; neither social difference nor modesty could keep him from her (ll.
9-10). Whatever the quality of the distance between them, he
speaks only of the physics of extension (l. 10)—and indirectly
of anatomy. He reveals very little of the experiential force of the
block. The interests of particular lovers and their circumstances
count for nothing, in this view. The iron wedges that bar him
from his beloved are impersonal and unaffected by metaphysics;
political change is exactly what they prevent (ll. 15-16).

V

And therefore her decrees of steel
Us as the distant poles have placed,

(Though Love's whole world on us doth wheel)
Not by themselves to be embraced: 20

VI

Unless the giddy heaven fall,
And earth some new convulsion tear;
And, us to join, the world should all
Be cramped into a planisphere.

The chances of these lovers coming together sound slim: Marvell has bent the syntax of the sole sentence stretched over two stanzas so that one must hear the violence done to natural affection by the contortions of fate and allowable grammar. The twists come with the entry into the poem of a first-person plural construction (l. 18). Marvell does not seek to conceal his tortuous craft: in line twenty-three he echoes the twist of line eighteen. This is also the song's only prosodic variation ("Us as," an inverted initial foot: to push the two beats of the first four syllables as far as possible from one another). The separation of the lovers is made to sound preposterous to a native English speaker, though the laws of syntax hold nonetheless as firm as Fate's steely decrees. Intellect or wit leads Marvell to the cosmic figures of the last two stanzas, but a conservative affection for traditional figures that have come from Italian poetry has him speak of "Love's whole world" in the fifth stanza (l. 19). The figure of Love as ruler of a realm is in some accord with the first sonnet of the *Vita Nuova*. But if Love has an entire world that wheels on poles, what is "the world" in the sixth stanza (l. 23)? The phrase "the world"—governed by Fate—seems to preclude the notion of multiple worlds. There is a fissure in the figurative structure that reveals the pressure intellectual knowledge puts on the terms received from poetic traditions that were still attractive to Marvell and his contemporaries in the mid-seventeenth century. He is unwilling to sacrifice one cosmology to another, so the strain shows.[63]

VII

As lines so loves oblique may well   25
Themselves in every angle greet:
But ours so truly parallel,
Though infinite, can never meet.

VIII

Therefore the love which us doth bind,
But Fate so enviously debars,   30
Is the conjunction of the mind,
And opposition of the stars.[64]

Lines twenty-five and twenty-six speak of kama sutra-like possibilities for most lovers. He has not said explicitly that mind is the basis of this love, but that much is implicit in the elaboration of figures from astronomy, geometry, and cosmology. The beloved addressed is sufficiently learned to find charm in this extremely intellectual love poem. Even though eroticism is not possible, their loves are called "perfect" (l. 14) not just in the general sense of ideal, but in the more particular sense of well-made. Love of this order is a construction, like art itself, but an achievement subordinate to a larger force. Love is not lord, as he is for the Tuscan poets. Fate rules, and does so jealously, meanly. In Dante's sonnet the paradoxes of love are displayed as features of Love's doings. Here even fine love is no match for Fate: there is no point in resistance. Insofar as the value of a love-ideology is its expansion of a field of autonomy or agency for lovers in a private sphere, Marvell's is a dark poem. Fate leaves so very little, beyond understanding and self-approval, for these lovers to enjoy in the light. How audacious to construct a philosophical definition of love that takes blockage and unfulfillment as absolute. Marvell's achievement is the construction of a poem that seems motivated by personal experience even though his idiom is so general that experience is barely implicit in his lines. The poem has two frames of reference, but the poet is thoroughly prudent about personal references (so different thereby from Wyatt and his master, Petrarch). The pleasure of the poem is in its display of rival power where acquiescence is expected. Fate is this love's opposite, but in his concise and forceful stanzas Marvell matches fate's force. These sentences demonstrate mastery and willfulness in emulation of fate's "iron wedges" (l. 11) and "decrees of steel" (l. 17).

Marvell's exposition of a lover's linguistic options is a brave pushing back against a long line of overpowered lovers. Just like fate, the lover aspires to "tyrannic power" (l. 16). His style is unencumbered by sentiment. This is an English poet up against continental literary obstacles to love. He may not get the girl, should there be a girl, but his words stand.

Marvell set a standard for speaking generally and analytically of love uncompromised by experience. The songs in the chapters that follow all speak generally of love, but recognizable experience is meant to authorize their statements. The challenge is Marvell's assertion that love is not the sum of various loves, that it is grander, stranger, and more constraining than experience. The quasi-religious vision of romance insists on the singularity of desire, or natural monogamy. The concept of a faithful, monogamous lover derives, I believe, from that of a loyal soldier. The case I make is that even the popular song displays the earnest intellectuality for which poets in English are known. From Provençe to Tuscany, Dante, Petrarch, Wyatt, then Rossetti, Yeats, Robert Duncan, and Frank Bidart, this tradition is intermittent and cultish, but more important woeful; it expresses horribly blocked desire. A constraining love-code that survives from medieval love poetry measures a lover's ardor not by its distinctiveness, but by its conformity to monogamous, high-minded, self-abnegating desire. There is a countertradition of love-lyrics, from Robert Herrick to many popular songs of the mid-twentieth century: a line of sunny sex that reaches back to pastoral poetry and eludes the torments of apparent intellectuality. It expresses neither frustration nor agony but delight in experience. One wants to think that these twin traditions are in balance, but they are not.

The values preserved by love poets and lyricists affect readers and listeners deeply. Which is not to say that love poems and songs add up to one thing: the commonplaces of chapters one and six contradict one another, as do chapters two and seven. The values and contradictions too are lodged deep in cultural memory. One wants to think that ideas of love derive from experience, that they are natural. The erotic experiences of readers and listeners range far more widely than do love poems; the latter derive principally from what we hear and read. Literary traditions change more by accretions than by displacements.[65] The esteem of loyalty in fine love was absorbed into a concept of monogamous devotion, and the militance of its origins has been preserved in figures more than doctrine. A romance ideology acquires ironies as it is variously bent by poets and lyricists; those ironies derive from a taste for contradiction. My selections are canonical, memorable; that is, not idiosyncratic. One may prefer other texts, other songs (less ironic ones, say), but these wield the authority that comes from having found, and over time maintained, diverse audiences.

1. Desire Is Monogamous

"Numbers" is an archaic term for verse. Proliferation is at the center of poetry: more, again. "Who is it *this* time?" Aphrodite asks Sappho, at the outset of western lyric. Poems move on syllable by syllable, to words, lines, and stanzas; and then even to another lover. And yet, what about the single, the one? That certainly has a place in numbers. Wyatt despises doubleness. His great power is in speaking for the one, broken off from a pair. Singularity, as he often says, is steadfast; it does not change. His master, Petrarch, prided himself on enduring devotion: he expressly counts the years in poems, as evidence that he was "still what I used to be, nor for a thousand turnings about have I yet moved."[1]

This ethos of romance is sharply gendered: although the cruel beloved remains chaste and unapproachable, she is figured as inconstant in character: moody, unpredictable. Catullus, traditional in his misogyny, says, "what a woman says to a passionate lover / ought to be scribbled on wind, on running water."[2] Petrarch, on the contrary, stands proudly steady: "I am still just what I was."[3] This is surprising because the chastity of men is anything but proverbial. And yet that is the authority of the male lyric of reproach: enduring sameness.

Poems of exclusive devotion and those of bitter recrimination
come from this single source: the idea of the one love.

Devotion is the central idea of romance. It names a differ-
ential of attention, behind which lies a judgment or finding
of exceptionality. Yet lyrics of ardent monogamous desire
describe devotion as an inevitable feature of the lover's life.
The devoté loves just one beloved; that is all there is in his
heart. He avows his devotion as evidence of his desire. He
is in control of his will and refers to the excellence of his
beloved as if his devotion were rationally motivated. Petrarch
says he was struck by a bolt from Laura's eyes on April 6,
1327. He had no choice in the matter. When the lead singer
of the Platters, Tony Williams, repeats "You are my destiny,"
in his 1955 version of Buck Ram's "Only You," he cracks his
voice a little to punctuate the claim that a force external to
the lover settles lives—when things work well.[4] When one's
own mere subjectivity prevails, one goes from love to love,
assessing how each one fits with what one imagines as desirable. If the fit seems less than perfect, as it ordinarily does, one
either copes with the contradictions between actuality and
imagination or, as a rational agent, moves on. The beauty of
destiny is that, without demanding any material judgment, it
sanctions one love above all others. Agency is then beside the
point—a great relief. A destined love may seem now and then
suitable or not, in one or another way; or not fully realized and
only a potential satisfaction. Ordinarily one labors through
dialogue and compromise to realize a potential satisfaction, or
otherwise transform a relationship. But the concept of destiny
renders that labor moot. This is the one, like it or not. These
songs of devotion come from a wish for release from seriality, from judgment. A wish for one lover is accompanied by
a claim or assertion that desire is exclusive: I have eyes for

only you. The song asserts that this wonder is a settled fact, that number holds nothing for the lover. No crowds, only the beloved. That is the dream, that desire were without contradiction, that love of the one might eliminate the distractions of the many.[5] Songs of exclusive love are deeply, willfully irrational. They teeter on the disputed boundary between honorable devotion and shameful obsession. Why is the apparent fact that desire is resilient and opportunistic vigorously disputed? That is the question addressed in this chapter.

The Platters often employed relatively grand orchestration by doo-wop standards; one may love their version of "Only You" (1955), as I do, but it is nothing if not overdone. Tony Williams caresses his own sonority, confident of the song's amplitude. He even adds a consonant to his articulation—a light "d" at some junctures between syllables. *On-dly* you *cand* make all this world seem right. This beloved is an enchantress, not an enlightener. She makes the darkness bright, the world right; counterfactuals, that is, not empirical reports. The program of this sort of love: deny the evident. Willfulness is everything. To exercise judgment, one must listen to the world. Will, on the contrary, resists whatever is put in its path. Will pushes; prudence pauses. Petrarch is lavishly imprudent. He took one look at Laura and resolved as an artist to write— over the course of twenty-one years—about her, and then for another decade after her death in 1348; not of the political and religious life of Avignon (of which he did write brilliantly in Poem 136), but of a blonde beauty he would never have in the flesh. He made himself an abstract poet. He simplified his art but concentrated and intensified it by exclusion—and countless European poets followed his example. Now his brilliant imaginative project is indissociable from lyric itself.

A devoted lover longs to escape subjectivity. "Only You" is sung by a promiscuous lover who wants to become monogamous.

> Only you, and you alone   5
> can thrill me like you do,
> And fill my heart with love for only you.
> Only you
> can make all this change in me,
> For it's true, you are my destiny.[6]   10

He speaks comparatively and exactly. Others can thrill him, but not in the beloved's particular way. Others can fill his heart with love, but not with an exclusive, monogamous love (l. 7). Pleasure in exclusive desire is new to him. The beloved can help him change into another *kind* of lover. That change is incomplete at the point of utterance; he needs her to complete this transformation (ll. 8-9). Lyrics of monogamous devotion constitute a utopian literature. A poet writes of how lovers might behave, not of their actual lives. This is a highly sophisticated art, meant for only those who already know that lovers degrade their desires, shame their spirits.

Songs of devotion rarely concern ordinary fidelity. Willed restraint or wrestling with Eros—this is irrelevant. The contrary assertion is that Eros has totally conquered these lovers: they are thralls. Devotion has been fully achieved by a force external to themselves. That conquest is in the past; Eros cannot lead them—as Sappho is led—from one to another beloved in a series. These songs celebrate the settling of desire. Monogamy as an elected form of social behavior, in support of which reasons can be adduced, is not the issue. By rendering desire itself as monogamous, as a fact of the lover's life, a single, exclusive marriage becomes a mere social adjustment to a natural phenomenon. From this point of view, alternative forms of romance are aberrant.

Eros's changes and surprises no longer affect those struck by monogamous desire; they are without stress or conflict. Devotés boast of immunity from machinations or novelty. The eyes are known as the sense of novelty; they roam. Eyes and want are the same. Carmen McRae describes a wonder when, in Harry Warren and Al Dubin's "I Only Have Eyes for You" (1934), she sings, "Maybe millions of people go by, / but they all disappear from view. / And I only have eyes for you."[7] That is devotion as an unsought fact of experience. Her version of the song is strong, athletic: she doesn't pace her force to an imagined narrative. The action is already complete, with nothing left for narrative. No questions are open at any point in the lyric. She's free to play with the tune, as she does, for instance, when she drops down a note on "*gar*den," for no semantic reason. The real joy of her song is exactly that she is free of a romance plot. Like Ella, she can work with the sounds without imitating romantic affect. The joy of monogamy is not that it fulfills but releases a lover from possessive desire. The objective is light-heartedness—just what Ella and Carmen display. But what is to be made of the repeated solecism, the misplaced "only." "Onlyness" is the key issue in this song, as in "It Only Happens Once" and "Only You." Is this what Yip Harburg meant by a "curved thought"? On an urbane style, this is a conspicuous blemish, sufficient to provoke irony concerning the boast.

A cruel, unattainable beloved generally presides over the monogamous lyric, but there is a counter-song too that tells of monogamy as a benign form of management. Neal Hefti's "Li'l Darlin'" (1957), for instance, to which Jon Hendricks wrote lyrics, is a boast of possession.[8] The beloved has eyes for only her lover: he enjoys the devotion of the blessed. That possession is the power to escape the pain, instability, and expense that attend a blocked beloved or promiscuity. This song begins with renunciation, or a *second* option: "Don't need no palace paved with gold . . ." An exclusive love is a renunciation of undisciplined desire, or multiple loves. These initial figures, though, are of material not sexual desire; ways of living, not just loving, are the topic. Walter Donaldson and Gus Kahn's "My Baby Just Cares for Me" (1930) is similarly domestic.[9] These songs distinguish the beloved from all contemporary socialized women who melt at Clark Gable's smile, or whatever mainstream media serve as fulfillment. Her monogamous desire is represented as unusual, not typical of the moment. She ignores social regard and measurement, and the lover is saved the cost of furs, laces, and "expensive things." "She's sensible as can be." Exclusivity is a kind of deal, and these songs, less ardent than other expressions of devotion, celebrate it as a good one. (The solecism of the misplaced modifier—"only loves me" and "just cares for me"—is less provocative in these lyrics, because the style is plainly vernacular rather than urbane.) Gains outweigh losses. One hears from both Mark Murphy and Kurt Elling that the chief gain is sustainability: repeatedly, they hold one note a very long time, as if to indicate that the tune is about that which can abide.

There are nonetheless losses, as everyone understands, and the lyric of "Li'l Darlin'" names what is given up for monogamy. The moment of desire begins in abundance. "When I get to feeling a feeling / For something there ain't too much of, / my sweet li'l darlin' gives me her love." If his feeling is one for love, as the rhyme (and common sense) leads one to infer, he holds by the notion that there is no such thing as too much love or lovemaking. His beloved, immediately accessible, does not withhold her favors. He boasts his satisfaction with her by saying twice, "Don't catch me chasing round at nights. / I'm not impressed by glamorous sights." He has given up the nightlife, and flashy women too. "Li'l darlin' may not be as pretty / as some of the girls you can see, / but my li'l darlin' only loves me." She is present and willing, however plain. If one thought that monogamy served the interests of the family or reproduction, there is no sign of those interests here. They are the social concerns that are hard to name in song, and this song represents male possession. This is a cool, superficial account of fidelity; the song insists on the calculating egotism of this male perspective. Neither lover says anything about his love or desire for his beloved; neither worries about missing a grander, deeper love—as Bidart does when he says, "*We could have had ecstasies.*"[10] Daily, selfish satisfaction is the subject. This is why Mark Murphy repeats the last line four times at the end and holds on the last syllable: me.

The term devotion suggests that having a love is like having a religion. Coltrane and Johnny Hartman draw out the Petrarchan sumptuosity of Robert Mellin and Guy Wood's "My One and Only Love" (1952).[11] Wood describes fulfillment in a zone of poetic diction, removed from familiar experience, like a magic garden: "an April breeze," the "wings of spring," "mystic charms." All that the lover says is sectarian: "the touch of your hand is like heaven." This is Poetry from old anthologies, without contact to speech. Ardent love songs are doctrinal, like monogamy; realism has little bearing. The doctrine is ample, beyond whatever confirmation or qualification might come from experience or dialectic; from a devoted monogamist's viewpoint there is no conflict, tension, or irony. A devoted lover readily acknowledges a moat separating

romantic love and actual experience. Petrarch's tightly bounded
sonnet (Poem 124) comes from deliberate disengagement that
is figured prosodically by repeated terms ("volta" and "mezzo,"
ll. 2-3, 11, 14) as exact rhymes and otherwise by exactly positioned links from stanza to stanza ("Amor," "Fortuna," and
"mente," ll. 1, 5, 6; "spero" and "speranza," ll. 9 & 13). Of
this self-aware turn away from ordinary, contemporary experience, Petrarch says that "his mind . . . avoids what it sees and
turns back to the past."[12] (Or, according to Wyatt: "my mind,
rememb'rer / Of that that is now with that that hath been.")[13]
Not that he expects to revive the past: he rather recoils from
his contemporaries and prefers to write within a fabricated
medieval court life. That this brings him no joy is a defining
feature of his project.

> Amor, Fortuna, et la mia mente, schiva
> di quel che vede et nel passato volta,
> m'affliggon sì ch' io porto alcuna volta
> invidia a quei che son su l'altra riva.
>
> Amor mi strugge 'l cor, Fortuna il priva   5
> d'ogni conforto, onde la mente stolta
> s'adira et piange; et cosi in pena molta
> sempre conven che combatiendo viva.
>
> Né spero i dolci dì tornino indietro,
> ma pur di male in peggio quel ch' avanza,   10
> et di mio corso ò già passato 'l mezzo.
>
> Lasso, non di diamante ma d'un vetro
> veggio di man cadermi ogni speranza
> et tutt' i miei pensier romper nel mezzo.[14]

Love, Fortune, and my mind—which now avoids
all that it sees and turns back to the past—
afflict me so that sometimes I must feel
envy for those who've reached the other shore.

Sir Love torments my heart, and Fortune   5
takes from it all its comforts, while my mind
weeps foolishly and pines; as a result,
I live at war, contending with my sorrow.

I do not hope that sweet days will return;
instead I think they'll go from bad to worse,   10
the midpoint of my course is now well past.

I see all hope, alas, crash through my hands;
it isn't made of diamond, merely glass,
and all my thoughts, I see, must break in two.

(trans. David Young)[15]

Monogamy is always meant to seem old-fashioned, as
though an archaic arrangement might release the spirit from
the instability of serial desire. Petrarch acknowledges—as Ezra
Pound and Robert Duncan later do—that his songs are imitations of something he never had, of a life not his own. He
frequently blames Eros or Amor for his obsessive desire, or he
blames Fortune for denying him a turn at satisfaction, but here
he says plainly that his own mind drew him to ersatz desire.
This is a scholar's love poetry: a project of the will, none of
it had to be; in retrospect, mere broken glass. A final sadness
seems right for an art that, with great persistence but little
struggle, honestly refuses a realistic basis.

What matters most is not how a lover loves—or ordinary agency—but how he or she writes. Making art is the real activity. A lover's praise is constitutive more than descriptive; Laura, more wonder than woman. A lover does not need to measure a beloved by comparison with other women—as in "Li'l Darlin'"; the beloved is a sign of surplus desire, a refusal of the adequacy of representation. Here is Petrarch 309:

> L'alto et novo miracol ch' a' dì nostri
> apparve al mondo et star seco no volse,
> che sol ne mostrò 'l Ciel, poi sel ritolse
> per adornarne i suoi stellanti chiostri,
>
> vuol ch' i' depinga a chi nol vide e 'l mostri
> Amor, che 'n prima la mia lingua sciolse;
> poi mille volte indarno a l'opra volse
> ingegno, tempo, penne, carte, enchiostri.
>
> Non son al sommo ancor giunte le rime,
> in me il conosco, et proval ben chiunque
> è 'nfin a qui che d'Amor parli o scriva;
>
> chi sa pensare, il ver tacito estime
> ch' ogni stil vince, et poi sospire: "Adunque
> beati gli occhi che la vider viva!"[16]

> The high, new miracle that in our time
> came to the world but did not wish to stay,
> whom Heaven merely showed us, then took back
> in order to adorn its starry cloisters:

Lord Love, who first set free my tongue, wants me
to show her to whoever didn't see her,
and to that end a thousand times he's worked
my wits, my time, my papers, pens, and inks.

But poetry has not attained its peak,
I know that well, and so does anyone
who's ever tried to write or speak of Love;

let thoughtful people love the silent truth
that passes anything in language, sighing:
"Blessed be the eyes that saw her while she lived!"

(trans. David Young)[17]

Devotion to a unique, transcendent idea, or beloved, is a condition of poetry. Poems come out of a gulf between value imagined (or supposed) and attained, or even analytically justified.
No poem will span that gulf, which is why another one can be
written. Poetic seriality, one sonnet or canzone after another,
instead of the erotic seriality of ordinary life, is paradoxically
a product of devotion. Petrarch proposes an intellectual cal-
culus. *Think* about it, he urges, and then acknowledge that,
yes, she was a wonder. If you yourself did not behold her value
realized, then the displacement of poetic art is for you. Her
presence was surrounded by a void: she existed, but he could
not have her, no one could; then she died. She lived, so that
artful approximations might come to exist.

The pun on "Laura" and "laurel" is constantly in view, as he
describes the comeliness of his tree; every unseemly reference to
birdlime suggests that she cannot be woman but must, oddly, be
the Tree of Fame: poetry itself, or more particularly his poetry
and fame. (This equation explains Rilke's peculiar tree that grows

in the ear.) Daphne, too: beloved and laurel tree, who resists, which is how she becomes laurel. Woman, poetry, eluder of the divine. Petrarch acknowledges that he too has resisted God in his devotion to Laura and poetry. He might have more wisely submitted. The last poem of the *Rime sparse* is devoted to the mother of God ("vera Beatrice," true bringer of happiness), not to Laura.[18] He turns away from his project (or "insanity"): "I consecrate and cleanse in your name my thought and wit and style, my tongue and heart, my tears and my sighs. Lead me to the better crossing and accept my changed desires."[19] The conclusion to his great book is renunciation of impious devotion.

One commonly thinks that monogamy facilitates social stability, that it's civilizing. Promiscuity and divorce divide families, households, inheritances. In the sense of above-all-others, devotion resolves contests among rival considerations. Yet one knows too that this turn of thought constrains deliberation, even communication. Yeats' "Adam's Curse," for instance, is enigmatic in that the devoté is at odds with his companions. In the first strophe, he rants in a familiar way against guardians of social order, "bankers, schoolmasters, and clergymen." The oddity is that he is addressing a silent Maud Gonne and her sister, Constance Gore-Booth, whom he twice identifies as that "beautiful mild woman" (ll. 2, 15). Despite his own harshness, he expressly admires a "sweet and low" voice (l. 17). He likens courtly love and poetry, in the third strophe, and that brings the conversation to a halt. The fourth and fifth stanzas reflect on that lapse.

> I had a thought for no one's but your ears:
> That you were beautiful, and that I strove   35
> To love you in the old high way of love;
> That it had all seemed happy, and yet we'd grown
> As weary-hearted as that hollow moon.[20]

He had focused his attention on Constance Gore-Booth for three strophes, but then at the end, against this silence, he addresses only Maud Gonne. Maud is silent, and Constance speaks softly; he vigorously explains poetry and the world. He asserts that all three characters grow piously quiet at the name of love, but his reference to courtly love seems to embarrass the women because of their awareness of his failed efforts to court Maud. (She would in fact marry Sgt. MacBride just a few months after Yeats wrote this poem in 1902.) The speaker is weirdly out of touch with his interlocutors, as Porphyria's lover is too. Devotion produces insensitivity to others, which Yeats and Browning understood. A devoted lover has but one subject; he only seems to speak of anything other than his love. That hollows out language. Sociality cannot withstand the intensity of devotion. Reproachful devotés want the last word. Yeats displays devotion to Maud, like a badge, as though to excuse an overbearing manner.

Those who can love only one are likely to suffer, and to discomfort others. Petrarch's Poem 124 and "Adam's Curse" suggest that devotion to the One brings estrangement from others. Equivalence facilitates recovery from loss, which is to say stability. From Sappho to Frank Bidart one lyric form triangulates lover, beloved, and *spectator*. When Sappho envies "that man" looking at her beloved, she recognizes an incompatibility of erotic devotion and sociality: she loves devotedly, and he presumably seeks a mate. The triangle structures observation and reflection. "That man" *looks* at the beloved; that is his entire act. He rivals the lover not in loving but in *looking*; she too is a spectator. Why is observation disruptive? One thinks that a look leads to a touch, but a look is distinct from sexual possession. Looking occurs in the condition of desire, not of possession. Acquisitiveness and possession are reasonably predictable and to that extent manageable. But a devoté is an outlier. Bidart analyzes the outsider-devoté as a gay male admirer in "Phenomenology of the Prick"—a fresh echo of Sappho's "That Man."

> You say, Let's get naked. It's 1962; the world
> is changing, or has changed, or is about to change;
> we want to get naked. Seven or eight old friends
>
> want to see certain bodies that for years we've
> guessed at, imagined. For me, not
> certain bodies: one. Yours. You know that.
>
> We get naked. The room
> is dark; shadows against the windows'
> light night sky; then you approach your wife. You light
>
> a cigarette, allowing me to see what is forbidden to see.
> You make sure I see it hard.
> You make sure I see it hard
>
> only once. *A year earlier, through the high partition
>   between cafeteria*
> *booths, invisible I hear you say you can get Frank's*
> *car keys tonight. Frank, you laugh, will do anything I want.*
>
> You seemed satisfied. This night, as they say,
> completed something. After five years of my
> obsession with you, without seeming to will it you
>
> managed to let me see it hard. Were you
> giving me a gift. Did you want fixed in my brain
> what I will not ever possess. Were you giving me
> a gift that cannot be possessed. You make sure

I see how hard
your wife makes it. You light a cigarette.[21]

Bidart's beloved presumably wants to shame the lover for his
desire: the lover is made to look at what he wants and will not
have. The lover's task is to recover pride from shame. He must
face the truth: that his objective is erotic possession, and that
devotion is an alternative, not a waystation, to possession. An
enlightened devoté recognizes that possession is not possible.
The difference from Sappho's poem is that Bidart's lover is
made to understand perfectly that devotion does not accommodate the stable business of social reproduction, though
monogamy does. Just when the friends purport to open up
to one another, the devoté is shamed into secrecy and resentment. Bidart echoes not only Sappho but Herodotus too. After
Gyges is made to observe the beauty of Candaules's naked wife,
he is required to conspire to kill the king. Just to see squarely
the object of devotion is to undermine social order, because
the beloved belongs to another; devotion requires blockage.
Sappho, Petrarch, Wyatt, and Bidart expose this dark truth.
    Devotion is a beautiful thing, for which sacrifices are will-
ingly endured. But from sacrifice to a claim on another is a
short step. Devotion places a beloved under obligation, with a
debt disguised as a gift. Of course a devoté wants reciprocity, a
consistency of affection between lovers—a modest, reasonable
expectation. But a lover's most bitter reproach is that of inconstancy—less for choosing another than for changing in time.
And people naturally change in time. Consider Wyatt's "When
first mine eyes," a strange but more conventional, abstract, and
impersonal poem than "Whoso list to hunt" and "They flee
from me." This poem obviously proceeds, stanza by stanza,
through a scheme—the eyes, the lips, the hands, and then
the mind; its rhetorical structure is prominent. The phrasing

at the outset is general ("fair beauty" [l. 2], "pleasant words" [l. 4]). Through line nine, the speaker is untroubled, coolly working schemes to invert the blazon. Then one senses a vein of very particular feeling. Without those schemes the poem's shift would be less dramatic. "They flee from me" and "Whoso list to hunt" develop too, but their emotional force is already gathered in their first lines.

> When first mine eyes did view and mark
> Thy fair beauty to behold
> And when mine ears listened to hark
> The pleasant words that thou me told,
> I would as then I had been free   5
> From ears to hear and eyes to see.
>
> And when my lips 'gan first to move,
> Whereby my heart to thee was known,
> And when my tongue did talk of love
> To thee that hast true love down thrown,   10
> I would my lips and tongue also
> Had then been dumb, no deal to go.
>
> And when my hands have handled aught
> That thee hath kept in memory
> And when my feet have gone and sought   15
> To find and get thy company,
> I would each hand a foot had been
> And I each foot a hand had seen.
>
> And when in mind I did consent
> To follow this my fancy's will   20
> And when my heart did first relent

To taste such bait my life to spill,
I would my heart had been as thine
Or else thy heart had been as mine.[22]

The poem develops a commonplace: Why did I choose you?—much later, a popular song title.[23] Poets make strange things of the familiar. Like Wyatt's more famous poems, this one reproaches a faithless beloved. To say that she threw down true love (l. 10) is to speak meaningfully, but impersonally, without suggestion of a rival, without adventitious address to a public personage. This is a general expression, and for that reason a poem harder to admire than "Whoso list to hunt" and "They flee from me." The specific historical context of these famous poems renders them paradoxically accessible. One marvels that Wyatt had the courage to shame Anne Boleyn by exposing their dalliance; the more his beloved is identified as a court figure, the more directly one senses her exposure and humiliation. And his figurative screens, in those poems, provide modern readers with an illusion of concreteness, as if "hind" as a sign for the beloved were more particular or sensual than "thou." But a sense too of drama in holding back more particular reproach and reference survives too for modern readers. That is one of the obvious sources of Wyatt's poetic power.[24]

The distinctive feature of "When first mine eyes" is that his wish for estrangement from his senses (ll. 5-6, 11-12) develops into a grotesque fantasy that his hands had been feet, or that his feet had seemed hands—and he had therefore been unable to seek out her company (ll. 17-18). How peculiar, this counter-blazon—of the lover rather than the beloved. The poem's imaginative arc peaks in the third stanza, in the middle of the poem, with its most musical and evasive line: "And when my hands have handled aught" (l. 13). That terminal word is

sufficiently vague to allow some conjecture. "Hand" appears
four times in this sestet; "memory," only once. Attention is
on touching. What might he have handled that would help
to keep her in his memory? Might he refer, in veiled fashion,
to handling her intimately? That his hand might then have
been a foot is a wicked way to express contempt: to touch her
so with his foot rather than his hand or tongue would be to
shame her. With pleasure, he imagines her allowing herself
to be treated without dignity by her lover. The trope of dis-
tortion that runs from lines five to eighteen implies a severe
judgment of devotion itself, for that is what led the speaker to
mean imaginings. He shamelessly reveals the cruelty of his own
fancies.[25] Strength of feeling, in particular of resentment, has
led to a bizarre, low figure distant from the conventional rhetorical structure with which he began. The ardor one admires
in a devoté has a flip side: contempt.

Self-judgment is implicit when he sees that his love has led
him where he had not thought to go (ll. 15-18). He imagines
a moment, in line eighteen, of critical self-regard: he might
have seen himself pursuing his beloved like a chimpanzee walking clownishly on its hands. The most obviously imaginative
flights of the poem suggest that, in retrospect, his devotion
had perverted his own nature. The last stanza is tighter, more
economical, more abstract than any other. The first in fact is
baggy: its verbs proliferate (view, mark, behold; listen, hark)
without any sharpening of sense. He writes loosely at the outset, as though with latitude to speak one way or another, and
some looseness persists (ll. 12, 15). In the third stanza he dou-
bles up on verbs again (ll. 15-16), as he had in the first stanza.
His style has already found economy, though, because the doubled verb in line fifteen does sharpen the sense by asserting
his intentionality. The double verb phrase of the next line is

still more forceful: he succeeded in getting her company. This single stylistic feature that had lacked point in stanza one has become penetrating a dozen lines later. In the end, no latitude.

The last stanza gathers the poem's intensity, but more than that: courage and candor too. He holds himself responsible for his plight in the most explicit terms possible, when he shifts from a catalogue of the senses to "mind" (l. 19). He *thought* about his love and against better judgment *relented*. He blames no one else, and refuses to say even that sensuality made him do it. "Destiny" is likewise irrelevant. The closing couplet of each tetrameter sestet expresses a wish to have been spared intimacy. The poem's most vigorous and memorable line is all self-reproach (l. 22). The toughness of lines ten through eighteen recalls his more famous poems of reproach, and then the tone obviously warms in the last line. He softens, wishing that she had loved him as he loved her. That too may be why this poem is neglected; Wyatt is treasured for recriminations, and warm second thoughts add only an unwelcome complication to his persona. The resilience of the last line reveals that his spirit is not irreversibly embittered: he would like another go at her still. His vulnerability is recognizable, familiar, human, we say, but not so tough as most readers want from this poet. It is courage, though, that allows him to qualify the toughness with a final wish that she too might have loved. And a challenging candor is required to show that this cruel shamer wishes at the end to be loved tenderly. That an angry lover wishes to humiliate a beloved and a moment later wants warmth in return is human nature, however undignified.[26]

The underside of devotion is degradation, as Wyatt, Petrarch, Sappho, and Bidart all show. A beloved is cherished and *served*; a lover's care is self-abnegating. For a courtly lover, service is honorable because required by a code, whereas for citizens of a republic, asymmetry is degrading. Billie Holiday's rendition of "My Man" (1948) tells of asymmetrical devotion without any redeeming frame, such as that of courtly love. The lover is merely abject, abused.

> Two or three girls has he,
> That he likes as well as me,
> But I love him.

> I don't know why I should,
> He isn't true,
> He beats me too.

> What can I do?

Modern romance rests on an understanding of autonomy: a lover *elects* to serve another. A lover's service ought not be conditional on a quid pro quo, though balance is the only honorable basis of stability. "My Man" is a version of "Mon Homme," a French song by Jacques Charles released in 1914 by Carmen Maria Vega. In the 1928 film *My Man* Fanny Brice's character sang about her fiancé Joe Halsey, a scoundrel caught making love to her sister. In the film, Fanny is on the street, under a lamp. Barbara Streisand, in *Funny Girl* (1965), left out the verse about being beaten. When Diana Ross sang it in Las Vegas in 1979, she said: "I hate that line." Relationships are generally held to a notion of justice. For what one gives, one is due a just response. In the event of a prolonged non-reciprocal devotion, on this view, one has *chosen* deprivation. Modern readers object to Shakespeare's servility in Sonnets 24, 35, and 49.[27] Those who in a republic embrace victimhood receive pity, not honor.

A forsaken devoté *knows* what a faithless beloved has not

guessed: that her life has peaked. He has given all there is.
He predicts, with conviction, that no future love can match
what she has lost. Pushkin, preternaturally generous, wishes
his beloved well: "I pray God grant another love you so."[28]
His meaning: that only God can bring her another such love.
Robert Lowell more frankly tells his beloved that that will
never happen.

> Dark swallows will doubtless come back killing
> the injudicious nightflies with a clack of the beak;
> but these that stopped full flight to see your beauty
> and my good fortune . . . as if they knew our names—
> they'll not come back. The thick lemony honeysuckle, 5
> climbing from the earthroot to your window,
> will open more beautiful blossoms to the evening;
> but these . . . like dewdrops, trembling, shining, falling,
> the tears of day—they'll not come back. . . .
> Some other love will sound his fireword for you   10
> and wake your heart, perhaps, from its cool sleep;
> but silent, absorbed, and on his knees,
> as men adore God at the altar, as I love you—
> don't blind yourself, you'll not be loved like that.[29]

This is a translation of a Spanish poem, "Rima 53," in six
quatrains, by Gustavo Adolfo Bécquer (1836-1870); it is now
one of the most memorable lyrics in English of the last half-
century. The lover tells the beloved that, although she does not
see her situation clearly, "las golondrinas *oscuras*" [dark, obscure
swallows], true love is leaving her behind. She'll be seduced
again, but not adored as a goddess. The poem has a sharp edge,
almost a curse, as does Keats's' "This Living Hand." Lowell's
poem brings to a fully traditional, even conventional account
of devotion (beauty, fortune, adoration) extraordinarily rich

descriptive terms and a master's ear. He displays delectation in
his choice of words: "doubtless" lands with rhetorical emphasis, a meaningful acknowledgment, because the word subtly
echoes "dark swallows" ("dark"→"doubt"; "-lows"→"less").
"Injudicious" too is a showy, perfect term because in this context it is inappropriately Latinate, and yet he knows he himself
has been an insufficiently intelligent lover. He renders the scene
with specific, concrete Anglo-Saxon words: clack and beak; the
kennings "nightflies," "earthroot," and "fireword" spaced out
neatly in lines 2, 6, and 10. The syntactic variations (clauses
opening out and then shutting down [ll. 4-5, 8-9, 12-14]) are
masterful too. These registers of English are brought to peace
in a framework that derives ultimately from Petrarch. Lowell
has no difficulty blending conventions; most of his lines are
rhythmically discrepant. The words and structures of his lines
display his freedom as a maker, his adaptability. The sonnet
form and the iambic pentameter are present, but subdued.
There are three "quatrains"—one on the swallows, one on the
honeysuckle, one on the rival—and an epigrammatic conclusion; no rhymes, though, and the boundaries of the quatrains
and couplet don't fall where they should.

The sonnet has less a prosodic than a rhetorical scheme of
expression. Lowell has roughed up the sonnet structure, but
it still resonates of love song beyond Bécquer. Lines one and
five faintly rhyme: *kill*ing/honeysu*ckle*; lines two and nine as
well: beak/back; seven and eight: even*ing*/fall*ing*; lines ten and
thirteen: you/you; and nine and fourteen too: back/that. These
lines are prosodically worked, but only so far. When he wishes,
as he does at the very end wish, to break through his own
artfulness, to speak plainly, he does, in perfectly regular iambic pentameter: "Don't blind yourself, you'll not be loved like
that." An emphatic, cutting conclusion to a luscious, caressing
praise poem. The point is that any prediction that love will

abandon the beloved, no matter how courteously expressed, retains its genealogy in the curse. The power of this poem comes from Lowell's having artfully established, through his syntax, rhythm, and figuration, the maturity and flexibility of the speaker before issuing a tough, memorable reproof.

Given this poet's control over his medium, it is unsettling that he gets to no more magnanimous utterance. He is closer to Wyatt than to Sappho. While Sappho and Lowell do recognize the seriality of desire, he does not acknowledge equivalence as she does. One love is not like another; the differences are crucial, he claims, and he intends for his expression, as Wyatt does, to injure the beloved. Lowell invokes the devotion of courtly love—its religiosity. Devotion is not affection, not desire; affection and desire recur serially, but not devotion. The tone of the translation shifts at the very end to a skeptical, vernacular idiom of pride and resentment, all the more cutting because he has moved to it slowly, from ardor. "Don't blind yourself," he says. That quick shift, like a splash of ice water, makes the poem unforgettable. Monogamous devotion seems here a reaction-formation. One recovers strength, in particular, after a loss, or in anticipation of rejection or failure. The forsaken male lover exploits devotion to affirm a higher standard. Reduced by rejection, he needs to speak down to his beloved. Monogamy authorizes the recriminations of these proud poets; Wyatt, Lowell, and Yeats, all masters of reproach. They sing for a severe, acidic art; their beloveds were not good enough for them.

Why should devotion lead to curses? "Time is the evil," Pound says. Wyatt does not inquire why his beloved has altered her affections. The answer is understood, or implied, by the *when*'s that structure his poem; now is not then, each stanza implies. The woeful fact is that time, for no deep reason, erodes devotion, and altogether unevenly. To a devoté who loves only one, nearly all pleasures seem promised; monogamy seeks to reconcile one and many, but two coincide in devotion only temporarily. "There was no end in those days to our pleasures," Catullus says, "when what you wished for was what she also wanted."[30] The paradoxical promise of monogamy is that so long as two are one in love, their pleasure is manifold, plural, unlimited. "Yes, there were days which shone with rare brightness." Rarity is a statistical term. As those days are plural, numerable, so this condition changes with the days that stretch beyond one's good fortune. A forsaken lover curses an inconstant beloved, but her heart has only moved on in time. "Now, she no longer wishes" (*nunc iam illa no uolt*).[31] That—a description, really—is all the explanation on offer. Roman toughness is in that firm bottom to Catullus' account of change. From denial of this fact come more words: either the lover asserts his constancy, or he assaults her moral character, as though that, not time, were the origin of his misery. Catullus acknowledges, unlike Wyatt, that he will love again, if only to survive, he implies, but not quite as he once loved her.

The standard lover's praise is that the beloved glows more brightly than all others. The blazon: her eyes . . . her lips . . . Of a male paragon the corresponding quality is devotion. Her beauty, his devotion.

> Nulla potest mulier tantum se dicere amatam
> Uere, quantum a me Lesbia amata mea est
> nulla fides ullo fuit umquam in foedere tanta,
> quanta in amore tuo ex parte reperta mea est.[32]

> No other woman can truthfully say she was cherished
> as much as Lesbia was when I was her lover.
> Never, in any such bond, was fidelity greater
> than mine, in my love for you, ever discovered.[33]

This implausible pose is traditional. Interestingly, the poem is saturated by comparison. Lesbia's qualities are compared to those of other women, and then she is said to enjoy an advantage not shared by them. Other comparisons are at work too. Boastful speech is compared with accurate representation: *dicere . . . uere*, to speak truly, becomes "verdict" in modern English. The idioms of litigation (as Peter Green's translation indicates) are implicitly compared to those of female speech.

> No woman can say she's truly been loved as much
> as my Lesbia has been loved by me: there's no
> guarantee so strong ever figured in any contract
> as that found, on my part, in my love for you.[34]

His devotion to her is compared as well to his devotion to other beloveds. The concept of incomparable love grows thinner with each comparison. Fidelity is a quality of behavior that admits of relative measurement. Have you been faithful, my dear? More than any of your other lovers has. More than I have been to any other lady. Catullus measures his claims carefully so that they might be tested empirically. Fidelity is not a metaphysical condition, but neither does the concept of plural lovers, of numbers, vacate that of fidelity.

Consider how devotion and plurality have more recently been reconciled in the Duke Ellington/Bob Russell collaboration "Do Nothing Till You Hear It from Me" (1940)—in particular its concessionary last two stanzas:

> True, I've been seen with someone new,
> But does that mean that I've been untrue?
> When we're apart,
> The words in my heart
> Reveal how I feel about you.

> Some kiss may cloud my memory,
> And other arms may hold a thrill,
> But please, do nothing till you hear it from me—
> And you never will.

This short poem moves past the contradictions confronted by Wyatt and Lowell. Frank thought is its beauty: the lover admits to roving. Devotion is nonetheless asserted without qualification—"And you never will." The first verses of the song are often dropped by performers. They refer to damaging gossip about the lover's apparent infidelity. But *how* the beloved learned of the lover's interest in someone new is insignificant. The problem is not to be resolved in social terms.[35] At first, one thinks that the lover is complaining of unjust accusations, but on the contrary he or she concedes having known another's arms. That leaves little room for denial. Yet the claim is to being true nonetheless. How does this lover explain infidelities? No effort is made to do so. Devotion is asserted as an enigma, specifically a matter of language retained—"the words in my heart"—not even of utterance. Petrarch insisted on his extraordinary chasteness: no part of his body touched any part of Laura's. Why should that claim be necessary to his version of devotion? Because it renders absolute the claim that sexuality and devotion are distinguishable. Devotion, on his account, has no bearing on physicality. Between language and action lies a gulf. Devotion is established through *words* not deeds. If the lover does not speak betrayal, none exists. What the beloved will never hear is renunciation. The lover will never deny his or her commitment to the beloved—no matter where the lover sleeps. The faith between them is no matter of lovemaking; it's a pledge. To what, then, does the lover adhere? To an *idea* of another. This is tantamount to making devotion a text, not a life. Petrarch had a daughter; for her and her mother, no poems.

My focus has been the under-songs of monogamous desire. Poets and songwriters have made critical instruments of these songs. And beyond criticism? At the end of the Introduction, I referred to a rift evident in Marvell's "Definition of Love" between intellectuality and experience. This song affirms a devotion not compromised by sexual acts. The lover conceives of devotion as willful and emotional, validated or invalidated only by avowals, and in that form devotion can survive corrosive experience and skeptical scrutiny. The commitment affirmed has no necessary sexual component. This song seems paradoxical to modern ears; it takes one back to Petrarch, or it projects a future in which a lover's devotion may be considered intact regardless of sexual activity. This, like Marvell's "Definition," presents an intellectual challenge. One normally thinks that commitment entails sexual fidelity and avowal. The point made here is that sexual fidelity without avowal does not constitute devotion, but avowal without sexual fidelity may constitute devotion. A lapse in fidelity does not always annul devotion, and many devoted lovers do not require sexual fidelity of one another. Avowal is the essential element of devotion; the lyric makes clear how strange and difficult devotion really is. However, in religious contexts, everyone is familiar with this distinction. One declares oneself Catholic, Protestant, Muslim, or Jew, though one's conduct routinely fails to conform to the precepts associated with one's avowal. One's conduct is only intermittently in conformity with one's declaration; nonetheless, one remains of a single faith. One pledges weekly not to renounce one's god, though life is a series of lapses. Faith is an element of aspiration. In romance, where the terms "faith," "devotion," and "vows" are borrowed, one commonly and naïvely expects conduct to mirror avowals. From the words themselves, one can learn.

2. Romance Is Mush

The grip of modernism relaxed in the late-1950s, when the Beats and then the Confessional poets recovered the pleasures of directly expressed feeling in poetry—warm feeling that a quarter-century earlier might have embarrassed Pound, Eliot, or Auden, say. But if one thinks broadly of poetry, including the popular song, one realizes that plain sentiment was enormously popular in the early-1940s and remained so through the next decade. Frank Sinatra was neither poet nor lyricist; he wrote lyrics to only two songs in his entire life. But from 1939 until 1994 he presented popular poetry to large numbers of listeners and television viewers. Like a rhapsode in ancient Greece, he became identified with a distinctive repertoire of songs. He was not a musical technician (he could not sight-read a score); he chose his songs on the basis of the words, not the tune. "I'll leave the music to somebody else," he said, "I pick the lyrics."[1] At the start of his career, his model was Bing Crosby, who was wrongly known as a crooner; Sinatra said that Crosby was instead a "troubadour. He tells a story in every song . . . He makes you feel like he's singing just for you. I bet I could do that."[2] It was Sinatra whose success effectively introduced, as Mel Tormé said, "a new era in popular music, a vocalist's era."[3] Before him, audiences came to hear the bands;

after him, they came to hear the singers. And the bands died.

His stardom began with a single performance, on December 31, 1942, at the Paramount theater in New York. He was added to a bill featuring the Benny Goodman band. When he came out on stage, the crowd let out a roar that stunned everyone, especially Benny Goodman, who said, "What the fuck was that?" With that performance, Sinatra became the biggest entertainer in the United States.[4] He had already left the Harry James band to join Tommy Dorsey in January 1940. James was a warm trumpeter who, according to Will Friedwald, taught Sinatra "not to be afraid of schmaltz."[5] Dorsey identified himself then as "The Sentimental Gentleman of Swing."[6] And, with The Voice, he recorded plainly sentimental tunes right from the start. "Polka Dots and Moonbeams," recorded in March 1940, is one the best of these early tunes. Dorsey and Sinatra had their first big hit with "I'll Never Smile Again," recorded by a small group from the band billed as "The Sentimentalists."[7] The word "sentiment" entered English from French in the twelfth century; the common verb *sentir* means to feel. Sentimental writers are commonly thought to be custodians of feelings. Which feelings? Familiar ones, "refined and tender" feelings, according to the *OED* (9, a). "Refined" is a surprising modifier. "A mental feeling, an emotion. Now chiefly applied . . . to those feelings which involve or are concerned with ideal objects" (*OED*, 7, a). Sentiments are known in relation to thinking; they are not thoughts, but they concern matters about which one might think as well as, or rather than, feel. The word itself helped to sell songs in the late 1930s and the 1940s.

But the literary culture was another matter. I. A. Richards said in 1929 that "among the politer terms of abuse there are few so effective as 'sentimental.'"[8] Intellectuals wanted no part of sentimental art. Following Eliot's effort in his essays of 1919 to urge English taste back to a standard established prior to the "sentimental age [that] began early in the eighteenth century," Richards, John Crowe Ransom, and Cleanth Brooks elaborated cognate critiques of sentimentality.[9] They argued that sentimentality simplifies the representation and interpretation of experience by stressing a single angle of vision—to the exclusion of others. As Brooks said, "The sentimentalist takes a short cut to intensity by removing all the elements of the experience which might conceivably militate against the intensity."[10] The sentimentalist constructs a thin representation of thought and experience. He had Popular Front poets in mind, and named Langston Hughes, Genevieve Taggard, and Don West in particular.[11]

The anti-sentimental critique was pitched against poets who tried to enlist their art in a struggle for social progress, and worse, against women poets in particular, as Ransom's blunt blast of Edna St. Vincent Millay reveals.[12] But the anti-sentimental critique drew justification from two vigorous and still-influential poetic principles expounded by Eliot. First is the anti-discursive idea that "permanent literature is always a presentation: either a presentation of thought, or a presentation of feeling by a statement of events in human action or objects in the external world. . . . The labor of the intellect consisted largely . . . in refraining from reflection, in putting into the statement enough to make reflection unnecessary."[13] An anti-sentimental or ironic poet is doubtful about the adequacy of reflective discourse. Second is the idea that great art encompasses deep heterogeneity. A poet's mind, according to Eliot, "is constantly amalgamating disparate experience; the ordinary man's experience is chaotic, irregular, fragmentary. The latter falls in love, or reads Spinoza, and the two experiences have nothing to do with each other, or with the noise of the typewriter or the smell of cooking; in the mind of the poet these experiences are always forming new wholes."[14] An ironic poet's subject includes disparities, and no single judgment consistently determines the poem's perspective. Ironic poets are heterodox in that they disagree even with themselves. Insofar as poets after Eliot represent experience in such detail that explicit interpretive reflection seems unnecessary to their purposes, encompass heterogeneous subject matter in their poems, and refrain as well from constructing a single angle of vision on their subjects, they have made their own the very objectives served by the anti-sentimental critique. Assessed by this measure, Eliot's influence has been far more extensive than poets realize. This chapter examines popular songs that bend sentiments.

When Sinatra began his career, Harry James, who first hired him, urged him to change his name, derived no doubt from *sinestro*, on the dark side, to Johnny Satin: he was so smooth. The direct, fluent expression of sensitivity: that was his art; struggle was never part of it. He started out with female fans and ended with males, as Pete Hamill observes.[15] How did that happen, and why? From the outset, young women went wild for him. Soon after he got started, young American men began to enlist and were inducted into the armed services. Other stars, like Clark Gable and James Stewart, went willingly to war, but not Sinatra; he had a punctured eardrum. (After the war he played a soldier in eleven films.)

> The male anger against Sinatra came to a head in October 1944, when he played the Paramount again and 30,000 mostly female fans erupted into a small

riot outside the theater. When a male dissenter in the Paramount balcony fired a tomato at the stage, he had to be rescued from women who were trying to beat him to death.[16]

William Manchester said that by the end of WWII Sinatra had become "the most hated man in the armed services."[17] And consider the competition! Sinatra recovered public authority after the war by performing the role of a soldier, in *From Here to Eternity* (1953), who is sacrificed. Sinatra had to die in the War, as Maggio, to make everything right again. He won an Academy Award for the part.

John Stuart Mill's paradox about lyric poetry has special bearing on the genre of sob-ballads: one *overhears* lyric, he said. But these songs are not only published, as poems routinely are, they are publicly and repeatedly performed before large audiences. Sinatra's sentimentality required a particular public display. He legitimated the expression of male tenderness, and a view of human nature, based on sentiment, that encouraged even hard-boiled types to display themselves as teary.[18] His social activities, widely reported in the press, were notorious: he kept the company of gangsters, and now and then engaged in fisticuffs in public, or had his bodyguards do so for him. He associated himself publicly with hypermasculinity, but on stage he was a strikingly tender, even slightly androgynous, lover, repeatedly forsaken by the ladies. His friend Noël Coward observed that he was "a remarkable personality— tough, vulnerable and somehow touching."[19] Another friend, Pete Hamill, developed the point:

> He could be tender and still be a tough guy . . . For men, whining or self- pity was not allowed; they were

forbidden by the male codes of the city. Sinatra slowly
found a way to allow tenderness into the performance
while remaining manly. When he finally took command of his own career, he perfected the role of the
Tender Tough Guy and passed it on to several generations of Americans. Before him, that archetype did not
exist in American popular culture. That is one reason
why he continues to matter; Frank Sinatra created a
new model for American masculinity.[20]

He has performed a vaguely feminine sort of persona on
stage, and in lyrics, but achieved remarkable success as an icon
of hypermasculinity; his grander aspiration being to propose
a model of sensibility that disregards gender and social distinction altogether. He challenged audiences to overlook the
psychic boundaries between men and women, the social ones
between black and white men, and the ethical ones between
law-abiding and law-evading entrepreneurs. Some features of
this challenge were drawn in the lyrics themselves, others in his
stage and television presentation with friends, still others in his
own social activities. It is conventional for singers to perform
the significance of the words they sing, to appear to live the
words of a song for the duration of a song. Sinatra went further than most other singers in presenting for consumption a
comprehensive image of his music. The covers of his albums
often represented him in the mood of the songs recorded. In
1942 he recorded the Jerome Kern/Oscar Hammerstein love
song "The Song Is You." The title seemed in retrospect to fit his
career. More than a half-century later the five-CD boxed set of
his recordings with the Tommy Dorsey band was released with
the same title. The following year, 1995, his best critic published the most extensive analysis of the music under the title

Sinatra! The Song is You. Sinatra did more than sing particular songs. He publicly represented the sentimental thematics of his music as a way of living. His aspiration to legitimate the social changes I have mentioned extended from vinyl recordings to televisions shows and concert stages, but it also included all his activities reported in the press, even his contact with politicians and mafiosi.

Of course, Sinatra was not the first to legitimate male weeping. Glenn Hendler tells of nineteenth-century temperance rallies at which great crowds of men gathered to weep. Sinatra's point is that human nature is universal, that no one is too tough for tears. The scandals about his infidelities, his friendship with Sam Giancana, and even the scuffles in restaurants—they all served to validate his sentimental art. His large point was that people are just people, that gender, class, and social distinctions (such as those between the legal and illegal economies) obscure our deep, reassuring sameness. This dream of universal manhood came apart spectacularly at the end of 1960, not because of the intransigence of racism or sexism, but because of the stigma of criminality. Anthony Summers explains that Sinatra served as a go-between from Giancana and associates to the presidential campaign of then-Senator John Kennedy. Giancana helped the Kennedy campaign win the elections in West Virginia and Illinois. When Robert Kennedy was appointed Attorney General, it was clear that the social distinction between licit and illicit businessmen was going to be strenuously enforced, not transcended, by the Kennedy administration. Sinatra was thought to have betrayed Giancana, and for a while he even feared for his life. The universality of sentimental art goes only so far.

American songwriters were evidently not indifferent

concerning sentimentality's corrupting effects, though they probably knew little of Ransom and Eliot. When Ransom accused sentimentalists of anti-intellectuality, he saw what some songwriters saw too. The more compelling sob-ballads are often explicitly framed as instructions.[21] Think of the tunes that propose something to be learned from the story of the gal that got away. Johnny Mercer's "One for My Baby" (1943), for instance, is set in a saloon. "So, set 'em up, Joe, / I've got a little story you ought to know." Why should Joe even hear, let alone know, one more story of forsaken love? Mercer imagines the song as a lesson, not just an expression; someone has to hear it, and benefit from the hearing. Philip Fisher says that compassion is the object of sentimental narrative.[22] But these sob-ballads suggest that compassion is not the end; enlightenment is the real objective. Just what can one learn from pain? From a sentimental point of view: that human life follows set patterns; that my romance resembles yours. As Fred Kaplan observes, "Dickens believed that there was an instinctive, irrepressible need for human beings to affirm both in private and in public that they possessed moral sentiments, that these sentiments were innate, that they best expressed themselves through spontaneous feelings, and that sentimentality in life and in art had a moral basis."[23] Mercer's song is ultimately ambiguous concerning the value of the lover's story. The "ought" in the lines I cited suggests that sentimental narrative has the didactic value that Kaplan describes, but Mercer presents this story oddly. He notes that a bartender is professionally obligated to listen and to maintain confidentiality ("to be true to your code"): Joe is a paid listener. What Mercer does not suggest is that the lover enlightened the bartender. "I hope you didn't mind my bending your ear," the lover says, as though the story may have had no value for the listener. More important, though, the story is not told in the song. "Well, that's how it goes," the lover enigmatically says, as though he has at this point completed his story; whereas in fact he has said nothing at all about his romance. A poet truly confident of the universal value of sentiment would provide the gist of the lover's experience, especially after such a build-up; Dickens or Hardy would have delivered what had been promised. Mercer prefers to pretend that he has told the tale. His subject is neither the lover's experience nor the enlightenment of others, but just the desire to speak to others. This lover needs to share words, though his only listener is a mute pro. Mercer presents a late moment in the decline of confidence in universal sentiments; his song is a shell where conviction once lived.

Sob-ballads begin in adversity; their first appeal is the performance of active, articulate melancholy, something more common in art than in life. It is certainly true that many great poems, whatever their actual sources, seem to derive from romantic melancholy. Heartbreak is a subject for all time, and the effort to recover sentiment is a recurrent impulse of literary culture.[24] "The Lord is with the broken-hearted," according to Psalm 34, and the poets are too. My subject is the recovery of sentiment in the popular song after Cole Porter, but also the apprehension concerning the limits of sentimentality, even among popular songwriters. Matthew Arnold warned that no poetical enjoyment can be derived from the representation of prolonged mental distress, a state in which "everything is to be endured, nothing to be done"; Yeats agreed with him.[25] The tin pan alley poets seem to have agreed as well. The great sob-ballads actually propose that one learn from loss, however hard that is to do. Ransom argued notoriously that sentimental poetry is relatively indifferent to intellectual matters.[26] The sob-ballads that interest me demonstrate, to the contrary, efforts to *think* one's way out of melancholy. Consider Ira Gershwin's lyric, "Someone to Watch over Me" (1926).

> There's a somebody I'm longing to see:
>
> I hope that she
> turns out to be
> Someone who'll watch over me.
> I'm a little lamb who's lost in a wood;   5
> I know I could
> always be good
> To one who'll watch over me.
> Although I may not be the man some
> Girls think of as handsome,   10
> To her heart I'll carry the key.
> Won't you tell her, please, to put on some speed,
> Follow my lead?
> Oh, how I need
>
> Someone to watch over me.[27]

Like many, many others, this song has Sinatra boldly expressing male tenderness: "Oh, how I need." The arrangement is especially saccharine from the opening notes on the celestina through the Viennese-style violin serenade before the last verses. Need and longing are repeatedly asserted, without embarrassment, in any number of his songs.

Yet what he longs for is subtle: a parental beloved to supervise him, but why? The second stanza is especially revealing. How does a man, in public, sing the effete line, "I'm a little lamb who's lost in a wood"? (Gershwin wrote the line for Gertrude Lawrence to perform in the musical. *Oh, Kay!*

[1926]; Sinatra might have revised it, as someone did lines nine through twelve, for gender conformity, but he preferred not to do so. He *wanted* the strangeness of a man likening himself to a little lamb.) Back to my question: how perform these lines? There's always just naïveté, but there is the more productive possibility of ironic, sophisticated role-playing: despite appearances, I'm a little lamb, and so on. Or more explicitly, I am not, as it appears, a wolf; instead I am a little lamb. Hastily one attributes the song to a neglected, forsaken lover who now yearns for attention. But instead, with a male voice, it expresses the situation of a chastised lover, one who has been caught not being good—the Wolf Exposed.[28] (Of a man singing as a lamb, one asks: if you are the lamb, who is the wolf?) A lamb might say that he is good to everyone. Instead Sinatra claims only that, given the right sort of partner, he "could always be good" *to her*, exactly because his goodness has come into question. The word "always" entails its contrary: the category of an exception, which may be how a chastised lover would designate an exposed violation of trust. That is, behind what the lyric says is an implicit narrative of betrayal and exposure. Overcome him with . . . not love, but supervision, and he will be a little lamb; he only appeared to be a wolf because his last lover neglected him. He has learned from loss that he needs a mother-lover. Or at least it's advisable to say so to the next woman. Sinatra's persona is obviously tender, apparently sweet, but also calculating, and resistant to the more difficult changes that self-knowledge might propose. The singer of this tune is less forlorn than self-reckoning, justifying. He is a proud lover, accustomed to such attention. Pride stabilizes.

The theme of Harold Arlen and Ira Gershwin's "The Gal that Got Away" (1953) is the education of the proud, and not, as it appears, mere forlornness. Nelson Riddle's arrangement

is forceful, driving, even melodramatic: it sets off with a blast
of horns. The same punctuating phrase—an aggressive, stagey
throb—returns after lines eight, twenty-eight, and at the end.
It's a relentless effect: the road is set, and the lover is pulled
along without ambiguity. Yet there is an oscillation between
two ostensible thematic poles, figured first in the emblematic frieze of the first three lines and the distinctive narrative that enters with a reference to the lover's age (as, later,
between the first- and second-person address). The lover is too
old for romantic failure. The emblematic landscape returns
as the "road" gets rougher, with each romantic failure (l. 23).
The beloved pursued and won the lover; she used to call him
eagerly. Now, so far as the singer understands, she has simply,
enigmatically run off. Or is that just how the lover understands
her? The singer dismisses any significance to the lover's experience of this "crazy game." No sense is to be had. The lover is
simply brought low, and then lower, a proud man reduced to
calling in the empty dark. This is "The Gal That Got Away"
(possibly in the sense of "escaped"), but it could be "The Guy
Who Doesn't Get It." Neither singer nor lover has a glimmer
about sustaining a relationship.

> The night is bitter.
> The stars have lost their glitter;
> The winds grow colder
> And suddenly you're older—
> And all because of the gal that got away.   5
> No more her eager call,
> The writing's on the wall;
> The dreams you dreamed have all
> gone astray.

The gal that won you   10
Has run off and undone you,
That great beginning
has seen the final inning.
Don't know what happened. It's all a crazy game.
No more that all-time thrill,   15
For you've been through the mill—
And never a new love will
be the same.
Good riddance, good-bye!
Ev'ry trick of hers you're on to.   20
But, fools will be fools
And where's she gone to?
The road gets rougher.
It's lonelier and tougher.
With hope you burn up—   25
Tomorrow she may turn up.
There's just no let-up the livelong night and day.
Ever since this world began
There is nothing sadder than
A lost, lost loser looking for   30
the gal that got away . . .

Please come back.
Won't you come back?
The gal that got away.[29]

    The singer's point of view is meant to seem transcendent. One understands his second-person self-address as a lover's effort to rise above personal suffering to the viewpoint of one who might use, say, the French third person *on* to express generality. He characterizes the forsaken lover so knowingly that he can foresee the future: "never a new love will be the same" (ll. 17-18). This is a special moment in Riddle's arrangement and in Gershwin's lyric. Riddle establishes a conclusion here, mid-song, by shifting to a slower tempo for lines nineteen through twenty-two. Lines seventeen and eighteen are also the most confident of the poem. The syntax is oddly inverted and remote from speech, but it is a variation on the structure of lines six and fifteen: lines seventeen and eighteen conclude a grammatical set of three with a prediction of what can never recur: romantic enthusiasm. In these two dramatic lines, the singer has his maximal authority, and the poem pauses.

The singer means to be a knower, like the singer of "In the Wee Small Hours," not a forsaken lover, but he wobbles repeatedly; these are the major terms of the oscillation I mentioned. A transcendent point of view should not be hampered by a forsaken lover's ignorance, but it is: "Don't know what happened; it's all a crazy game" (l. 14). This sounds like a line not for a knowing singer but for a benighted, forsaken lover, though there is no marker of such a shift. Two lines later the singer must be the source of the line "For you've been through the mill."[30] The conventionality of the figure itself transcends any one lover's experience; this voice rises to proverbial understanding, but that level cannot be held. The singer, in his impersonal mode, actually knows no more than the lover; there is nothing to be had beyond plaintive, passive suffering. The singer narrates a familiar story, but without distinctive comprehension, and this, for him, is an intellectual failure. The oscillation between first- and second-person address expresses a desire, failed in the end, to get beyond the prolonged mental distress of which Arnold warned. The lover cannot retain an impersonal viewpoint, though he tries repeatedly. The transition from an uncomprehending, forsaken lover to a knowing explainer is what lovers, especially mature ones, should want to master. Without that mastery, there is only the deterministic drive of Riddle's arrangement—into the night, as Sinatra fans like to say.

Song lyrics have been written with full awareness of exactly the hazards of sentimentality that Eliot, Richards, Ransom, and Brooks described. These songs appeal to sentiment, but with stories about learning lessons from loss: they have an intellectual objective. Ransom thought that sentimental poetry tends toward abstraction, by selecting from the rich texture of experience only those elements that suit a single view. But the songs I am discussing are thick with complicating narrative. The third quatrain of Bob Hilliard's iambic pentameter lyric, "In the Wee Small Hours of the Morning" (1955), draws one to the view that feelings are governed by thoughts and ideas, that a life of feeling best answers to the needs of the mind, that familiar sentiment alone is insufficient to romance and to art.

> When your lonely heart has learned its lesson,
> You'd be hers if only she would call.
> In the wee small hours of the morning,
> That's the time you miss her most of all.[31]

The phrase "you'd be hers" suggests that her desire for him has already been established; she wanted him in some contractual way, as a suitor for his hand might. He's ready to accede to her wish, now that "his lonely heart has learned its lesson." (And he waits for her call, as a woman conventionally waits for a man's call.) The lesson learned? He did something that drove her away, though she had been asking for more. He has learned not to take her for granted. He is chastened. The song is uttered in a stable second-person address, it is far from a sentimental moan.

The correction of lovers is a recurrent feature of the great sob-ballads. In 1947 Sinatra recorded a medley of "The Gal that Got Away" (originally "The Man that Got Away," performed memorably by Judy Garland) and "It Never Entered My Mind." This last tune, extraordinary by any measure, is a revealing instance of a sob-ballad about a lesson learned.[32] Rather than discuss Sinatra's performance of the tune, I prefer to consider Sarah Vaughan's unbeatable version. But I want also to make the point that there is no necessary gender-orientation to the recovery of sentimentality. Male sentimentality makes better stage action because it resists a stereotype of masculine restraint. The real point, though, is the public expression of warm feeling, by men or women, which is why these songs often represent scenes of public statement—as at a bar.

Sinatra is the Wordsworth of popular song. As in poetry, so in song: the convention of sincerity is closely bound to the imitation of speech. He would not work without a proper microphone, a black one that would not be much noticed against his dinner jacket. A good microphone enables you, he said, to "sing as if you're singing in someone's ear, you can talk to a buddy at the bar, you can whisper sweet nothings to a woman."[33] His objective was to depart only inconspicuously from intimate speech. His enunciation is especially clear and careful, so that he can always be easily understood. He learned from Tommy Dorsey to sing in long breaths, without an audible pause for breath within a sentence. He used to swim underwater to enhance his lung capacity. One should think that he really means what he says; Bob Dylan referred to "the truth of things in his voice."[34] Consider Sinatra's 1945 version of Eric Maschwitz's "These Foolish Things." He sings at a very slow tempo and without much volume, as though he meant to conceal altogether his effort to perform. Almost speech, from his mouth to your ear.

Sinatra's is an anti-theatrical style that remained effective for decades after this recording. But in the early 1950s he lost young audiences, and he was bitter about it (rock n' roll, in 1957, was "the most brutal, ugly, degenerate, vicious form of expression it has been my displeasure to hear").[35] Clyde McPhatter also performed "These Foolish Things," in 1953, at his last recording date with Billy Ward and the Dominoes; then he left Ward and founded the Drifters. Speech was one prominent coordinate of the doo-wop style, as one hears at the start; spoken monologues were a staple, but so too were the screams, the *oohs* and *ahs* (here: the bass moans following lines one, four, nine, seventeen, and twenty-two). This is body music, beyond social conventions. An appearance of sincerity and sentiment survived in the doo-wop style, but as theatrical pretense, or camp.

> Darling, you've gone and left me.
> And now all I have left are memories,
> Memories like
>
> A cigarette that bears a lipstick's traces,
> An airline ticket to romantic places,   5
> And still my heart has wings.
> These foolish things
> Remind me of you.
> A tinkling piano in the next, next apartment,
> Those stumbling words that told you what my
>   heart meant,   10
> A fairground's painted swings,
> These foolish things
> Remind me of you.
> You came, you saw, you conquered me;
> When you did that to me,   15

I knew somehow this had to be.
The winds of March that make my heart a dancer,
A telephone that rings, but who's to answer?
Oh, how the ghost of you clings!
These foolish things   20
Remind me of you.

Now, Darling, you know how much I've missed you,
And how much I long for the day that you return,
Return to my arms.
But until that day: 25

Oh, how the ghost of you clings!
These foolish things
Reminds me of you.[36]

Sentimental songs often project sensibility onto landscape; this is Maschwitz' single trope. A sentimental poet overwhelms an external scene. Paul Fussell spoke of this as "poetic indulgence of more emotion (often self-regarding) than seems warranted by the stimulus."[37] After three lines of frame-monologue (lines not written by Eric Maschwitz), Clyde McPhatter reaches his ecstatic manner in contemplation of a cigarette butt. There is a less censorious way than Fussell's to think about this. The immoderate coloring of a sentimental scene expresses a great wish to affect things, to make a world. That is, sentimental poetry begins less in grief or romantic ardor than in estrangement from material circumstances, or some version of poverty. There's a sense in which sob-ballads express enormous pleasure: the world of objects comes alive for the forsaken lover who, while bemoaning absence, celebrates the presence of a felt world. These objects tell a story only because the beloved is gone. Until he or she left, they were trivial, or inert, there for use. But a lonely lover reads them as relics of a lost presence. They have no utility for a forsaken one beyond their signification; they are immaterial. The forsaken lover has been transformed, made a visionary, just by abandonment: he or she lives in an incarnational world where objects radiate significance. Listen to the end of McPhatter's "These Foolish Things." When the Dominoes chime through a scale, they take credit for something grand that no one would wish to change. After saying three times "remind me of you," at the end McPhatter inserts a dialect touch: "reminds me of you." At this point he can claim this standard as a black achievement, a moment of proud possession. He assures the beloved that he awaits her return (ll. 22-24) in a speech that is obvious hokum (also these lines were not written by Maschwitz). The interesting revelation is that the possible return of the beloved is a potential embarrassment to the forsaken lover. What the lover really wants can be heard in McPhatter's voice: the glorious consolation of art celebrating a religious sense of the material world.[38]

"I knew somehow this had to be," he says. An eager lover wants not happy circumstance, but a determined life. He had to be the lover, and now he has to be forsaken—"somehow." The determinative force is only incidentally his faithless beloved. The real cause is mysterious, grand, and holy. All is in its place, even the beloved belongs somewhere else, so that this music can ascend like a host. "Still," he says, "my heart has wings." One recognizes the gospel choral backing of doo-wop arrangements, but it is nonetheless stunning that McPhatter has transformed this sob-ballad into a hymn. He has gone to another level in the effort to learn from loss. He understood that the making of art is the thing. The beloved is needed, for *sacrifice*: she must be lost, like Poe's dead girl, so that the spirit may climb higher. Sentimental song craves a sacrament. The song is more ritual than report. No need to say anything particular about the beloved. This is the key to sentimentality: it leaves the thickness of contingency for a set of abstract concerns aimed at release, transcendence, transformation—affirmation of the spirit.

A final point: Sinatra's sentimental manner was recognized in the late-1930s as an alternative to secular sophistication. Cole Porter had mastered an urbane style, but earlier, in 1925, he had said that he wished he could write sobs.[39] He is known instead for a witty, cosmopolitan, brittle manner (revived decades later by James Merrill, Turner Cassity, and others). Philip Furia argues that for all Porter's aplomb, he could not manage warm, romantic art of the sort that made Oscar Hammerstein's career. "When he abandoned the list," Furia says, Porter "frequently slipped into sentimentality."[40] This stylistic contest bears directly on gender. Sinatra stresses the femininity of sentiment in Hammerstein's "Someone to Watch over Me." "A Fine Romance" is a song of failing, not failed, love, sung by a woman with a will of her own and a range of worldly interests. Dorothy Fields (1904-1974) wrote it as a poem before Jerome Kern had a melody: alternating quatrains and cinquains.[41] Thirty-six lines for the new year of 1936; form affirms—and lightens. Both songs push, from different directions, against gender proscriptions, and each needs a particular style to do so. The speaker is annoyed by her partner's indifference, but not despondent, and she is more than content in her moment and milieu.

> A fine romance! With no quarrels!
> With no insults, and all morals!   15

I've never mussed the crease in your blue serge pants,
I never get the chance.
This is a fine romance.

A fine romance, with no kisses!
A fine romance, my friend, this is!   20
We should be like clams in a dish of chowder;
But we just "fizz" like parts of a Seidlitz powder.

A fine romance, with no clinches!
A fine romance, with no pinches!
You're just as hard to land as the "Ile de France,"   25
I haven't got a chance,
This is a fine romance![42]

The lyricist Sheldon Harnick praised Fields' "unusual sense of selectivity."[43] This feature of craft counted for a lot among her contemporaries. The heterogeneous terms evoke a sensibility admirably mobile in face of social distinctions. Ocean liners were for one setting, Seidlitz powders (drugstore laxatives) for another. After Cole Porter, the urbane style seemed to belong to the "upper sets." But here is a less classed freedom from inhibition, sexual and social, in an outspoken woman. She registers distinctions and judgments but does not inquire into the cause of her partner's coolness, because she is pragmatic and means to enjoy, not explain, her life. She confirms widely avowed American values: opportunity and liberty. Hers is a complaint of a libidinous woman who wants intimacy, but this ample style suggests that a particularly inclusive perspective goes with her erotic desire. That is, she knows the world is full.

Songs should seem simple to make an impact right away. And love songs are supposed to appeal to warm sentiments;

hence the term of art "sob-songs." Familiar sentiment provides reliable allure for a love song: the pathos of forlorn lovers. The success of sobs reminds poets that boldly expressed feelings attract a crowd. Cole Porter amuses, impresses, and encourages listeners; all good things, but the emotionality and simplicity of sobs are a coveted resource. Poets and lyricists enjoy various kinds of success, but when they touch hearts they appeal to a gold standard. Pope is a great poet, but not because he touches the hearts of many. Herbert, Wordsworth, Dickinson, and Eliot do better in this way, which directly affects literary judgments. One understands why many critics consider Bishop's "One Art" her greatest poem. The pain of losing, as Poe said, is essential to romantic art.

This nexus of simplicity and sentiment accounts for the common understanding of love songs as affecting but minor. Sinatra understood this, as most lyricists do too. His innovation was to complicate the character of the lover. "Simple" means guileless (*OED*, I), not composite, of one substance (*OED*, II). Sincere, yes, certainly; but guileless, no. That, he is not. Of one substance? Nor that. He mixed genders to claim range: the sentiments conventionally associated with femininity; the corresponding toughness and solitariness gendered male. He performed love songs of a mixed character: melancholy. The songs affect the sentiments without being of one substance. He found ways to get more than expected out of a ballad. That is a jongleur's ambition. Of Clyde McPhatter the same should be said. The stories of these ballads are not entirely what they may first appear. Once one unravels their details, "sentimental" is not an apt term. The jongleurs are concerned about control; their pleas manipulative. The words "kinky" and "cunning" come to mind.

The best sob-writers sought enlightenment in pain. Loving,

losing, then thinking. Even sob-ballads may pull in two directions, and are thus ironic in that sense. The popular song made an effective peace with sentimentality by absorbing other feelings. David Lehman speaks well of doubled love song as "Jewish lyric," a song written "against the grain of [its] assertions."[44] Songwriters, without apparent awareness of the controversies among literary intellectuals, worried about sentimental writing in the ways that modernist critics had warned of. Eliot, Richards, Ransom, and Brooks had clear eyes on this issue. These lyricists sought correlatives, in Eliot's terms—some narrative context behind their words. Ballads relate or imply a narrative. Sinatra admired Crosby, remember, as a troubadour who "tells a story in every song." Those correlatives are often ill-proportioned to the emotions expressed, even in the great songs. Yet disproportion has some legitimate uses. Sentimental song moves easily toward religious ecstasy exactly because all that is material does not measure up to the imaginable grandeur of the unseen. There is a point at which what one draws from loss is not judicious inference from human events but religious affirmation. Some great sob-ballads propose adjustment to the facts of life, but the genre evolved toward McPhatter's ecstatic refusal of justness or realism of any sort. There is a hymn inside the sob-ballad.

3. No Love, No Life

Like a blow from behind, heartbreak, and long pain. Thought and analysis come too, if only in the form of blame. Was it that thing in me, or her, or him? This is a primitive form of self-scrutiny. Love songs constantly measure: her beauty, his devotion, its depth and duration. Songs of abandonment measure loss and wrongdoing, injustice, inequity. They moralize and often end harshly. But, eventually, one wants whatever peace can realistically follow heartbreak. Love begins with sudden joy and change. One wants to be all in, with abandon, as in to enter a dominion. When love goes, one is alone with oneself, inert, not as one might be: suddenly an exile, as if one had crossed a boundary, surprised to hear strange words spoken. True abandonment is the end of a series: the loss, not of one more lover, but of love itself. Those songs are rarer, darker, and more thoughtful than sob-ballads. Their topic: an irrevocably altered life. Resilience, the alternative, is shameful, unworthy. Why? That is the focus of this chapter.

First, then, blame. Forsaken lovers curse faithless beloveds. Understandable, and ancient: Archilochus, Catullus. Dryden took the voice of a forsaken woman in "Farewell, Ungrateful Traitor" who rails, as she puts it, not that her faithless beloved did not marry her, but that he left in a hurry. Men lose interest after the conquest. Her reproach is based entirely on common-places, without suggestion of individual experience or feeling. It shows only what needs no explanation. Blame is the under-side of devotion. A forsaken lover transforms him- or herself from an object of pity to an aggrieved party seeking dam-ages. These lovers refuse to be ashamed, pitied for their failure. In an art-court, they sue for justice. For Provençal poets and then their Tuscan interpreters, justice was irrelevant. Lover and beloved alike were vassals of the Lord of Love, without agency or responsibility. Like ancient Greeks, they were serious about erotic possession. Wyatt's sense of justice (later Robert Lowell's too) derives from the alternative idea that lover and beloved are civil agents, not vassals, with a capacity, if not always a will, to deal fairly with one another.

Wyatt is the acknowledged master of reproach, of returning in words to close proximity—in-fighting. A sense of fettered utterance intensifies the feelings expressed. He will not or dares not reproach the former beloved altogether expressly. Political prudence or a sense of his own dignity prevents him from saying all that might be said. In lines one through ten he uses the third-person plural as if describing multiple beloveds who came to his room; no one in particular. In line 11, after this gradual approach, he drops the plural reference for a third-person singular. She who spoke boldly to him can now be des-ignated only in figure. The beauty of the poem is that he says much and gives one to believe that he is nonetheless exercising restraint. As his first three sentences gather clauses, overriding proprieties, he gradually exposes her more fully (ll. 1-14).

> They flee from me that sometime did me seek
> With naked foot stalking in my chamber.
> I have seen them gentle, tame, and meek

That now are wild and do not remember
That sometime they put themself in danger   5
To take bread at my hand; and now they range
Busily seeking with a continual change.

Thanked be fortune, it hath been otherwise
Twenty times better, but once in special,
In thin array after a pleasant guise,   10
When her loose gown from her shoulders did fall
And she me caught in her arms long and small,
Therewithal sweetly did me kiss
And softly said, 'Dear heart, how like you this?'

It was no dream: I lay broad waking.   15
But all is turned thorough my gentleness
Into a strange fashion of forsaking.
And I have leave to go of her goodness
And she also to use newfangleness.
But since that I so kindly am served   20
I would fain know what she hath deserved.[1]

However constrained, his language is specific—and thereby convincing. No question, he was there.[2] But it is inexact to speak of his expression as constrained. Constraints present occasions for inventiveness. The sonic structure of the first stanza makes evident that he can express just what he wishes within the constraints of his seven-line rhymed stanzas of iambic pentameter. The rhyme scheme is ABABBCC. In this stanza, however, the third B-rhyme ("danger") is just off the first two ("chamber," "remember"), and at the same time it is a C-rhyme ("*danger*," "range," "change"). Danger, he can handle variously, the rhyme suggests—can she? She has gone wild, he says in line four. He makes that line stand alone by saying less than expected. (The mind easily imagines a wild beloved more aggressive than "do not remember" indicates.) This is a subtle technique, but its effect is felt. There is a vowel-music in lines one to three and five to seven on long-ē and long-ā. But line four has no instance of either. In terms of this music, it's an anomaly, or wild line. I have said nothing of Wyatt's display of liberty in torsions of his iambic pentameter lines. The first line is regular, the second and many after that are irregular. He frequently exploits the play of trochaic words against the iambic meter, putting stresses side by side, like spondees, and loosening his pace with unstressed syllables next to each other. The instances of prosodic surprise are too numerous in this one stanza to track here. With constraints, he toys.

From a serial approach to romance, no progress is envisaged. One affair is more or less like another, none inherently better or worse. But Wyatt is a moralist for whom people have not only experiences but deserts. He criticizes his beloved for her "continual change" (l. 7), whereas Yeats prided himself on his ability to love Maud Gonne's "changing face." Wyatt's beloved fails to remember, he says, how she had trusted him. His lines question fit, how her recent treatment of him corresponds to their past. Responsive lovers match one another. A concept of balance or justice is implicit. (A lover's reproach of the beloved's inconsistency is traditional, but usually uttered by a ruined maid on behalf of all womankind, as in Dryden's "Farewell Ungrateful Traitor.") Wyatt's fondest memory of his beloved is when she kissed him and asked, "how like you this?" Or, does this suit you, does my kiss meet your expectation, your pleasure? She asks him to measure his pleasure. He narrates the "once," presumably their first intimacy, and refers to "twenty times," without saying explicitly that they slept

together repeatedly, only that she initiated their first encounter. He does not name her; she is a hind in "Whoso List to
Hunt" and perhaps also in stanza 1 of "They Flee from Me."
He withholds her name, with the innuendo that he might
have retaliated with exposure. The plural pronoun in the first
stanza displays a gloved hand: ten lines boast of forbearance.
Wyatt regards the beloved's inconstancy as deliberate duplicity, masked by euphemisms. She is inconstant in this case; her
nature does not require duplicity. A worse curse would malign
her nature, not just her acts. In the first and second stanzas
he contrasts nakedness and drapery. In the third he objects to
her effort to present her release of him as an act of "goodness."
His own doubled language keeps in view his contempt for
disguises. He offends her, but only to a certain point—partly
because she is powerful. He waits for justice to prevail.

Justice requires impersonality, whereas blame issues invec-
tive. "They Flee from Me," despite its reticence, is specific and
personal. "Patience, Though I Have Not" is a charm recited by
the lover to himself, against his own appetite for vengeance. He
proudly maintains continuity with the past, while his beloved
is blown about by fortune. Unlike a ruined maid, the male
lover claims no cost to his reputation. He complains instead
that the beloved has betrayed not just him but common concepts of reciprocity and good faith. Her offense is metaphysical. "Patience, Though I Have Not" is focused entirely on
himself. Of her character, nearly nothing is said; a cipher.

> Patience, though I have not
> The thing that I require!
> I must of force, God wot,
> Forbear my most desire
> For no ways can I find   5

To sail against the wind.
Patience, do what they will
To work me woe or spite!
I shall content me still
To think both day and night,   10
To think and hold my peace,
Since there is no redress.

Patience, withouten blame,
For I offended naught!
I know they know the same   15
Though they have changed their thought.
Was ever thought so moved
To hate that it hath loved?

Patience of all my harm
For Fortune is my foe!   20
Patience must be the charm
To heal me of my woe.
Patience without offence
Is a painful patience.[3]

The initial circumlocution, "the thing that I require" (l. 2), may refer to his beloved's attention: a conventional lover's plea for pity. More likely, though, he refers to justice. Patience is a strategical resource, an instrument for healing, not an inherent virtue. Wyatt writes from within an ongoing game. He is not done yet. That is the emotional vigor of his poems. Redress (l. 12), blame (l. 13), offence (l. 23) are terms more for a court-room than a bedroom. The implication is that the affairs of lovers are governed, not random.

Patience is reasonable insofar as the future is predictable.

He pledges to remain rational day and night, on the assumption that reason is a sound guide to romance (l. 10). Patience is not peace: a patient lover does not merely reconcile himself to rejection, he waits for something—for justice or a turn of fortune. Wyatt gives no suggestion that he waits for love. He sees himself beset by plural adversaries (l. 7)—overpowered and outnumbered. His engagement must therefore remain nearly private and intellectual; he consoles himself with freedom of thought (ll. 10-11), not of action. The injustice done to him, on his own representation, was not necessarily abandonment. This is the ambiguity that the third-person plural permits: did he lose the political favor of some others or of just one who is better not more closely identified: "they have changed their thought" (l. 16)? (He may have in mind the loose sense of the third-person plural pronoun that is commonly advocated now.) This language makes it difficult to distinguish sharply between romantic and political adversity. Fortune, who traditionally governs worldly matters, has turned on him (l. 20). His only power is to write of his adversity in this abstract, hedging manner—and to wait.

Remembrance is owed to values insufficiently honored—not only to the wounded. "Patience," he repeats at the outset of each of four stanzas, but in the fourth he says it four times in six lines. This is his charm: to repeat his need, in hope that he can hold on to some little patience. The last line is uttered through clenched teeth. Sophisticated lovers accept changes and move on to new romance. Moralists stick on the wound. Their poems aspire to intense economy, as if to honor the site of injury. Wyatt's verse, especially in the fourth stanza, is insistently regular iambic trimeter. There is nothing like the sonic variety of "They Flee from Me." As the representation of the experience of romance recedes in favor of metaphysical norms, the verse itself becomes relentless. The poem tends inevitably

toward tight, unqualified expression—words for the stonecut-
ters, manly complaint.

I said at the outset of this chapter that analysis begins when
blame no longer satisfies. I had in mind a turn (after blam-
ing a faithless beloved) toward oneself. Wyatt goes very far in
reproach of his beloved without imagining his own failures.
There is another phase of understanding—beyond blame—at
which only a few poems arrive. With it comes some peace,
though no joy. When self-understanding is represented as
arriving quickly, poems seem schematic, insufficiently steeped
in loss.[4] This is an issue in Wyatt's "Patience," and more obviously in Gascoigne's "And If I Did, What Then," which is certainly not about the agony of abandonment, though it begins
apparently just after the speaker has accused his beloved of
"new fangleness," or taking another lover. Wyatt reproaches
his beloved for a lack of candor and steadfastness. But is it
reasonable or naïve to expect such candor from a beloved? Is
that what lovers require? Not right away: his beloved stuns him
with a ready admission of infidelity. He goes right to the point
without citing his accusation; she dispenses with intrigue and
deception and addresses herself directly to his understanding—
forget about his feelings: sudden candor.

> "And if I did, what then?
> Are you aggrieved therefore?
> The sea hath fish for every man,
> And what would you have more?"

> Thus did my mistress once
> Amaze my mind with doubt,
> And popped a question for the nonce
> To beat my brains about.

Whereto I thus replied:
"Each fisherman can wish
That all the sea at every tide
Were his alone to fish.

And so did I, in vain;
But since it may not be,
Let such fish there as find the gain,
And leave the loss for me.

And with such luck and loss
I will content myself.
Till tides of turning time may toss
Such fishers on the shelf.

And when they stick on sands,
That every man may see,
Then will I laugh and clap my hands,
As they do now at me."[5]

Her question challenges him, without breaking his heart. His adjustment is intellectual. He is an atheist at the temple of love who will take candor, utility, logic, and arithmetic in place of patter of consistency and devotion. Gladly will he satisfy himself with what others leave behind—the greater part. When they find themselves depleted, revenge will be his. That resilience, and its basis is clear thinking.

This low-down poem gains force from its easy manner. The apparently effortless syntax conforms to the simple prosodic structure of these quatrains (trimeter, trimeter, tetrameter, trimeter, set to alternating rhyme). It could be sung. Concision is the central resource of lyric poetry. One feels the pressure of economy in the beloved's initial directness: she avoids complications by self-confidently conceding infidelities. In a quick four quatrains, he offers intelligence, enlightenment—never mind the raunchy innuendo about women and fish. Gascoigne devotes one stanza, the second, to saying that her bluntness confused him, then immediately follows his formulation of policy in stanzas three and four. This form suggests that with candor and intelligence life can be simpler than lovers' credos customarily propose. Only in the last stanza is one given to realize that the speaker has struggled with shame, and that male rivalry and humiliation are easily disguised as romantic agony. One might have realized sooner that heartache was not his problem. He is a cool customer. The trick to sustaining a relationship is to lower the temperature to a point where actual experience is sustainable. Love is an intellectual and sexual matter for him, not a sentimental one. This is comic verse, not an essay, yet it is uttered in a voice heard—however often in blues lyrics—only rarely in love poetry, because sophistication is chilly.

All forsaken love poems—sobs included—are character studies. They exhibit persons paying with pain for intimacy. Losing is ordinary, common; lowered expectations anaesthetize. The grandest expectation is fidelity, only because infidelity is indissociable from abandonment. How lovers find resilience is of interest to everyone. In political philosophy the displacement of vengeance by impersonal justice is recognized as a great step in social progress—the rule of law—but not in poetry. Wyatt's greatest poem is his most vengeful. In "They Flee from Me" one hears a larger voice—a fuller humanity—than in "Patience." Songs of abandonment show lovers more deeply injured than even they realize. Forsaken lovers pushed to the periphery may expect that the cycle will start up again. This is a source of dramatic pathos, when listeners are

given to think that the situation is worse still. Think of Billy
Strayhorn's saloon-song "Lush Life," uttered by a weak-willed
lover—wounded, but not definitively abandoned. When love
leaves forever, that's real abandonment. The speaker doesn't
imagine another love entering the bar, but he does think that
he has time left on his clock.

> I used to visit all the very gay places,
> Those come-what-may places,
> Where one relaxes on the axis
> Of the wheel of life
> To get the feel of life   5
> From jazz and cocktails.
>
> The girls I knew had sad and sullen gray faces,
> With distingué traces
> That used to be there, you could see where
> They'd been washed away   10
> By too many through the day
> Twelve o'clock tails.
>
> Then you came along with your siren song
> To tempt me to madness.
> I thought for a while that your poignant smile   15
> Was tinged with the sadness of a great love for me.
> Ah, yes, I was wrong,
> Again, I was wrong.
>
> Life is lonely again,
> And only last year   20
> Ev'rything seemed so sure.
> Now life is awful again,

A trough full of hearts
Could only be a bore.

A week in Paris will ease the bite of it.   25
All I care is to smile in spite of it.
I'll forget you, I will,
While yet you are still
Burning inside my brain.

Romance is mush,   30
Stifling those who strive.
I'll live a lush life in some small dive,
And there I'll be, while I rot with the rest
Of those whose lives are lonely too.[6]

Strayhorn composed this song well before he was twenty-one; his friends heard it in 1933, when he was seventeen or eighteen. He completed it two years later. He presented it to his partner, Duke Ellington, who did not record it for a decade; it seemed not right for the band, but Strayhorn liked to perform it privately, at parties. (He was annoyed when Nat King Cole released it in 1949, because Cole did not accurately perform what Strayhorn had written.)[7] The cover on the sheet music for the tune shows a spilled cocktail glass. The song examines the conventional, self-serving pathos of substance-abuse and rejection. You turned out not to love me, so I drink myself into oblivion. Paris as a site of release is much-worn ("I was a free man in Paris, I felt unfettered and alive"). Listeners are meant to know better than the speaker. Sentimentality is his vulnerability, though the song has redeeming complications. First, the lover admits he was a barfly before he met his beloved. He does not claim that a cold woman drove him to drink. He says instead that bar-life normally wears people down in time anyway, and that needs repeating. Second, the failure of this love affair is treated abstractly insofar as he says: "Ah, yes, I was wrong. / Again, I was wrong" (ll. 17-18). He repeated an old error; that is self-understanding. He presents himself less as a tender heart than as a thinking person whose judgment fails him, as it has before. Rejection, like desire, is a serial experience. It matters that his failure is a lapse of judgment, because that—not the cosmos—can be corrected. Intellectuality is an unexpected feature of the poetry of forsaken lovers.

Sophistication Displayed is a major feature of American popular song of the 1930s. Strayhorn's song is youthful: ostentation is the opposite of sophistication. He imagines rejuvenation (l. 25), but eventually claims, hollowly, to have seen beyond romance (l. 30), as if cynicism were an adequate substitute for love. The allure of sophistication is ancient; its purpose is not just display. Sappho's Aphrodite smiles knowingly: Sappho will go through the rounds of seduction and farewell again and again. Because she suffers an excess of desire, she must do that, even though they both know how it will end, "this want past bearing." Not everyone needs romantic sophistication, but those may whose desire repeatedly leads to disappointment. The lover goes through it all again in Carmen McRae's great version of "I Have the Feeling I've Been Here Before," because the "carpet-ride is always worth a try," not because she expects anything to change.[8] Her life, like Sappho's, is a string of goodbyes, a corollary of serial desire. Dull pathos is part of Carmen's performance: she is emerging from a fog as the end approaches. The signs are becoming legible. There is even some pleasure for her in resignation: that is the song's modest modern element. Strayhorn has his character grasping at just that (ll. 27-34). Both songs express a clear sense of failure, and a dim sense of their lovers' chances having run out. Most poems of abandonment try to imagine a future beyond the pain of the forsaken. Remember, in the Hymn to Aphrodite, only Aphrodite is amused; it's not hard to imagine that as wickedly knowing. Sappho has boundless resilience, but her path is circular, as readers sense, even though the speaker makes no issue of it. That's a serious problem with resilience: it means survival but also repetition, like breathing.

The greatest abandonment song, "It Never Entered My Mind," focuses more realistically on the subtractions of a life after romance has failed, and in that way moves more deeply into the subject. This song and the three that follow in this chapter are mature in their implication that losses are not to be recovered—no circling back. One's life and losses stand revealed in maturity. The song was written by Richard Rodgers and Lorenz Hart for the musical *Higher and Higher* (1940). Sinatra (1947), Ella Fitzgerald (1956), Anita O'Day (1960), Johnny Hartman (1966), Leontyne Price (1967), Linda Ronstadt (1984) and many others have recorded their versions; I take Sarah Vaughan's (1958) performance as canonical. In chapters four and five I will examine songs and poems about the joy and suddenness of love's approach. At this far side of my subject is ordinary *material* existence without the beloved. The state of abandonment is characterized, of course, by lack—of metaphysical depth or richness in particular.

> I don't care if there's powder on my nose,
> I don't care if my hairdo is in place,
> I've lost the very meaning of repose.
> I never put a mud pack on my face.
> Oh, who'd have thought   5
> That I'd walk in a daze now?

I never go to shows at night,
But just to matinees now.
I see the show
And home I go.   10

Once I laughed when I heard you saying
That I'd be playing solitaire,
Uneasy in my easy chair.
It never entered my mind,
Once you told me I was mistaken,   15
That I'd awaken with the sun
And order orange juice for one.
It never entered my mind.
You have what I lack myself.
And now I even have to scratch my back myself.   20
Once you warned me that if you scorned me

I'd sing the maiden's prayer again
And wish that you were there again
To get into my hair again.
It never entered my mind.[9]   25

This is a rare song of reasoned self-reproach, sober retrospection—contrary to Wyatt, and yet also piercing.[10] The lover
understands something distinct about herself that she had formerly failed to understand. Her sense of sophistication and
social well-being depended on her lover's presence. She overlooked this simple fact. Only when her beloved left was her
obtuseness apparent. The song's thematic strength derives from
self-analysis: she has been made to feel the limits of her former
self-assurance, made to adjust to a reduced life. She presents
a type of abandoned lover who learns only by losing. Johnny

Hartman altered the lyric by rendering "maiden's prayer" as "loser's song."

She has come to cold terms with her loss. The title is every-thing, but she is incapable of uttering it until the fourteenth line. ("What was I thinking?" is a fair paraphrase.) First, she sings a more general account: "Oh, who'd have thought . . .?" (l. 5) The implication is that no one would reasonably have thought that *she* would be so upset by the loss of her beloved. But this is not adequate to the situation she goes on to describe in the next strophe. The suggestion that no one predicted her suffering is false. Her beloved predicted just that, as the next strophe says. She was a cool one before he left: concerned about her makeup, hair, and complexion. The last four lines of the first strophe (ll. 7-10) say exactly how she has adjusted to her loss:

> I never go to shows at night,
> But just to matinees now.
> I see the show
> And home I go.

She has a life, gets out, is not despondent. One modest adjust-ment confirms her self-control: afternoon shows, because she can go unescorted. An evening show would attract the social scrutiny she prefers to avoid. This is important, because the opening lines assert her indifference to her physical appear-ance, but social status is another matter. Her life is thinner, but not nothing. Self-possession abides. But so too does her lack of self-awareness. She still refuses to admit to herself the extent of her own adversity.

The second and third strophes (ll. 11-25) are richest. She describes a beloved who warned her that she had not fathomed her own involvement. His warning may have sounded cruel, like a threat to leave. But he cleverly addressed her remoteness: she would play solitaire, wake early, and order room-service for one. Classy, cool. Working people have no leisure to sleep late, nor funds for hotel rooms. Finally, he warned her that she would "sing the maiden's prayer," presumably for a lover. Three ways, then, to say she was a stranger to her own heart. The last is explicitly archaic: only old poems spoke of maidens' prayers in 1946 (Wordsworth referred to a maiden's *song* actually). Hers is a sensibility attuned to irony. He knew that if she lost him, her cushion would not preserve her comfort, and he told her so judiciously, playfully. What might his intention have been? To solicit acknowledgment from an egotist. She neglected three gentle warnings.

Speakers say one thing or another of an experience, and one draws inferences; here, about the character of the speaker: her coolness, pride, need for mastery. And there is significance to her manner of expression. She takes credit for the poem. Her mastery is heard in the elaborately rhymed and plotted verse. However distraught one imagines her, her ability to make words serve her well and intricately is evident. She has her language by the throat, no syllable out of place. "It never entered my mind," she sings three times in these strophes. The first sense of the title is that this came as a complete surprise, a blow from behind; but that is much qualified by her realization that she had been warned of exactly what would happen if she lost her beloved. The second sense is that the warnings never got through to her. This self-criticism runs deeper. The tug between these two senses is the point of the song. The title line resists all the rhyme schemes of the poem. Line eleven rhymes with the penultimate word of line twelve; the end-rhyme of line twelve links to the end-rhyme of the next line.

Two rhymes bind three lines together quite tightly by this arrangement. Line fifteen repeats this scheme by rhyming with the third word of line sixteen. The rhyme linking lines eleven and twelve is disyllabic, as is the one linking lines fifteen and sixteen. This rhyming fit intensifies as the strophe proceeds. The end rhyme of line sixteen is linked to line seventeen, as lines twelve and thirteen are linked by simple monosyllabic rhymes. Lines nineteen and twenty, however, are linked by an extraordinary end-rhyme of four syllables. Line twenty-two has an internal trisyllabic rhyme. Lines twenty-two and twenty-three are linked by a trisyllabic end rhyme. Lines five, seven, fourteen, eighteen, and twenty-five, as I said, are unrhymed, the only unrhymed lines in this web of emphatic rhymes. The beauty of this form—as obsessive as a sestina or villanelle—is that the reason for her own uncoupling is indicated in these repeated unrhymed lines: *thought, night,* and *mind.* The obvious and suppressed rhyme for the refrain: *blind.* I've said that this is an especially intellectual, analytical song. The elaborate rhyme scheme is an expression, certainly, of control, and so in character with the singer. But it also suggests that she is thoroughly ensnared by her own efforts to construct a presentation of self. This is the song's pathos. She goes on to make rhymes and matinees. But she cannot see beyond the title and refrain.

One speaks of being in love as if it were a known, settled state of feeling—like being left-handed. The speaker is maximally aware of her love only in a state of abandonment. I have spoken of the character of the speaker, because the song is a revelation of character, but in fact its focus is a state of loving and delusion. Martha Nussbaum has written about cataleptic knowledge: one comes to know as a consequence of strong impressions; pain is a forceful instructor. She makes the point that a lover loves all along, but only recognizes that love when strong impressions make themselves felt.[11] Before those impressions register, a lover dwells in habit. This has much to do with domesticity: the backscratching, the breakfasts seem small, ordinary; one does not adequately attend to the state of feeling in which they take place. One may acknowledge that one "loves" one's daily partner but then deny "being in love" with that person. Until one is alone at breakfast, that benighted semantic distinction will serve. Then comes the revelation of what being in love entails. The song is a profound representation of coming to knowledge through feeling. Moreover, the lesson learned is not provisional. Her beloved is gone, and in his place she has firm self-knowledge, but no reason to expect another chance at love. Resilience gets her to a matinee, but not to another lover.

The failure of relationships once vowed to be one of a kind, life choices—that seems tragic. But a darker realization comes when one's failures gather into a pattern. The notion of an episodic love life becomes obvious to one after several crashes. Pick yourself up, dust yourself off . . . What are the imaginative possibilities of a second or third love? Lorenz Hart wrote "I Wish I Were in Love Again" about three years before "It Never Entered My Mind." They are both constructions of sophistication; both explore a connection between willfulness and self-knowledge. Here are the first ten lines of the second refrain of "I Wish I Were in Love Again":

> The furtive sigh,
> The blackened eye,
> The words "I'll love you till the day I die,"
> The self-deception that believes the lie—
> I wish I were in love again.
> When love congeals

It soon reveals
The faint aroma of performing seals,
The double-crossing of a pair of heels.
I wish I were in love again!

Furtive glances are familiar, but Hart's phrase suggests some exactness. Does that sigh express disdain, fear or despair? A punch in the eye brutally dismisses distinctions and ends inquiry. He is writing of extreme differences between lovers—and of eager roughness. "Congeals" is a verb for coming together, solidifying, but by freezing. A coldness, that is, from the outset. The next two lines coarsely refer to the odors of sex. How peculiar that a Broadway love song takes up that topic.[12] And the rhyme of seals and heels: why are lovers so quickly called heels—unless they are an illicit pair? This is a song about the desire to fight and fail *again*. Songs of devotion gather around the term *only*. The opposite is asserted here: plural nouns of all sorts. One repeatedly collides with another, both urged by eros. And a life of that is intense, engaging, if also degrading of one's ability to love. The song at first seems amusing, partly because of Hart's torrent of terms. His fluency is impressive, though different from Cole Porter's. Hart's words are driven by an unattractive severity, by self-loathing. The masochistic call, *again*, is ugly. Nelson Riddle's arrangement of Sinatra's 1957 version accentuates that force, though Sinatra lightens it with a sweet caress of "love" in the last line. The song exposes erotic contradictions, the attraction of opposites, the appeal of conflict. A match made in hell: perfect, just what I want, difference. Isn't the appeal of difference at the base of many abandonments? And how resilient of Hart to imagine starting again with such self-knowledge.

Bishop's justly famous villanelle "One Art" expresses fear of

the sort of abandonment that Sarah Vaughan seems to accept.
Bishop's friend the poet Lloyd Schwartz says that its "real audience" is Bishop herself.[13] He recognizes, as others have, that
the poem comes directly from her love life, that it is intended
to be understood as sincere. My sense is that the intended
audience of the entire poem (not just of its final quatrain) is
her actual beloved, Alice Methfessel, who was considering a
marriage proposal to a man when Bishop worked on the poem
in October, November, and early December 1975. Alice had
separated herself from Elizabeth by early October.[14] These inci-
dentals seem to have had an effect on the way Bishop addresses
abandonment.

> The art of losing isn't hard to master;
> so many things seem filled with the intent
> to be lost that their loss is no disaster.

> Lose something every day. Accept the fluster
> of lost door keys, the hour badly spent.
> The art of losing isn't hard to master.

> Then practice losing farther, losing faster:
> Places, and names, and where it was you meant
> to travel. None of these will bring disaster.

> I lost my mother's watch. And look! my last, or
> next-to-last, of three loved houses went.
> The art of losing isn't hard to master.

> I lost two cities, lovely ones. And, vaster,
> some realms I owned, two rivers, a continent.
> I miss them, but it wasn't a disaster.

Even losing you (the joking voice, a gesture
I love) I shan't have lied. It's evident
the art of losing's not too hard to master
though it may look like (*Write* it!) like disaster.[15]

In December Bishop, depressed over Alice's absence, took
sleeping pills with alcohol and passed out on the floor; it is
uncertain whether this was a suicide attempt. In March 1976,
after Elizabeth injured her ankle and needed assistance, she
and Alice were reconciled, and nothing more came of the marriage proposal. The poem displays art and ardor for a young
woman who seemed then to be leaving Bishop. Poetry is traditionally an art for gaining renown; the "art of losing" is a clever
formulation, a "perverse rejection" of the desire to win, as Susan
McCabe puts it.[16] The poet is witty, charming from the outset.
The notion of things that "seem filled with the intent / to be
lost" is amusing too. The second tercet begins a drill: "Lose
something every day. Accept the fluster / of lost door keys, the
hour badly spent." A little Popean, that combination of unlike
particulars (or one may recall Dorothy Fields and Cole Porter).

Loss of spirit is the great fear. That is why the poem pre-
tends to be concerned with material losses. The truth is otherwise. One notes too that only one beloved is mentioned
among Bishop's losses. She does not present her life as a series
of loves. As her drill proceeds—farther, faster—the pathos of
ageing begins to displace the humor. Only the closing quatrain reveals the drive behind the poem: not the car-keys, not
a continent, but the beloved who seems filled with an intent
to leave, though "I shan't have lied" indicates that the beloved
has not yet definitively left the lover (she had not married). The
prosody emphasizes feminine endings (thirteen of them): that
is her grand concern. Only the B-rhymes are masculine—fewer

than half so many. He has little chance in this poem. Bishop's biographer, Brett Millier, observes that this future-perfect clause entered the poem in the sixteenth and final draft; it means, as she says, "Even if I lose you."[17] Bishop's friends told her that Alice would probably return. The poem appeals to a beloved to rescue Bishop from a once-in-a-lifetime disaster. This is a praise-poem based on a hope that willfulness can prevent a disaster; it is not as dark as Bishop herself had become in December 1975.[18]

Christina Rossetti's "Mirage" (1860) is a comparable but more austere poem. No displays for her; she is all sincerity. The contrast with "One Art" concerns rhetorical address, prosody, and diction: the differences in these elements are necessary to write *after* hope. Hers is almost a different topic. No one else is blamed for her suffering, and lasting gloom follows the shock.

> The hope I dreamed of was a dream,
> Was but a dream; and now I wake
> Exceeding comfortless, and worn, and old,
> For a dream's sake.
>
> I hang my harp upon a tree,   5
> A weeping willow in a lake;
> I hang my silenced harp there, wrung and snapt
> For a dream's sake.
>
> Lie still, lie still, my breaking heart;
> My silent heart, lie still and break: 10
> Life, and the world, and mine own self, are changed
> For a dream's sake.[19]

She speaks from the end of romance generally. The clauses hold their darkest terms for the end, and then greater darkness pulls the syntax into further gloom. The pattern is clearest in the first stanza. The last line of each quatrain thuds closed: two unstressed syllables, then two stressed. The poem does not develop intellectually or emotionally; no consolation is found or sought. Her main clauses come first, then follow dark phrases to fill out the sentences. The rhythm of the sentences establishes that supplements will come, and they will be gloomy. The exact nature of the loss is not characterized. Part is a romantic loss; that much is implied by reference to her breaking heart. The harp in a tree connects the speaker to the art of poetry generally, and more particularly to Psalm 137, which concerns the Babylonian captivity. The psalmist says that the harps were abandoned in response to the captors' request that the poets sing a song of Zion. The defeated would not betray their memory of Zion. The children of Edom said, "Raze it, raze it [meaning Jerusalem], even to the foundations thereof"—lest the city provide their enemies any comfort at all. Rossetti does not directly reproach her beloved. She appears to blame only the emptiness of her dream, or mirage—which the psalmist never does. But Psalm 137 is her collaborative text. The psalmist directly addresses the Babylonian captors. The last line:

> Happy shall he be, that taketh and dasheth thy little
> ones against the stones.

At first one puts oneself at a beloved's disposal. A *bandon* is a jurisdiction. Cast out, one relinquishes the protection and constraints of love's laws. Abandonment nudges one toward lawlessness. Not said, by Rossetti, but not far below her allusive lines.

Their songs address an abusive, faithless beloved, even when they appear aloof, as Rossetti surely does. The art of such song depends on the complaining lover's proximity to the curse. The great beauty of this poem is its austerity. She does not say what the psalmist does. Her style, stoical, taciturn. The poem's artfulness is minimal: one feels her spirit move less in her words than in the caesura's shifts, particularly in lines three, seven (inside the fourth foot), and eleven. Prosodically, the poem is regular (tetrameter, tetrameter, pentameter, dimeter). Her only thumbprints are the caesura in line seven and a reversed initial foot in the penultimate line. Poems by lovers left behind may curse the beloved, even when that utterance is kept from the poet's mouth. The curse here is silent; the power, subtraction, cancellation. Artistic mastery is exactly what Rossetti renounces as pretense. Hers is the deeper poem because she sees that eloquence without a viable vision is not enough. That is why she hangs up her harp.

Her speaker has been remade by experiences that have come to nothing in the end. Hope, harp, and heart are all broken, stanza by stanza. Song makes none of it better. She urges her heart to be silent in the last stanza. The loss of the beloved entails silence because a poet with a mirage for a vision ought not to speak at all. Though the poem does not say so explicitly, she has been a captive of her love. The poem's intellectual vigor comes from an unflinching articulation of loss without comfort, without even that of reproach. Only the dream can be blamed—her Zion. This is to say that her judgment failed her, and she is left with herself, alone and silent. Her terms remain traditional, abstract: hope, dream, life, world, self. She declines to base the poem on a distinctive experience. Its hardiness is in that insistence on general concepts.

Compare "Mirage" to "This Is My Last Affair" (1936),

Haven Johnson's cognate song about the consequences of failed romance—made famous by Billie Holiday's 1937 performance.

> Can't you see
>
> What love and romance have done to me?
> I'm not the same as I used to be.
> This is my last affair.
>
> Tragedy just seems to be the end of me.
> My happiness is misery.
> This is my last affair.
>
> Right from the start
> You took my love,
> Tore my heart apart.
> Now there's nothing new to look forward to.
> My dreams won't come true.
>
> So I'll make a vow, make a vow:
> No more to love's line will I bow
> I cross my heart and seal it now.
> This is my last affair.[20]

The speaker is a serial lover who sees what should be apparent to her insensitive beloved: that she has been permanently damaged by disappointment. This is not about only one failure, as Rossetti's poem is, though this was the decisive one. The song is more meaningful for the suggestion that the speaker is a serial lover. She does not say, though she implies, that all her affairs contributed to her present state. Somehow, she has

become one whose function is misery. Failure is not an acci-
dent but the objective of her life; without intending to fail,
she was headed toward failure all along. Love and romance
have corrupted her being. "My dreams won't come true"—a
simple, devastatingly frank line. A report of fact, the same one
Rossetti made.

Popular songs are obviously full of pain. But the pitiless clarity of Rossetti's poem and of Billie's version of Haven Johnson's
song are rare. Not that people don't get past their griefs. They
do, but in time. The best of these songs are of a moment and
articulate a just estimation of a speaker's resources. Despite
heartache, a will that is firm; that is the basis of Rossetti's and
Billie's honor. All the poems I have cited (except "And If I Did
What Then?") concern long pain, the dues paid for bad ideas.
The idea under examination is that the loss of the One is the
loss of all. This is a rich idea for poets, but it's murder on lovers. The speakers have found costly ways past their pain. Songs
of abandonment are especially courageous when the speakers
decline comfort. These are character-portraits of strength without hope. Gascoigne's poem has it that resilience—the ability
to bounce back after loss—requires of a lover only clear thinking and some range of imagination. Clarity is not the issue
for these last two poems discussed, but Haven Johnson does
say that losses eventually narrow one's ability to hope. "Time
is the evil," Pound says. Matthew Arnold argued famously,
you'll recall, that no poetic pleasure can be derived from the
representation of situations "in which the suffering finds no
vent in action; in which a continuous state of mental distress
is prolonged, . . . in which there is everything to be endured,
nothing to be done."[21] These poems and songs show the great
critic to have been, as Lorenz Hart said, *mistaken.*

4. Love Rushes

The best-known topos of love poetry is *carpe diem*: Seize the day. To the beloved, one says: Since this passing moment will not return, take the pleasure on offer now; opportunities grow rare as beauty fades. Graceless, to propose that the beloved may not see another chance to be loved. And ill-considered: to scare her into bed. Amazing then that so many poems propose this implausible brief for love-making. Crosby, Stills, and Nash say instead: "if you can't be with the one you love, honey, love the one you're with." Their point is presence, not promiscuity: love your moment well because it will be taken from you. Which is an inversion of the case for plural joys. These poems only seem to be addressed to naïve maidens. They speak to all who lose sight of life's instability—and more narrowly to those who treasure the topoi. Like most canonical poems, spoken by men for other men's consideration. Nigel Smith leaves no doubt that Marvell's "To His Coy Mistress," the most admired *carpe diem* poem, is a compendium of allusions to the writings of his contemporaries. *Carpe diem* is the most illiberal topos because it invokes a regime of force that reduces individual autonomy. Devotion is a promise of constancy in an indefinite future—something altogether different. And the following chapters analyze what can be said when devotion is not part of the promise.

A pastoral setting is meant to render imaginable a love unaffected by time. In the last stanza of Marlowe's "The Passionate Shepherd to His Love," the speaker says that "swains shall dance and sing / For thy delight each May morning" (ll. 21-22). The scene of pleasures taken just continues, one spring day after the next. Should the beloved accept his proposition, she would enjoy gentle pleasure every day. Time does not fly in this literary countryside, and lovers live on love. Ralegh replies that she knows better.

> If all the world and love were young,
> And truth in every shepherd's tongue,
> These pretty pleasures might me move
> To live with thee and be thy love.
>
> Time drives the flocks from field to fold   5
> When rivers rage and rocks grow cold,
> And Philomel becometh dumb;
> The rest complains of cares to come.
>
> The flowers do fade, and wanton fields
> To wayward winter reckoning yields;   10
> A honey tongue, a heart of gall,
> Is fancy's spring, but sorrow's fall.
>
> Thy gowns, thy shoes, thy beds of roses,
> Thy cap, thy kirtle, and thy posies
> Soon break, soon wither, soon forgotten—   15
> In folly ripe, in reason rotten.

Thy belt of straw and ivy buds,
Thy coral clasps and amber studs,
All these in me no means can move
To come to thee and be thy love.   20

But could youth last and love still breed,
Had joys no date nor age no need,
Then these delights my mind might move
To live with thee and be thy love.[1]

It is an art-game, revising a rival. Wit and concision make for victory. Some rhymes alone trounce the rival: young tongue (ll. 1-2), buds studs (ll. 17-18). Line sixteen is especially shapely (even with its extra syllable, hinting at decline). One notices the phrase "in reason rotten," just a little off from now-current idioms. The familiar phrase "within reason" expresses slighter esteem for this faculty. Ralegh's usage is unremarkable in the sixteenth century but reminds one that this term had the broad currency and prestige that a term like "creativity" now has. The notion that "rotten" might modify reason makes clear the moral expectations associated with rationality. This modifier indicates that where reason leads one astray, one would feel *betrayed*. In this way Ralegh's world seems young. These two poets playfully debate intimacy on rational, empirical ground. They pretend to present lovemaking as a consequence of rational choice in pursuit of recognized ends. That pretense of extending reason toward the zone where its sovereignty is least secure still gives pleasure. Ralegh in particular celebrates the mobility of pragmatic analysis: he can speak for the nymphs. Poetry allows one liberty to assume voices, to imagine a rational woman coolly assessing the value of desire. And yet her rationality is only frank, not surprising. She alludes to topoi

that contravene the shepherd's pitch. Conventions allow a poet
to move swiftly through a controversy with terms that already
commanded the attention and feelings of an audience: shep-
herds, nymphs, caps, coral, amber, roses, and ivory, but then
the tough and lucid "breed" and "need." Both poems are all
neatness and closure; neither moving nor unsettling, unless
one finds the link between urgency and predation surprising.

Ralegh's reply, in Marlowe's tetrameter quatrains (AABB),
raises two points of contestation. Temporality and treachery
count against Marlowe's case for pleasure. In the last stanza
Ralegh returns to his subjunctive mood.

> But could youth last and love still breed,
> Had joys no date nor age no need . . .

The contrary is the case: youth does not last; fecundity expires;
joys fade. Age requires constancy. The inevitability of change
is the lesson of the seasons. "Time drives the flock from field
to fold" as winter approaches. Marlowe's "pretty lambs" need
shelter from the storms, as do women, Ralegh implies.

Reason and mindfulness are attributed to Ralegh's speaking maid; she needs less protection than the lambs exactly
because of her wit. From time's depredations, everyone needs
protection, but little is to be had. Several poets, as I'll now
show, write less of the charm of *carpe diem* than of its brutal-
ity. They see this corruption of desire as male and shameful.
Women need to guard well against predatory admirers. "So
rudely forc'd. / Tereu," as the *Waste Land* has it (ll. 205-6). The
sentence in the second stanza about birds ceasing their songs
as winter approaches alludes to the grisly tale of Procne and
Philomela. King Tereus, Procne's husband, raped his sister-in-
law Philomela. In order to prevent Philomela from exposing

his treachery, he extracted her tongue. For Procne, she wove a picture of her abuse. The sisters, changed into nightingales, fled from Tereus. This story is about betrayal and misrepresentation, not temporality. "A honey tongue, a heart of gall, / Is fancy's spring, but sorrow's fall" (ll. 11-12). Men lie to women, and women need protection against seduction itself, not just against time's changes. They need above all their own tongues, as Ralegh indicates.

Petrarch, paragon of patience, praised Laura over decades and well after her death, in constant awareness that his suit would bring him no carnal satisfaction. Yet he so successfully expressed extreme feelings that his figures of ice and fire still stand for the instability of a lover's feelings. To urge is to press, drive, or compel. Another's urge renders one object-like, reduces one's autonomy. One receives another's force. An urgent petition is uttered by one who claims to feel that push. He is a receiver then and recruits another for his release from the moment's power. Extremity and urgency are at the heart of romance. Thomas Carew's tetrameter sonnet, "Song: Mediocrity in Love Rejected" (1640), affirms the view that fire and ice are preferable to medial points in between.

> Give me more love, or more disdain;
> The torrid or the frozen zone
> Bring equal ease unto my pain;
> The temperate affords me none;
> Either extreme, of love or hate,   5
> Is sweeter than a calm estate.
>
> Give me a storm; if it be love,
> Like Danaë in that golden shower,
> I swim in pleasure; if it prove

Disdain, that torrent will devour   10
My vulture hopes; and he's possessed
Of heaven that's but from hell released.
Then crown my joys, or cure my pain;
Give me more love or more disdain.[2]

Urgency is made to carry a sense of excess, or quantity. At a certain point desire cannot be withstood; a threshold is reached, and the urge to act is irresistible. This notion underlies the elaborate descriptions and repetitions of love poetry. A muchness exists not for itself but as justification of aggression; such thinking is evident in Marvell's later "To His Coy Mistress." The first three words of Carew's poem are among the most erotic in English. Lines seven to twelve alter the pace by playing syntax against line breaks. Take me to the limit, these lines cry. There is where pain and gender flip to their contraries. Lines eight and nine flamboyantly assert that he will receive penetration as a treasure: "I swim in pleasure." A storm of disdain might eliminate all hope of the beloved, and that could be a great pleasure, for his "vulture hopes" seem to wait for him to die. Being consumed by desire is a familiar expression, as in Sonnet 73, when Shakespeare famously says: "consumed with that which it was nourished by," and in Petrarch's Rime 364. Carew complicates this with a notion of predatory hope. The most memorable lines are the last clause of this chiseled sentence (ll. 11-12). The shapely syntax takes one to an ironic but familiar truth handsomely expressed.

Morbidity and sexual aggression are entangled with the urgency of love poetry. Although a bright sun is a traditional figure of an idealized beloved, Thomas Campion's "Follow Thy Fair Sun" (1601) does not directly refer to sexual desire; it focusses abstractly on the exhaustion of long pursuit, the alternative to urgency. The imperative title urges auditors to pursue

ideas of beauty and glory, no matter how unlikely realization
may be; no mention here of seizing a beloved. These are the
last two of the poem's five quatrains:

> Follow her while yet her glory shineth;
> There comes a luckless night,
> That will dim all her light;   15
> And this the black unhappy shade divineth.

> Follow still since so thy fates ordained;
> The sun must have his shade,
> Till both at once do fade;
> The sun still proved, the shadow still disdained.[3]   20

The contrast between the honored beloved and her merely
actual lover does not warrant withdrawal from the chase,
though a long pursuit wears on the pursuer. He is said to be
unhappy, deprived, disgraced, scorched, and disdained. That
is determined by sustained pursuit itself, Campion claims; its
end, not a happy pairing of contraries, but the imposition
of darkness on sun and shade. Mortality ends the struggle,
without reconciliation. The beloved light deprives the shade/
lover of honor as well as satisfaction (ll. 5-6). This is a tough
poem about an urgent expectation of change (predatory hope).
Admirers burn to ashes with desire; the beloved burns up too,
merely with years. Mutual intense desire is out of the question.

And the appeal, then, of urgency? To the beseeched: being
intensely desired. To the beseecher: liberation from circuitous-
ness. To both: the charm of an extraordinary moment of abandon—the most ephemeral phase of romance. Both imagine a
force beyond themselves—a kind fate pulling them together,
not apart. Recall film scenes of two lovers quickly entering a
private room and crashing against a wall. These scenes insist

that urgent romance is not predatory; that, contra Campion, both may feel so moved simultaneously. Force, though, is always implicit. The alternative to this magic moment is rape. And for the dark side, consider James Shirley's "Cupid's Call":

> Ho! Cupid calls; come, lovers, come,
> Bring his wanton harvest home;
> The west wind blows, the birds do sing,
> The earth's enameled, 'tis high spring;
>   Let hinds whose soul is corn and hay   5
>   Expect their crop another day.
>
> Into Love's spring-garden walk,
> Virgins dangle on their stalk,
> Full-blown, and playing at fifteen;
> Come, bring your amorous sickles then!   10
>   See, they are pointing to their beds,
>   And call to reap their maidenheads.
>
> Hark, how in yonder shady grove
> Sweet Philomel is warbling love,
> And with her voice is courting kings;   15
> For since she was a bird, she sings,
>   "There is no pleasure but in men;
>   Oh, come and ravish me again."
>
> Virgins that are young and fair
> May kiss, and grow into a pair;   20
> Then warm and active use your blood,
> No sad thought congeal the flood;
>   Nature no med'cine can impart
>   When age once snows upon our heart.[4]

This is a web of traditional phrases. At the level of diction and syntax, a verse exercise, like Ralegh's "The Nymph's Reply to the Shepherd." The terms "enameled," "spring-garden," "shady grove," "warbling," "bird," "sings" invoke a timeless pastoral setting, a traditional exception to temporality. This literariness is evident in the first stanza, though its last couplet bears the pertinent innuendo that, while hinds live on grain, the men to whom the stanza is addressed want their meat (ll. 5-6). Spring is the season of courtship, but the second stanza presents a call to rape, or "reap their maidenheads" (l. 12). Line nine nicely characterizes what is meant by the conventional phrase "young maid": a fifteen-year-old girl playing in perilous proximity to men who are serious. The third stanza is more outrageous still in asserting that Philomel, "since she was a bird" (i.e. after suffering rape and mutilation), wishes only to be raped again (ll. 14-18). The poem claims that predation is natural, inevitable, comes with the seasons, rather than with malefactors. As hinds are hunted, so are maids. It's a poem to be uttered by a man to other men. Locker-room, we say, meaning vulgar, shameful, but boyish too. Playful too, provocative, not entirely in earnest, though meant to assert an account of male desire too frank for mixed company. I cite it here to identify one destination of the logic of urgency.

Suddenness and romance are closely connected. Jim Powell's "Song" is a figure of abrupt sex, or the anticipation of that at a dance club. Powell sets emphasis on *knowing*, not just imagining. An exchanged look establishes mutual attraction, full awareness, without coyness. Eros appears with certainty, as if a switch had been flipped. Whatever follows begins in mutuality.

Dear eyes, slut eyes
my angel for tonight

suddenly your glance
above a hand cupped full of matchlight
across the roaring room   5

and now this compact
of our locked gazes—promises,
frank craving:

Powell is a subtle prosodist: the array of stresses among the
syllables, however variable, is heard as definite. The first line
is trochaic and symmetrical—just two balanced feet putting
the hammer up front. Lines two and five are regular iambic
trimeter. Slight rhythmic variations occur in lines three and
four. Line three lacks an initial unstressed syllable to make a
regular iambic trimeter line. That feels right, because the initial stress is all about quick change, surprise. The fourth line,
iambic tetrameter, is irregular only in its feminine ending. This
first stanza is shapely and settled in form; the later stanzas, by
contrast, are especially adventurous. One senses that both parties enter this liaison wanting the same thing; that they desire
equally. But that's probably not the case.

once, I saw this same lust at first sight
in the blank marble stare   10

of a Roman statuette,
the god Pan sodomizing
a billy goat:
a fixed, feral leer so naked
it looks innocent—Pan's thighs   15

intent; the kid's beard
pinched in the god's right hand

and his head tilted
back to return that gaze, a mixed
look on the goat's wise face   20

of quizzical
detachment, and some
curiosity
to contemplate these ephemeral
ecstasies in the god's eyes.[5]   25

    Powell gathers stresses into pairs, beginning in the second stanza. The first two syllables of line eight constitute a spondee. And in line ten the third and fourth syllables are stressed. Spondees also tighten the verse in lines twelve, fourteen, and fifteen. The other variation that runs through the poem is a four-syllable unit with stress on the first and fourth syllables. This pattern is first heard in line nine, with the phrase "lust at first sight" (and recurs in lines 16, 17, 19, 20, 22, and 24). This variation loosens the iambic verse and orients one's ear on phrasal music. The many variations complicate the sound and feeling of the poem, which is stormy after the first stanza, as if Powell were stirred up by the implications of the initial encounter. The narrative of lines one through eight is small. With line nine he moves the scene to a museum gallery and never returns to the night club. The grandeur of the poem is the curated comparison and analysis of the art-work that mediates between present ("now" in line 6) and the imagination of millenia past. The suddenness of the encounter diminishes in the passage that follows. Reflection and analysis are mightier, subtler than immediate presentation.

    The theme of promiscuity is announced in the opening eight lines: a sexual attraction between strangers in a public place. Whatever draws them to one another has little to do with family background, social status, ideas about life or such. One says, raw nature, but mutual, and presumably egalitarian; neither is pursuer nor pursued. This is eros, bold, unencumbered, unresisted. But Pan is dominant, an intent top, and the goat, an uncomplaining bottom. Domination is represented as ancient and natural, given the identity of the top. If the speaker thought at first of fraternal sex as egalitarian—suddenness as an aid to equity—he cannot maintain that view after recalling the statuette. How wise can a goat be?

One is asked to see in "slut" eyes a window onto ephemeral ecstasies. Here is a liaison without obligation or consequence, but the speaker understands how solitary an experience is on offer. Pan is utterly alone. Ephemeridae are insects that live for one day. The descriptive language of stanzas three and four is exact and surprising. "Sodomizing / a billy goat" leaves no doubt around this statuette. "Pan's thighs // intent" is a fine suggestion: that one could see mind and body in a thigh. The expression on the face of Pan is emphatic, felt on the lips and tongue. "Fixed, feral leer" is a memorable epithet: three of its four syllables stressed, and the second and third words echo one another with "l" and "r" sounds. "Leer" derives from Old English, a "side glance; . . . expressive of slyness, malignity, immodest desire." His ecstasy leaves his partner uncomprehending—merely quizzical. The last stanza gathers a series of polysyllabic terms (quizzical, curiosity, contemplate, ephemeral ecstasies) suggesting something less decisive and definite than the rough, monosyllabic terms of possession (locked, lust, fixed, pinched) that preceded them. The judgment that generated the term "slut" has turned after twenty-five lines. Nature is a slut and a god, Powell insists. Consent, mutuality—they are irrelevant to the greedy Pan. Nature, not negligence, not evil, underlies the vagaries of desire. Even bestiality is part of what one likes to think of as natural. Pleasure is to be had where offered. Pan means all.

Lyric poetry has always shown romance to be damaging, anything but innocent. The concept of crazy love implies sincerity, because it so obviously runs counter to the lover's interest. Seduction poems are often conniving, and that compromises consent. Sappho's reference to "my / raving heart" is self-aware and candid, a convincing expression of feeling. In the first stanza Aphrodite is said to be "artfully adorned," rather than, say, naturally beautiful; like Odysseus and Hermes, a "weaver of wiles," or trickster. The memorable account of her, pulled around in a Love-Chariot by sparrows rather than steeds, is pastiche or mock-epic, an imitation of grandness; animals can be made to bear burdens counter to their nature. Her sophistication derives from eros's ability to render trivial what one says or thinks or wills. A beloved may be bamboozled into submission. Long before, Homer had said that Helen was drugged by Aphrodite. Think of the Johnny Mercer lyric "That Old Black Magic" (1942). Sappho wants compliance more than consent.

> That old black magic has me in its spell.
> That old black magic that you weave so well.
> Those icy fingers up and down my spine.
> The same old witchcraft when your eyes meet mine.
>
> The same old tingle that I feel inside
> And then that elevator starts its ride
> And down and down I go,
> 'Round and 'round I go
> Like a leaf that's caught in the tide.

I should stay away,
But what can I do?
I hear your name
And I'm aflame,
Aflame with such a burning desire
That only your kiss
Can put out the fire.

For you're the lover I have waited for,
The mate that fate had me created for,
And ev'ry time your lips meet mine
Darling, down and down I go,
'Round and 'round I go
In a spin,
Loving the spin I'm in,
Under that old black magic called love![6]

The deterministic version of consanguinity proposes that
some lovers are made to be together, that ultimately they can
only acquiesce. This song combines monogamous desire and
fate. "You do something to me," as Cole Porter had put it.
You demon, you. My agency shrinks in your presence. Mercer
identifies intensity and depth of feeling with surrender. In the
presence of such desire, lovers cannot answer for their acts.
"The Devil made me do it." To which Ralegh's maid could only
smile. Druggy eros, for the addict. "Come to me again, and
release me from this / want past bearing," Sappho says. Louis
Prima and Keely Smith gave a famous comic interpretation
to the song in 1958. Their dialogue featured the voice and
expressions of an ironic nymph, rather than, as Ralegh had it,
a rational skeptic. But Ralegh heard the suppressed undertone
of Marlowe's shepherd song, as Louis Prima and Keely Smith

heard it in Sinatra's 1954 version of Mercer's song. This is not a coincidence. Songs of love's urgency are recognized by all parties to be not reports of psychological states but art-games within familiar conventions. Sincere deterministic songs beg for parody, because they so underestimate individual responsibility. The more familiar the conventions, the more plausible the irony.

Poets borrow each other's successes, and thereby extend traditions. Marvell writes in tetrameter couplets, as did Marlowe and Ralegh (who combined them into quatrains); they address one another on that channel. Marvell gives over the first five couplets of "To His Coy Mistress" to a good-natured pastiche of Petrarchan conceits about the beauties of the beloved.

> Had we but world enough, and time,
> This coyness lady were no crime,
> We would sit down, and think which way
> To walk, and pass our long love's day.
> Thou by the Indian Ganges' side   5
> Shouldst rubies find: I by the tide
> Of Humber would complain. I would
> Love you ten years before the flood:
> And you should, if you please, refuse
> Till the conversion of the Jews.   10
> My vegetable love should grow
> Vaster than empires, and more slow.
> An hundred years should go to praise
> Thine eyes, and on thy forehead gaze.
> Two hundred to adore each breast: 15
> But thirty thousand to the rest.
> An age at least to every part,
> And the last age should show your heart.

> For Lady you deserve this state;
> Nor would I love at lower rate.   20

The first line proposes, in the subjunctive, a condition that cannot be met: easy enough to imagine longevity, but "world enough"? However much impatience, even exasperation, the poem expresses no world-weariness. The paragraph luxuriates in the safety of slowness and great distance (ll. 3-7). He jokes that before choosing where to walk they would suspend their movement altogether and devote the day to deliberation as to a direction; that's how slowly they *would* proceed. He jokes too about their being, in that case, safely positioned on different continents: she in India, he in homely Hull—her virtue thoroughly secure at that distance. But the wide-ranging references to Hindus, Jews, and Christians evoke conjunctions of people from far away, as in an imperial metropolis. The hypothetical slow and compliant lover is figured as grandly acquisitive, fond of all the world, in that sense no different from a quick, rapacious lover. The poet's imagination tracks magnitude and diversity. Given time, he would make love to his beloved interminably, "Nor would I love at lower rate." But who has time? He will have her fast and hard—at the higher rate.

This too is a brief for sudden sex. Tarry in neither the approach nor the act, for the world is full. Places and things and women are many, wondrously distinct. A baroque sensibility is there still, as witness Johnny Mercer's "The Midnight Sun" (1954), surely affected by Marvell's poem.

> Your lips were like a red and ruby chalice,
> Warmer than the summer night,
> The clouds were like an alabaster palace
> Rising to a snowy height.

Each star its own aurora borealis,   5
Suddenly you held me tight.
I could see the midnight sun.[7]

Suddenness follows delightful delay. Sarah Vaughan chews
the phrase "Aurora borealis": a delectation of languorous love.
Mercer stretches out the terminal phrases of lines one, three,
and five to tantalize (as Marvell does in lines 1-20) before
the disturbance of line six. The figurative elaboration of both
these poems tests credulity, though seduction is not the actual
objective. The ladies are mannequins draped with phrases to
render visible familiar forms of loving. The genuine praise is
that the beloved provokes writers to extravagant elaboration.
To speak of her is delicious, no labor at all. Samuel Johnson
felt, in writing "On the Death of Dr. Robert Levet," an obligation to describe and praise the deceased justly and exactly; a
poet's labor and invention constitute tribute paid to his subject.
A lover displays delight in describing the beloved. Marvell's
extravagance is in the figures, but also in his manipulation of
familiar words. The phrase "vegetable love" is odd now, as it was
then too. The *OED* cites no comparable usage before him. He
insists that his love is not sudden and predatory, as tumescent
organs may be, but accretive, as a vegetable grows. He com-
pares his love to the growth of empires. However, they grow
rapidly, as the Athenian and British empires did, by conquest,
not accretion. He compels his words to take the sense he wills,
and the strain is meant to show: text and subtext. The extravagant style is dramatic, reflexive.

The tone shifts in the second verse-paragraph; playfulness
famously recedes. "Always" indicates a general metaphysical
issue, not a local circumstance.

But at my back I always hear
Time's wingèd chariot hurrying near:
And yonder all before us lie
Deserts of vast eternity.
Thy beauty shall no more be found;   25
Nor, in thy marble vault, shall sound
My echoing song: then worms shall try
That long preserved virginity:
And your quaint honour turn to dust;
And into ashes all my lust.   30
The grave's a fine and private place,
But none I think do there embrace.

The change does not occur right away: the first couplet of the paragraph remains within conventional figures of seduction poetry. The somber and stately phrase "deserts of vast eternity" seems earnest, metaphysical. Beginning with line twenty-five he warns the beloved of the consequences of delay: his imagination penetrates her "marble vault" or chilling cavity to predict that "worms shall try / That long-preserved virginity." This is a strikingly genital site of contemplation. After he has adored each breast, this grim, anatomical passage is intrusive, rough. (His description of his own decomposition, on the contrary, is summary and abstract.) The phrase "quaint honor" is especially mean. The note in the *Norton Anthology of Poetry* directs students toward a pun on Middle English *quaynte* for female genitalia—presumably related to modern "cunt." The common senses of "quaint" are clever, cunning, scheming. The term is sharply disparaging from at least two directions. Any sense of the poem's charm falters here. The close of the paragraph is smug ("I think"), like a schoolboy with a clever rhyme. Had the poem ended here, as it might have, it would not be read

now. The last paragraph makes it. The tone is so labile, one
moves clause by clause.

> Now, therefore, while the youthful glew
> Sits on thy skin like morning dew,
> And while thy willing soul transpires   35
> At every pore with instant fires,
> Now let us sport us while we may;
> And now, like am'rous birds of prey,
> Rather at once our Time devour,
> Than languish in his slow-chapped power.   40
> Let us roll all our strength, and all
> Our sweetness, up into one ball:
> And tear our pleasures with rough strife,
> Thorough the iron gates of life.
> Thus, though we cannot make our sun   45
> Stand still, yet we will make him run.[8]

At first, he returns to the mode of praise, as if his auditor
might, after listening to lines twenty-five through thirty-two,
still be charmed. He proposes that the soul is expressed by the
body: her spirit escapes through her pores; she is hot and "willing." This is an audacious, implausible representation of his
supposed auditor, as he and she would surely know, were they
actual, and that irony summons again a sophisticated bond
between them. So long as she is aroused, he proposes that they
"sport" themselves. This word is familiar from Jonson's "Song
to Celia," and Nigel Smith cites other relevant uses; the word
refers to vigorous sex, but also to entertainment. He proposes
that they join as athletes, peers in pleasure-taking. Although
he refers to her soul escaping in line thirty-five, no suggestion
is offered that lovemaking is soulful; it is sport and aggression.

Time is a predator, as are the amorous birds. He advocates devouring it quickly rather than being slowly devoured by it. The slowness of "long love's day" (l. 4) has doubled back as languishing in mortality (l. 40). He will kick back against age. To get the tone of the conclusion (ll. 38-46), note the rhymes: may [May]/prey, devour/power, strife/life, sun/run. He wants a fight. Marlowe's shepherd offers the beloved a diverse array of gentle pleasures. Marvell wants to "tear our pleasures with rough strife / Thorough the iron gates of life." These densely emphatic, forbidding lines cannot be intended to entice a woman to bed. He has collapsed all distinction between sex and death. The "gates of life" refer to her body, but indirectly to the end of life. He is motivated less by a desire for pleasure than by rage against the dying of light. The linkage of athletic sex and aggression (ll. 37-38) has taken the poem to morbidity.

The seduction poem is grand in Marvell's hands because he has so little concern for seduction. The poem is a meditation on will and mortality in inappropriate circumstances. The word "extravagant" has the sense of wandering away. "To His Coy Mistress" was a favorite of the New Critics, but it is neither tightly organized nor unified in texture. This poem gives meaning to the appreciation of figurative texture, and to the poetic value of heterogeneity. Marvell wanders out and back: seduction is an intermittent focus. Line nine proposes the one act by the beloved that might be directly represented by the poem: she might speak and thereby refuse his proposition, as Ralegh's maid is made to speak. But no indication is given of her refusal. As to consent: he refers to her "willing soul" at just the point where consent is hardest to imagine (l. 35). Consent is as remote as her voice. "Coy" means quiet, still. An actual woman hearing his recitation might well excuse herself, when he refers to crashing through the gates of life. J. B. Leishman notes that Donne writes about experiences of love; Marvell, about lovemaking.[9] I described prosodic and thematic connections among Marlowe, Ralegh, and Marvell; they speak of wooing in a single sonic form, though their differences are great. Marlowe and Ralegh are charming, amusing, sophisticated. Marvell is astonishing and rude. He takes an ostensible seduction poem to genital decomposition, to predation, and struggles for physical survival. The passage of time, in his great poem, is conducive more to terror than to pleasure. In a seduction poem he pursues the effects of the sublime, and this is more bewildering than amusing. Urgency comes to aggression and, for Shirley, rape. For Powell, not rape, but bestiality. The truth is that male sexuality entails aggression, whether the object of desire is female or male. One listens to songs of urgency alert to the violence solicited, to the mutuality of desire. Violation is at the periphery of urgency. That is what requires scrutiny.

The impulse to push back against urgent art has survived Ralegh, of course. Lew Spence, Marilyn and Alan Bergman's "Nice 'n' Easy" is one such modern inversion.

> Let's take it nice 'n' easy.
> It's gonna be so easy
> For us to fall in love.
> Hey, baby, what's your hurry?
> Relax and don't you worry.
> We're gonna fall in love.
> We're on the road to romance—that's safe to say—
> But let's make all the stops along the way.
>
> The problem now of course is
> To simply hold your horses.

To rush would be a crime,
'Cause nice and easy does it every time.[10]

Sinatra is slowing down a lady, as if in answer to Marvell. The perspective is that of the much-romanced lover who can say "every time" without embarrassment. He's a connoisseur: love-making to be savored slowly, like wine or food. No crisis is felt, no climax sought, no singularity asserted. This perspective is legible in the style. "Hold your horses" is usually a dead metaphor, too familiar to be figurative. It's reinvigorated, though, with a sense of rightness and surprise, confirmed by an amusing disyllabic rhyme. Rhyming across grammatical categories is a measure of craft, control. The poem is fresh at this level of prosody, not at the more vulgar level of figure; everyone notices a bright figure. A connoisseur winks at the aptness of the rhyme: sophistication in small things. This love doesn't change the lovers; it enhances the quality of their experience— an aesthetic effect. "Let's make all the stops along the way" refers to the social phases of courtship, but with an innuendo too concerning erotic activity. Even in this tantric alternative to urgency, I have to add, one hears lexical indications of risk concerning force and consent, not in the sentences sung but in individual phrases and words: "worry," "safe," "stops," "problems," "hold your horses," "crime." Urgency songs are heavy on double entendres. Billy Ward and the Dominoes boasted in 1951 of Lovin' Dan, a sixty-minute man. Three decades later the Pointer Sisters sought a lover with a slow hand. From Ralegh to Louis Prima and Keely Smith, those who resist panting gratification affirm geniality and humor.

Urgent and joyful songs speak of a moment's impact, as one does of *finding* a wife or husband, of a consequential encounter. But one also hears incessant counsel that good relationships are *made* not discovered. One is advised to *work* on a relationship over time. Laura Kipnis notes that, in our readiness to think all good things rationally constructed, we conceive of a relationship as a workplace, a salt mine.[11] Urgent, joyful poems discount deliberation, foresight, care, and persistence, and celebrate surprises. In esteeming those poems one wishes for release from discipline and long durations. They express a secular sense of temporality, even when gods are said to intervene. Time repeats, and then stops—without qualitative progression: plural love affairs, moments, one much like its predecessors. From this viewpoint, no progress, only oblivion. A love that deepens gradually finds no words here. A human love modeled on divine love: no, certainly not. Carnality is urgent; its measure, clock-time. With the feeling that some particular thing needs to be done goes the corollary that something else will be needed in the future. Urgency comes and goes, possibly soon. Intense desire is its fair face. Aggression is its dark one, a mean endpoint of seriality. Expressions of urgency concern presence, not constancy. Devotion promises soldierly loyalty in absence, love over distance. The Book of Love was never, for Dante and Petrarch, cheerful. The "old high way of love," as Yeats put it, is a waning moon.

5. Love Is Joyful

Plato banished poets from the Republic—but not hymnists. Joyful poems seem small to critics, which is why one does not bother to say that he banished all but praise poets. This subject is a little off to the side of traditions of love poetry. "The innovation of happy love," Laura Kipnis remarks, "didn't even enter the vocabulary of romance until the seventeenth century."[1] Listening to someone else express joy is a test of patience. Why care about joy? Of all love poetry, it is the necessary horizon—either ahead or behind. More particularly its songs call for another way to love: with relaxed expectations of duration, because joy is at best intermittent. Joys have beginnings and ends, boundaries, as many loves do too. For repetition, another joy, one hopes: multiple joys, beloveds, and relationships, after monogamy. These poems' real subject is not steadiness but transformation, from indifference or even grief to pleasure. They are curative. Behind them is an implicit deprivation. What one wants to understand are the conditions or terms of a cure. That is the topic of this chapter.

A rift lies between joyful love-songs and most serious love poetry, because the latter examines joy-in-time. Shelley's "Mutability" confirms what a clear eye eventually reveals.

What is this world's delight?
Lightning that mocks the night,
    Brief even as bright.[2]

Things flicker—delight, light-, night, bright—but joyful songs refuse all dark. The commonplace that all clocks wind down is what joyful songs aggressively resist. "Mocks" is the active verb, the threat of a retrospective of joy. One expects joyful songs and poems to be of the You-Make-Me-Feel-So-Young, or Oh-What-a-Night! variety. Popular songwriters do not even consider a theological basis for hope; joy requires less support in song than in verse. Songwriters claim instead that one already controls one's life: no hostages to fortune. This is their didacticism. As Buddy deSylva says: "So always look for / The silver lining / And try to find the sunny side of life."[3] Dark times, he acknowledges, but not their inevitability. "There's a way to make your very biggest troubles small, / Here's the happy secret of it all." When that works, one may boast of making one's own way.

Happiness is a product of the will. Johnny Mercer is direct about this: "You've got to spread joy / Up to the maximum."[4] "The attitude of doin' right" is at one's disposal, same as it ever was. Joyful writers urge one to change entirely, from dark to bright. Just do it. In "Blue Skies" (1926) Irving Berlin makes the point subtly. In the first line of the verse, he wrote simply: "I was blue."[5] Then the refrain opens: "Blue skies / Smiling at me." From blue to blue, then. An easy transit by renaming: blue-as-gloom to blue-as-bright. "If they say it can't be true," he writes at the end, "I should smile. / That's exactly what I do." No reasons or arguments proffered, except that it is in one's control to be happy. A difference in being derives from a difference in *doing*. Joyful songs propose a radically individualist approach to difficulty. Their severity is heard in Mercer's rhyme: "Don't mess with Mr. In-between." "Have faith, or pandemonium liable to walk upon the scene." All qualification, refinement of measure, negotiated resolution or compromise—that way lies chaos. Intellectuality and its complications are ushered out of the song. The play of mind seems at odds with the ascent of spirit. Mercer imagines the fruits of analysis to be thoroughly disruptive. Joy is armor strapped on against the uncertainties of reflection. No one is urged to find joy in the spirit, or to seek it in another. Instead, one must make a joyful sound, as Mercer himself does memorably: a song of will triumphant. One can admit, he has a point. Intellectuality is conducive to love poems, but less so to joyful ones. Marvell's "Definition of Love" begins in despair and impossibility, and it never gets to fulfillment.

Joy brings exhilaration more than satisfaction. Its songs celebrate flashes of love. Many songs pledge ongoing devotion, as if effort effectively sustains love.[6] Willful songs presume not thralldom but autonomy, an ethical love. Momentary joy is different from the love into which one falls, as into a trance. Duration and number are the issues raised by songs of joy: longevity or brevity; one moment or many. And about that one can learn from Wordsworth's "I Wandered Lonely as a Cloud," not a love poem, but the canonical analysis of an extraordinary moment. He starts off blue, or lonely, disconnected from his surroundings, undirected in his movements.

> I wandered lonely as a cloud
> That floats on high o'er vales and hills,
> When all at once I saw a crowd,
> A host, of golden daffodils;
> Beside the lake, beneath the trees,   5
> Fluttering and dancing in the breeze.

Continuous as the stars that shine
And twinkle on the milky way,
They stretched in never-ending line
Along the margin of a bay: 10
Ten thousand saw I at a glance,
Tossing their heads in sprightly dance.[7]

The flowers are many, while he is one; they dance, he wanders.
They are rooted in a locale; he floats above everything. Those
contrasts seem to present an antidote to his condition, but the
opposed terms bleed into one another. At first, he is on high,
cloud-like over a crowd. But then the flowers are characterized as angelic, a fluttering host (ll. 4 and 6). This account of
a country walk seems strenuously secular, until his diction
becomes Christian. A "crowd" is a term of secular, urban multiplicity, closely associated with labor, whereas one speaks of
an angelic host in a faith-community, not on the street. This
apposition of "crowd" and "host," over a line break, sounds
like a thoughtful correction. The second two stanzas focus on
a concept of surplus.

The waves beside them danced; but they
Outdid the sparkling waves in glee;
A poet could not but be gay,   15
In such a jocund company;
I gazed—and gazed—but little thought
What wealth the show to me had brought:

For oft, when on my couch I lie
In vacant or in pensive mood,   20
They flash upon that inward eye
Which is the bliss of solitude;

> And then my heart with pleasure fills,
> And dances with the daffodils.

Daffodils bloom suddenly—"They flash"—and change a view
entirely. Here their number arouses an excess of joy. They "outdid" the innumerable waves in their glee. And plenitude allows
him to think of continuity (ll. 7 and 9), particularly in the final
stanza. The poem links a sudden joy to a long duration, largely
by reference to number. So *many* flowers!

The metrically regular (but rhythmically tricky) line fifteen—"A poet could not but be gay"—expresses the common
notion that poets, generally morose, require a good deal to
cheer them. The daffodils overwhelm that resistance. The second half of the poem is all about outdoing. The last stanza
explains the *use* to which a poet may put surplus. He details
a distinctive emotional economy: the daffodils return to him
in "vacant or in pensive mood" and provide new bliss. The
surprise is that he wishes *not* to escape but to enjoy solitude.
Presumably, then, excess finds its balance in time. His objective is not to be with the daffodils nor to live gleefully, as one
might expect, but to retain memory of them for what one may
call an intellectual joy. This is an unconventional, paradoxical
approach to joy: the vision of the daffodils did not stimulate
him to thought (though the *poem* is an intellectual product).
In line seventeen, he says, "I gazed—and gazed—but little
thought." It was appreciation of them as emblems of joy that
made an impression on him, even though they would later
enable a mental more than an experiential recovery; memory sequesters excess to enrich later solitude. At all points
Wordsworth celebrates a joy not of action but of observation,
as if looking and remembering were the essential channels of
joy. Contemplation is another thing, more analytical than the

poem allows. His subject is the discipline that allows him to draw sustenance from the flowers. The joy of flowers in bloom is of course transitory. One does not complain that they perish. But when, in *Casablanca*, Humphrey Bogart tells Ingrid Bergman: "We'll always have Paris," one realizes that memory is an imperfect substitute for certain experiences.

Joy comes apparently unbidden to Wordsworth. He had only to be on his feet, out walking; he didn't have to fall in love. Songs like "Accentuate the Positive" and "Look for the Silver Lining" insist instead on a lover's willfulness. They conceive of transformation as hard-won, thoughtfully acquired. English love poetry is generally intellectual, reflective and analytical, more than presentational. Wordsworth is certainly reflective, but *after* seeing the daffodils. He separates the experience from his own reflection on its effect. Consider Shakespeare's Sonnet 29, about getting out of a funk induced by wrong-headed self-reflection. It too is about transformation: what love *does* to experience.

> When, in disgrace with Fortune and men's eyes,
> I all alone beweep my outcast state,
> And trouble deaf heaven with my bootless cries,
> And look upon myself and curse my fate,
> Wishing me like to one more rich in hope,   5
> Featured like him, like him with friends possessed,
> Desiring this man's art, and that man's scope,
> With what I most enjoy contented least;
> Yet in these thoughts myself almost despising,
> Haply I think on thee, and then my state,   10
> Like to the lark at break of day arising
> From sullen earth, sings hymns at heaven's gate;
>   For thy sweet love rememb'red such wealth brings,
>   That then I scorn to change my state with kings.[8]

The word "joy" is placed at the center of the poem, however inconspicuously: "With what I most enjoy contented least" (l. 8). This handsomely shaped line draws on an elaborate syntactic structure to express a cutting irony at the speaker's expense. What happens eventually to the experience of joy? A greedy ego obscures it from view. This strong eighth line, as Helen Vendler observes, "yields . . . a stunning moment of self-analysis."⁹ That which has been *enjoyed* entails responsibility. One answers finally for all that is received: his hopefulness (l. 5), his good looks and companions (l. 6), his art or range of vision (l. 7). Shakespeare's nature is such that he wants still more of the goods of life, and the sight of peers enjoying any arouses his envy. The joys he has known have left him to respond, as here in line eight, to the dark moments of egotism. The vigorous structure of this one clause is an adequate assertion of the poet's sanity: he understands his vanity. Beyond that, he's amused by it, as readers are too.

The sestet is joined to the octave by a delicate semicolon that leaves the relation of the eighth and ninth lines a little uncertain. The word "almost," a faint modifier—not an obvious one for poets; here, an expression of sophistication—affirms a sense of mere humanity. For Shakespeare to envy another's art or scope is ridiculous, as this word suggests. This ordinarily overused adverb, "almost," uttered here with a wink of admission lightens the tone to indicate that he cannot reasonably despise himself. He recognizes his own gifts and is able then to turn the poem to praise of another (l. 10). Congeniality requires a sense of self-worth. He can only "think on thee" once he has refused self-loathing. To think of another is then likened to the sound of irrepressible birdsong, to the echoing of cognate tones: "Like to the lark." Those simple, liquid but clipped syllables seem to sound praise of God's blessings. "It is right to give thanks and praise." The syntactic structures that expose paradox, contradiction, "with what I most enjoy contented least," reveal the folly of self-regard.[10] From that awareness comes not only openness to a beloved, but access to the meaning of analogies among natural phenomena. Birdsong in the pre-dawn dark is a call to prayer. The poet hears that call because he has properly understood his own excesses and confusions. The song of the four syllables opening line eleven has been prepared by self-awareness: reasonably he can only *almost* despise himself. The poet who wrote the first word, "When," had already understood the process described by the poem, written in a continual present-tense: the joys brought by the beloved are not continuous, but they recur, as birdsong and dawn do.

Wordsworth and Shakespeare produced models of *change*. "The notion of love as transformative," as Troy Jollimore notes, "the idea that love initiates a new stage of life and that after falling in love things will never be the same, is . . . common."[11] Wordsworth, on a walk, inadvertently comes upon an impetus to change, though he seeks none. Shakespeare recalls his beloved, and that pulls him out of self-concern. "Continuous" is the word that begins Wordsworth's second stanza, and continuity is the topic of his concluding stanza. Shakespeare does not need to address this topic, because the proverb "Count your blessings" so obviously suits the narrative he has constructed. He needs only to recognize the existence of his beloved in order to see that all along he has had more than enough. He had momentarily overlooked the all-along. There is a semantic (not an etymological) link between counting, arranging in sequence, and continuity, holding together. The master sustainer of upbeat songs is Cole Porter, who wrote five refrains for "Let's Do It" (1928). As he proceeds through a long list of animals, fish, and insects that "do it," he displays, above all, writerly invention. The joyfulness of the song is in the abundance of reproduction, "surplus," as Wordsworth says; but still more in the skills of the lyricist who marshals these words to the tune. Torch-songs, blues, longing, and regret seem remote distractions; romantic desire, absurd. Life is enough; besides, artifice works. No fuss.

> Romantic sponges, they say, do it,
> Oysters, down in Oyster Bay, do it,
> Let's do it, let's fall in love.
> Cold Cape Cod clams, 'gainst their wish, do it.
> Even lazy jellyfish do it,
> Let's do it, let's fall in love.
> Electric eels, I might add, do it,
> Though it shocks 'em, I know.
> Why ask if shad do it?
> Waiter, bring me shad roe.
> In shallow shoals, English soles do it,
> Goldfish, in the privacy of bowls, do it,
> Let's do it, let's fall in love.[12]

The joy proposed is simple and evidently universal: call copulation love; close enough. Cole Porter, like Johnny Mercer, takes seriously the idea of *making* love, of assuming responsibility for one's own joy. Those who wait for some real thing to come along evade life itself. Fish and crustaceans come to the lyricist in no particular sequence. He makes do with what he has to fill out the form of a song, and that constraint is thoroughly manageable: no straining or complaining from him. Surprising turns and rhymes ("know" and "roe," for instance) inhere in the sounds. The phrase "cold Cape Cod clams" packs four hard c's in as many syllables, and the adverbial phrase ("'gainst their wish") exactly accounts for the one hard c that was not inevitable ("cold"). The progress of sounds is stunning: shad→shad roe→shallow; shallow→shoals→soles→bowls. Billie Holiday paces her phrasing not to the syntax of Porter's sentences but to the track of consonance. From "shad roe" to "In shallow shoals" is delivered as a single sentence. It is not just rhymes that Porter is after, but echoes, strong and surprising, that can take the poem to fresh water, so to speak. Most of what he needs is in the words at their sensual surfaces; the rest is in well-known customs of class signage. Can it be so much harder for lovers to feel satisfaction, if he can harness art and exuberance in a list? Make the changes you can.

Originality is an unreasonable measure of joyous poets. The pleasures of love song and poetry are largely traditional. Joyful songs in particular have a conspicuous sameness about them. Their terms are conventional, parts of a code: blue, clouds, rain, sun, love, marry, paradise, heaven. When Buddy deSylva and Jerome Kern collaborated on "Look for the Silver Lining" in 1920, they probably started from a World War I poem by Lena Guilbert Ford, "Keep the Home Fires Burning" (1915): "There's a silver lining / Through the dark cloud shining; / Turn the dark cloud inside out, / Till the boys come home." Irving Berlin cannot have thought that he was being fresh or surprising when in 1935 he wrote, "Heaven, / I'm in heaven."[13] In "Cloudburst" Leroy Kirkland in the mid-1950s was obviously taking up the terms—clouds and blue skies— made famous by Irving Berlin in "Blue Skies," and by Buddy deSylva in "Look for the Silver Lining."[14] These are deliberate revisions of predecessor songs adequately explained as the topoi and copia of the genre. But it is not just that it is hard to express joy in a fresh way; the issue goes deeper.

Ease with conventional values and experiences, with life as it is said to be—not what it actually is—this is what troubles many critics and poets. Many memorable love songs express that ease. In Mitchell Parrish's "Sweet Lorraine" (1928), Nat King Cole sings, "Just to think that / I'm the lucky one / Who will lead her / Down the aisle."[15] The diction, figuration, and avowals of "Sweet Lorraine" are utterly conventional; that is the point. There is no apparent irony in Parrish's lyric, nor in Cole's performance. In "Cloudburst" Jon Hendricks says, "I won't be satisfied / 'till I hear 'em play 'Here Comes the Bride.'" One must take pleasure in the simple expectation of marriage in order to perform this song appropriately. One may well do so in a sophisticated manner, with recognition of the comforts of conventionality. The song is prefaced, in a sense, by a subjunctive. If only this were life: that the groom were a lucky guy, that he would never miss the sun, that his sweetie would smile steadily. All obviously unlikely (as is the notion that a black male lover might publicly celebrate his love of a blue-eyed sweetie (though Nat King Cole famously overcame racial interdictions). For the duration of a lovesong, one finds joy in an ostensible, implausible fit between what is commonly proposed and what is actually done. But then how does one explain to another the value of the song?

If by irony one means saying one thing but meaning something more or less antithetical, "Sweet Lorraine" is not ironic. The words alone—their paraphrasable sense—are without surprise. When does a sophisticated sensibility such as Parrish's or yours or mine take pleasure in a naïve account of romance and marriage as luck? Cole's rendition is elegant, full of musical surprises, though its literal sense is slight. Its terms are understood to be deliberately conventional: the walk down the aisle, the picket fence leave fulfillment as a sign, an abstraction.

The terms on which lovers live with the erosions that come in time are not stated, because the song is too hip to address the matter. Conventions serve the song and may serve lovers too; actual experience is too various for the song. The gap between the lyrics and the musical performance makes one ask how to reconcile aesthetic judgment with the norms of one's chosen contemporaries. I nonetheless admire this song's geniality (a kindliness that derives etymologically from wedding feasts). An audience recognizes dramatic irony when a character's expression does not fit known facts. This song and others like it display a sincerity that presents the singer as a willful character, plainly trying to grasp at something only apparently simple. William Empson spoke of the social leveling that is part of the traditions of love poetry. The genre of pastoral, he argued, advocates humility by focusing, as troubadours did too, on those moments when a lover pines. The hearts of those high and low are broken by deprivation. "Sweet Lorraine" turns this just a little: lovers hip and square want the same thing, to hold on tight to their honeys. The song helps one recognize that ordinary impulse that cuts across boundaries of taste between audiences.

Brevity is a formal or rhetorical characteristic: a poet declines to elaborate. A bolt of lightning is Shelley's figure for "delight" in "Mutability." One does not argue with lightning. One sees what one can in the flash. Some matters require no analysis or explanation; simplicity is enough. The poems and songs discussed above in this chapter make the point, if implicitly, that elaboration is dubious. They are poems, as I've indicated, of accommodation. They urge acceptance of immediate circumstances or familiar structures of imagination—weddings, picket fences, blue-eyed honeys—a white happiness. I turn now to some longer poems that focus on problems of continuity, exactly that which brevity cannot achieve. These poems claim that economic forces make joy seem unsustainable. They imagine a distant, external source of joy and some traditional figures of mediation: birds and angels more or less above human activity. Apostrophe is one of the techniques of these ambitious poems. It urges one, as Jonathan Culler has shown, to understand such address less as a "relic of archaic beliefs" than as a claim to the authority of a "poetical and prophetic voice."[16]

Czeslaw Milosz wrote a twenty-five-line poem (not a song), explicitly addressed to angels, that includes these lines:

> Short is your stay here:
> now and then at a matinal hour, if the sky is clear,
> in a melody repeated by a bird,
> or in the smell of apples at the close of day
> when the light makes the orchards magic.[17](ll. 8-12)

The pressure of economy is not apparent. His choice of words seems casual, loose: "now and then"; "at the close of day when the light . . ." In this manner, significance can be indefinitely insinuated more than stated. "Angels" and "matinal" evoke traditions of worship without insisting that the remnants of Christian belief properly govern our lives. He has little to predicate of these magical moments, only that they arrive.

> I have heard that voice many a time when asleep
> and, what is strange, I understood more or less
> an order or an appeal in an unearthly tongue:
>
> day draws near
> another one
> do what you can. (ll. 20-25)

Those last three dimeters, stitched together from a displaced source, express conviction that truth is brief, modest; the relaxed style of the earlier lines can accommodate religious feelings outside of a theological frame. This conclusion is cast in a taciturn form, but it addresses the continuity of one's days.

Poems of ostensible wisdom often derive from conviction that ordinary life is enlightened by singular moments. Elizabeth Bishop's "The Fish" (1946) is a masterpiece of this kind. Where that conviction loosens its grip on form and joyful poems are given greater length, intellectual analysis becomes more prominent—and suspect. In 1951 Allen Tate wrote an essay arguing that poetry loses contact with objects, or nature, as it commits to rational analysis; he titled the essay in which he discusses Poe in particular "The Angelic Imagination." Rationality is angelic, in his view, because it operates *above* the complications of material existence. "Man as angel," he wrote, "becomes a demon who cannot initiate the first motion of love."[18] The angels of poetry are attracted by love and intimacy, but only as observers, like surveillance agents. Robert Hass has them captivated but also desolate at the sight of lovemaking.[19] Efforts to approximate the supposed ways of angels entail abstraction from material experience. What one wants is not wings but enlightenment *and* the "smell of apples"—or magical orchards. Is a disciplined, rational mind compatible with love and joy—and creation—is a question, in Traherne's view.

Analysis is more conducive to doubt than to joy. Gravity comes easily to poets. Think of Frost's famous sonnet on birds, "Never Again Would Birds' Song Be the Same," that wobbles between critique and admiration.

> He would declare and could himself believe
> That the birds there in all the garden round

> From having heard the daylong voice of Eve
> Had added to their own an oversound,
> Her tone of meaning but without the words.   5
> Admittedly an eloquence so soft
> Could only have had an influence on birds
> When call or laughter carried it aloft.
> Be that as may be, she was in their song.
> Moreover her voice upon their voices crossed   10
> Had now persisted in the woods so long
> That probably it never would be lost.
> Never again would birds' song be the same.
> And to do that to birds was why she came.[20]

Eve knew joy (l. 8), but the speaker admires that only from an explainer's distance; he resembles the speaker of Browning's "My Last Duchess." The first five lines express admiration of tenderness, but a skeptical undertone is audible in the first line. The syntax of the first sentence spills out of the quatrain, confirming a sense of excess like Eve's overtone. Even the sweet third line insinuates that she talked constantly. His words are prosaic—"would declare," "Admittedly," "moreover," "be that as may be," "probably"—appropriate to doubt-driven inquiry, not birds' song. His is the voice of a disciplined intellectual. The contrast of these two conceptions of utterance concerns the power of sonority. Where does that come from, one wants to know. From the first woman.

This poem proposes an apocryphal Bible story or folk-belief within the idioms of uncertainty. The first word refers to an obscure origin. The pronoun identifies the first human, the most contested antecedent of all—maybe only a suppressed name. The initial verbs are in a conditional mode and recommend Adam's belief that the indefinite "tone of meaning" of birds' song originated in his mate's voice. What conditions need to be met before *would declare* and *could believe* might become indicative? If Adam *existed*, he would declare . . . ? Or more likely the line means only that, if he could be asked, he would so declare, and that he was able to believe that quaint account of birds' song. But the distinction between declaration and belief itself is postlapsarian and basic to skeptical inquiry; it admits the possibility of deliberate misrepresentation. Adam does not believe that their song derives wholly from her voice—only partly. She had an influence, as we say, that is distinguishable from the meaning of her words (ll. 4-8). She contributed a *part* to bird's song. And to Adam?

The claim of the second sentence (ll. 6-8) is the speaker's, or Frost's, not Adam's; it is firmer than the hypothesis of the first sentence about another mind. This claim concerns the two *parts* of Eve's spirit that must have affected birds' song: her joyfulness and desire for companionship—a wish not to live apart (l. 8). Ambition, will-to-knowledge, disobedience—all such is evidently irrelevant to birds' song. The last line, secure in its syntax, sounds assured of its assertion, though again a pronoun, or retrospective reference, is conspicuous. The word "that" refers to her abiding but indefinite effect on birds' song, as if that were sufficiently clear for this modest pronoun to do its conclusive work. The poem does not try to circumscribe her effect sharply, only to say that it pertains to sound rather than sense. The force of the conclusion is to distinguish among reasons for her presence in the garden. She did not come to comfort Adam, as Milton claims, nor to propagate the species, as Genesis has it.

She came to add a joyful tone to birds' song, according to the wry and skeptical speaker. Wry, because this Eve came of her own volition, not as an instrument of a Christian God's will, and because she came as a designing, restless aesthete. This also seems to be what Adam believed of his beloved, and what explains the compelling plaintiveness of birds' song. Line thirteen might suggest regret insofar as it begins "Never again." The poem strikes even critical readers as sad.[21] A sense of loss is implied by the bold use of pronouns in the first and last lines: a reader is sent looking for an antecedent. Her contribution to birds' song is enduring testimony of an elusive spirit. Birds' song will never again be without this record of her soft, joyful being, which is something for her progeny to appreciate. The poem is melancholy in that the inscrutability of birds' song is a sign less of surviving joy than of meaning lost to mortal life—and of a human presence flown away. Adam may seem to listen to the birds as a widower might—after a loss, that is. Their songs summon one to a lost elsewhere of gentle collaboration that one wants to understand. One senses that the poem is threatened finally not by melancholy but by supercilious humor. Pound and Eliot characterized the influence of poets in terms of the revision of semantic forms: poets purify the dialect of the tribe. But Frost imagines instead an influence above semantics. Poets too convey something joyous but not paraphrasable. In the idioms of explanation, where terms can have grammatical sense without semantic exactness, one settles for amusement and admiration.

It's easy enough for lovers to attribute their joy to their beloveds. But the great poems about birds' song (Johnny Mercer's "Skylark" is another) speak of obscure origins of joy. One wants to know: where is that bird, where is its home? Mercer begins with apostrophe: the motive of strong figuration is not ornamentation but confidence that connections of tenor and vehicle are cognitive. To feel the greatest joy, according to Thomas Traherne, one needs a deep account of the meaning and value of sense-experience. Mid-seventeenth century poets celebrated the sensual joy of romance. Traherne constructed an economic and religious analysis of sense-experience. What he wanted was unlikely to come from a short lyric to a beloved. Longer forms speak of joy and love beyond romance, mediated by angels and birds as instruments of greater powers.

1
How like an Angel came I down!
How Bright are all Things here!
When first among his Works I did appear
O how their GLORY me did Crown?
The World resembled his *Eternitie*,   5
In which my Soul did Walk;
And evry Thing that I did see,
Did with me talk.

2
The Skies in their Magnificence,
The Lively, Lovely Air;   10
Oh how Divine, how Soft, how Sweet, how fair!
The Stars did entertain my Sence,
And all the Works of GOD so Bright and pure,
So Rich and Great did seem,
As if they ever must endure,   15
In my Esteem.[22]

Traherne attributes intelligence to objects: his chief figure is animation. This is the obverse of apostrophe: as poets speak to birds, birds may speak to poets.[23] The term *bright* means shining (*OED*, 1a), but it also indicates brilliance in conversation (*OED*, 7a). This pun is evident at the end of the opening stanza, in the claim that objects talked with him. The idea of bright conversation with physical objects is in accord with these two initial stanzas. If they talked, they had agency as well as intelligence, which renders significant the apposition "lively, lovely" concerning the air (line 10). But Traherne makes no effort to represent the substance of this talk. His only concern is that creation communicated with him.[24] This is the point of animation: that in a state of innocence no matter is inert. Things and people correspond to one another without any concept of ownership.

Nearly all of "Wonder" (ca. 1665) is retrospective. The one clear exception, a main clause in the present indicative, is that second line: "How Bright are all Things here!" The oscillation from past to present and back to past in the first three lines establishes instability between a vision at the start of life and later adult utterances. Moments come and go. The oscillating line-lengths keep instability in the ear as well. The basis of wonder is recollection of objects charged with spirit—rather like Wordsworth's angelic flowers. When Traherne says, "The World resembled his *Eternitie*" (l. 5), he affirms an enduring meaning of mortal life generally, and a holy ground for poetic figuration. In a state of innocence, worldly objects are expressive: "And evry Thing that I did see / Did with me talk" (ll. 7-8). The skies then seemed "divine" and "soft" and "fair," like a beloved. "Divine" is meant literally, whereas now one would have to mean it figuratively, if one were speaking of the *appearance* of the skies. His is a radical incarnational view, oriented on a single tenet of Christian theology: "I nothing in the World did know / But 'twas Divine" (ll. 23-24). Aristotle understood poetry to be the construction of surprising connections, and most later poets remember this claim well. Traherne insists that joy derives from a distinct relation to physical experience. He affirms that sensual pleasure is more than mundane. This is to say that allegory is indistinguishable from realistic representation: objects *possess* (not just stand for) metaphysical qualities.

The word "sence" is repeated in the third stanza in exactly the position where it appears in the second; a few other words are repeated (*bright* twice; *bliss* twice; *joy* four times), but none is comparably positioned. The primary meaning of *sence* in line twelve refers to that which is received by the organs of physical perception: "The bodily senses considered as a single faculty in contrast to intellect, reason, will, etc." (*OED*, 12b) This usage is first dated to 1533 and pertains to Traherne's usage. He is intent to represent a state of innocence as, above all, a physical scenario into which he dropped, as if from the sky. More than that, he did not do. The stars entertained *him*. Here is the third stanza:

3

A Native Health and Innocence
   Within my Bones did grow;
And while my GOD did all his *Glories* shew,
   I felt a Vigour in my Sence   20
That was all SPIRIT. I within did flow
   With Seas of Life, like Wine;
   I nothing in the World did know,
      But 'twas Divine.

When *sence* reappears in line twenty, its primary meaning is different; line twenty-one says that this *sence* was "all spirit," which means that the primary meaning cannot be the organs of physical perception. These organs are surely relevant to the usage in lines twenty and twenty-one, but in a secondary manner. My point is that Traherne employs this famously polysemic term, sence, in ways that indicate that some words must be turned one way and another in order to convey the variousness of God's ways. Another way to put this is that, like many other poets, though not all, Traherne mines the semantic density of words.[25]

God's manifold presence bears on the poem at the level of syllable, line, and stanza. Formally, the poem is intricate, though thoroughly regular: eight eight-line stanzas fall in three thematic groups (incarnation: sts. 1-3; ornamentation: 4-6; and private property: 7-8). Yet all sixty-four lines reiterate one thing: I saw the world did shine. The poem urges one, by formal means, to attend to the variety and intricacy of God's presence in creation. The first quatrain of each stanza (rhymed ABBA) has an iambic tetrameter line, then a trimeter, a pentameter, and another tetrameter; the second quatrain (rhymed CDCD) is comprised of a pentameter followed by a trimeter, a tetrameter, and finally a dimeter. This shape is elaborate and instantiated eight times with few departures. The syntax begins (ll. 1-4) in an exclamatory voice to which the poet returns in later stanzas (ll. 11, 35 and 48). That register of utterance is familiar to joyous poetry generally. But the grammatical structures otherwise extend freely and variously over line-breaks. His only formal experimentation is in the array of nouns and adjectives in some of the long lines of the poem.

> Sins, Griefs, Complaints, Dissentions, Weeping Eys,
> (l. 27)
> Rare Splendors, Yellow, Blew, Red, White and Green,
> (l. 43)
> And so did Hedges, Ditches, Limits, Bounds, (l. 53)
> Clothes, Ribbans, Jewels, Laces, I esteemed (l. 61)

He draws out the prescriptive effect of iambic pentameter; as the lines grow dense with specificity, the determinative force of prosodic convention must increase. Only the prosodic norm stipulates that "Griefs" takes more stress than "Sins," and "Red" less than "White." These lines are strung with the beads of what Traherne understands as the world, and Richard Wilbur would later nicely call "the world's hunks and colors." Traherne invents a stanza form without inhibition. All elements of language can be exuberantly turned to a new shape, because each word, like each thing, bears into the world the richest of all meanings. The joy of his poem is apparent in his prosodic invention, as Cole Porter's is in his lists. All that the world contains—things, names, sounds—is perfectly suited to human desire. And none of this depends on romance.

Traherne understood that in order to live in joy one needs to quarantine pain and deprivation, restrict the prerogatives of private property, and live independently of others. Stanza four says bluntly that in a state of health and innocence he could not see all the evil he would later comprehend.

4

Harsh ragged Objects were concealed;   25
    Oppressions Tears and Cries,
Sins, Griefs, Complaints, Dissensions, weeping Eyes,
    Were hid: and only Things reveald,
Which Heavnly Spirits, and the Angels prize.
    The State of Innocence   30
    And Bliss, not Trades and Poverties,
        Did fill my Sence.

Half the nouns in series in lines twenty-five and twenty-six refer to intentions, ideas, feelings, things of the spirit, not to objects. Corruption of people is part of the hidden harshness of economic activity. Political, personal, and financial suffering were present in his youth, but obscured from his view. In the last two stanzas, he reasserts the notion that, when innocent, he was formerly blind in particular to the adversity caused by the severing of public and private parcels of land: "Hedges, Ditches, Limits, Bounds" (l. 53)—which were used to keep grazing animals from trespassing on private estate lands.

7

Cursd and Devisd Proprieties,
    With Envy, Avarice   50
And Fraud, those Feinds that Spoyl even Paradice,
    Flew from the Splendor of mine Eys,
And so did Hedges, Ditches, Limits, Bounds . . .

Since the fourteenth century "devise" has meant to divide, then to bequeath, and then to contrive or invent (*OED*, 1a, 4, 5a). In the sixteenth century it came to mean to contrive deceitfully (*OED*, 7b). Proprieties referred to properties owned by someone; the two words were formerly one. (The sense of social or moral propriety is an eighteenth century usage.) The density of reference of some of Traherne's key terms—*bliss, sence, devise*—reveal his exactness. He pulls together some of the distinct, even disparate senses of single words. He speaks not only out of his own convictions but out of the gathered experiences and insights of English-speakers generally. Barbara Lewalski concluded that Traherne approached "language as a transparent medium pointing to essences rather than as a densely and complexly suggestive poetic matrix."[26] In this great poem, the opposite seems to be the case. The poem's innocent joy is a state of *seeming* (l. 63). The greatest joy ("No joy to this!" [l. 48]) is to move freely over terrain, to go where one wishes, and to see the wealth of others as a show intended to please oneself. No obstructions in one's path, no covetousness within oneself. Such joy was unattainable by nearly everyone in seventeenth-century England, according to Traherne, because of an economic system whereby private property could be held indefinitely.

8

Proprieties themselves were mine,
      And Hedges Ornaments;
Walls, Boxes, Coffers, and their rich Contents
      Did not divide my joys, but all shine.   60
Clothes, Ribbans, Jewels, Laces, I esteemd
      My Joys by others worn:
For me they all to wear them seem'd
      When I was born.

Traherne asserts that there is no satisfactory way to reconcile, in the sense of legitimate, incarnationist doctrine and the worldly suffering of poor people. Insofar as perceptible objects are charged with God's presence, any notion of private property is absurd. One does not *own* pieces of Christ. To live in joy, one must see with the partiality of an angel, or be blind to oppression. His poem is structured insistently around the depredations of temporality. The creation, he implies, as the instability of the subjunctive creeps into the second stanza, does not retain its value for mortals living in time. One expects him to press a distinction between God's creation and the devices of mortals, but he sees that temporality corrupts experience. Creation itself changes in time.

And all the Works of GOD so Bright and pure,
   So Rich and Great did seem,
As if they ever must endure,   15
   In my Esteem.

He felt himself to be spirit, not just sense, only so long as God
revealed to him His glories (l. 19). Because his vision so closely
concerns temporality, the shifts of tense in the first three lines
and throughout matter greatly. He sees the beauty of Christ
only *while* suffering is hid from his eyes (ll. 25-29), or *while*
God revealed His glories (l. 19), *while* he saw like an angel (l.
39). These temporal markers gather force that is fulfilled in
the last line that identifies the specific moment of the vision,
"When I was born." The innocence and spirit he felt at birth
passed from him, as youth did. Although the poem insists that
the institution of private property is the dominant error of the
fallen world, he is not denouncing *other* people's bad behavior.
In sixty-four lines, he has thirty first-person singular pronouns,
and twelve of those indicate possession, including the phrase
"my wealth"; the point is implicitly made that Traherne feels
the allure of possession. This is to say not only that the greatest joy is incompatible with private property and secular time,
but further that one inevitably surrenders innocence and the
life of a full spirit.

    Moments of recovery, when body and spirit come together
again, are out of the question; economic relations, enforced
by law, rule that out. Recent poets, however, adhere to a more
optimistic sense of temporality. Wordsworth's "I Wandered
Lonely as a Cloud" is a model of the exceptional moment that
alters a future. Richard Wilbur's "Love Calls Us to the Things
of the World" (1956) is a particularly distinguished example
of this type of poem, and one that acknowledges economic
constraints on the life of spirit.

The eyes open to a cry of pulleys,
And spirited from sleep, the astounded soul
Hangs for a moment bodiless and simple
As false dawn.
                        Outside the open window
The morning air is all awash with angels.   5

Some are in bed-sheets, some are in blouses,
Some are in smocks: but truly there they are.
Now they are rising together in calm swells
Of halcyon feeling, filling whatever they wear
With the deep joy of their impersonal breathing;   10

Now they are flying in place, conveying
The terrible speed of their omnipresence, moving
And staying like white water; and now of a sudden
They swoon down into so rapt a quiet
That nobody seems to be there.
                                        The soul shrinks   15

From all that it is about to remember,
From the punctual rape of every blessed day,
And cries,
            "Oh, let there be nothing on earth but laundry,
Nothing but rosy hands in the rising steam
And clear dances done in the sight of heaven."   20

Yet, as the sun acknowledges
With a warm look the world's hunks and colors,
The soul descends once more in bitter love
To accept the waking body, saying now
In a changed voice as the man yawns and rises,   25

> "Bring them down from their ruddy gallows;
> Let there be clean linen for the backs of thieves;
> Let lovers go fresh and sweet to be undone,
> And the heaviest nuns walk in a pure floating
> Of dark habits,
>   Keeping their difficult balance."   30

Wilbur too has seen the world shine ("All things bright and beautiful," as the hymn has it) and, like Traherne, been astonished: "but truly there they are" (l. 7), he says. This is a forceful declaration from the mouth of a doubter in the presence of spirit in the things of the world. The adversative "but" signals resistance not to the inertness of matter but to the fancifulness of Wilbur's own idioms. His inventiveness dazzles, as Porter's does, but in a lexical zone removed from contemporary city life; only the first line refers explicitly (and beneath its vowel music) to an urban setting ("cry of [clothesline] pulleys"). The *sine qua non* of his art: distance and a changeable rhythm. The folds of his poem are patted down gently; it alters more in mood than substance. He shows some delicacy in not stating the conditions of modern labor from which the soul shrinks. (Traherne is less concerned with consensus with his audience, and much more doctrinal.) Certain flights of phrasing refer to antique conventions of feeling: "calm swells of halcyon feeling," for instance, is a phrase that resists currency and the instrumentality of ordinary discourse. The poem's approved norms of feeling are displaced from the mid-century American language Wilbur shared with his first readers. Angels, laundresses, and nuns. When the poem closes with reference to the sisters' "dark habits" and "difficult balance," one infers that "the man's" estrangement from his own labor—that which he awakens to—has something to do with insidious procedures and dubious accounting; that is, Wilbur's wordplay is rather differently expressive than his literal statements. "Rapt" (l. 14), for example, is part of an exuberant sentence about flights of spirit. It is a word familiar from recorded accounts of intense concentration; like "halcyon" (l. 9), it is immediately known to readers, but just outside vernacular currency. To a native speaker of American English, such words are signs of casual, comfortable, harmlessly arch periphrasis. One may be aware already that "rapt" derives from "rapture," and that both terms indicate not only the transport of one's spirit but the abduction, or rape, of a woman as well, but "rapt" is the word that seems to awaken the speaker to the brutal reality of urban life, its "punctual rape of every blessed day" three lines later. "Rapt" presents a veiled vision of "rape," as Wilbur's style more generally might seem to elude the roughness of material and spiritual life in a modern economy, were the sonic and figurative texture of his words less intricate.

The poem's style insinuates duplicity or divided signification: "bodiless and simple / As a false dawn" (ll. 3-4). False dawn is a glow in the sky about an hour before true dawn. Can anything so called be known for simplicity?[27] The simile opens a track for reading against the express sense of Wilbur's sentences. Consider the soul's final speech: a magnanimous blessing on thieves, lovers, and nuns in their "dark habits" (ll. 26-30). (There can be, incidentally, no *pure* floating of *dark* habits, as there is nothing simple about a false dawn.) Beneath the intricate figures and sounds of this poem about angels is an ultimately illegible subtext concerning women, theft, and deception. The formal dynamic is unlike that of poems that employ sonic resources to enforce an express theme. This poem's first term is "eyes," and they are immediately said to open, as three lines later a window is said to be open. Several words recur, suggesting non-syntactic links among the poem's terms, as is altogether common in lyric poetry. "Eyes" half-rhymes with the "cry" of the pulleys, also in the first line. Sonically, the eyes cry, despite a later reference to "deep joy" (l. 10). The eyes rhyme as well with angels "rising together in calm swells" in line eight. This matters because the central action of the poem is a man, apparently alone, rising with difficulty from bed, mysteriously reluctant to begin another workday. He will actually rise, yawning, in line thirty-five. But between the rising angels of line eight and his later rising is a prayer uttered by the soul that refers warmly to "rosy hands in the rising steam" (l. 19). Rosy . . . rising, or maybe a Rosie rising with "the man," as the angels rise "together in calm swells" (l. 8). The sonic texture works at an oblique angle to the paraphrasable sense of this ostensibly joyful poem. The pleasure of this art is in such indirect, sprightly engagement with an unspeakably leaden reality.

Two of Wilbur's intellectual words, "impersonal" (l. 10) and "omnipresence" (l.12), stand out from their companions, like a thumbprint on a clear window; they reveal the press of mind on the vision he imagines. In a modern intellectual context, they are familiar; they identify the notion that souls are not tied to distinct personalities, that spirit is everywhere at once. Wilbur's engagement with love is abstract. This speaker's willfully impersonal voice is somehow dissociated from "the man," but for no apparent reason: "the eyes open" are the words that open the poem without any indication just who is waking. Impersonality is a condition of the opening of a window onto a flock of angels—emblems of spirit and "deep joy" (l. 10). *Opening* is the point: without that impersonality one more person might once again wake to make his or her way to work, and a smaller sense of the world. Wilbur's analytical categories are not so specific or acute as Traherne's: the modern poet accepts, with some lightness, the inevitability of

the "punctual rape of every blessèd day." The surprise is less
that poets write of the inconvenient fact that life is everywhere
and always a mix of innocence and evil, surface and depth,
body and soul, joy and pain, than that they wish, after all, to
have it no other way. Traherne certainly wished to live free of
private property, in the joy of Christ incarnate, "the grandeur
of God," as Hopkins says. Wilbur's poem instead resolves a
different dilemma: how to transform indefinite terror of the
approaching day into a celebration of the adversity that characterizes every day. The older poet was less easily satisfied that
resistance is feckless. This is a political difference, and it derives
from Traherne's particular theological bearings.

His poem begins with a connection between angelic and
joyous human being: "How like an angel came I down!" The
hymnus angelicus, or "Gloria in Excelsis Deo," is sung by a chorus of angels announcing the birth of Christ—one of two psalms
included in the Roman Catholic liturgy but not taken from the
Bible. Someone invented the hymn, as Milosz would say, and
the *Te Deum* too; they are called *psalmi idiotici*. ("Idiot" meant
someone lacking in learning, then a layperson.) That inven-
tor began with Luke 2:14, and then went beyond the gospel.
Wilbur and Milosz do not write as straightforward believers
in the presence of Christ in the material world. They instead
maintain a bifocal perspective on the aspiration toward spirit
and purity, on one side, and the fallenness of a city life without
belief, on the other. Christian tenets are memories and fancies
for secular intellectuals; they can't be articles of faith. Poets tease
the remnants of Christian faith in the intellectual classes in order
to construct figurative accounts of joy taken in the presence of
spirit in the world. Were angels in the air, rather than laundry
on the lines, would that not be joyful? The results are beautiful,
but hesitant, nostalgic. The poems register a comprehensive joy
that is to be had in no other way in a secular milieu.

Joyful songs celebrate the adequacy of all that love daily provides. A dawn song, for instance, reflects on a night of lovemaking; it derives from the plain physical facts of a loving life. It sets lovemaking against the rising sun, which keeps on rising. That is a wake-up call to understand love in relation to the days ahead. A poet-lover in the dawn puts some punctuation on the act of love. Some lovers name a value as they leave the bed; that is an act of mind. Here is a supposed late Roman aubade, actually an excerpt from Petronius' prose translated by Kenneth Rexroth.

> Good God, what a night that was,
> The bed was so soft, and how we clung,
> Burning together, lying this way and that,
> Our uncontrollable passions
> Flowing through our mouths.
> If I could only die that way,
> I'd say goodbye to the business of living.[28]

Lovemaking reveals something missing from ordinary existence, which Rexroth calls "the business of living." It is not that one ordinarily pines for sexual intensity. One forgets the pleasures of love while negotiating the exchanges and arrangements that underlie everyday calm. Eventually amnesia permits one to speak plausibly but wrongly of living as a "business," or challenge to management. What flows through the lovers' mouths is unmanaged and warrants another kind of living. Herodotus said that no life can be justly assessed before its end. Rexroth's closing couplet proposes that unmanaged passionate expression is a justification of life itself. Realized passion permits lovers to die satisfied that their lives have been truly revealed—if only to each other. That is its clarity.

Even so short and apparently simple a poem as Rexroth's responds to the intellectual tradition of love poetry in English. All the poems and songs discussed above aspire to general statement about love. But Milosz, Traherne, and Wilbur suggest that joy thrives most grandly with support of a metaphysics. Traherne is most ambitious in examining the relation of love to ordinary existence; Wilbur similarly speaks of love in a life of daily labor. Rexroth's Petronius poem is obviously simpler than those of Milosz, Traherne, and Wilbur. Vision, Christianity, labor—these topics are displaced by a mattress and a lively partner. Yet one notices that this short poem is peppered with words that have been altered by Christian worship: "burning," "passions," and "die." They implicate a night of good sex in a tradition of religious thought. "Good God," the poem begins, because what English-speaking lovers know of transcendence, or rising above their workaday activities, derives from Christianity. Lawrence Lipking describes the end of Samuel Johnson's literary career as a retreat "into the language that everyone shares."[29] That was the express aspiration—indefinite as it sounds—of poets such as Pound and Eliot whose use of English is now preserved in words used by countless speakers without awareness of a debt owed to poetry. Joyful poems seem more skeptical and secular than those extolling undying romantic devotion, but that impression is mistaken. "Rejoice evermore" (1 Thessalonians 5:16). "Joy," "rejoice," and "joyful" appear more than 400 times in the Bible. The poems discussed above (but not the songs) all come at the topic with idioms that derive from Christian usage. The language has been so affected by Christian utterance that even Rexroth's version of an ancient Roman passage must speak with anachronistically enhanced terms.

I usually think that poetry resists conventions, that

intellectuals unsettle common thought, but then also that joyful poems are not for critics. Pound once said that it is the work of a poet to encourage readers to go on living, as elegies traditionally do. Samuel Johnson had said this too.[30] But not all poems are written in the shadow of loss, as Shelley suggests. In proximity to a corpse, one is not going to protest some uplift, but otherwise one may feel that no one comes to art entitled to encouragement. The notion that one must *work through* the pain to get to a resolution is conscientious, grievous. Joy comes not from labor or analysis; it may be a product of will, as Johnny Mercer said. The two longer poems above—by Traherne and Wilbur—speak to the relations between joy and the daily lives we share with many. They remind us that joy is commonly accessible only to individuals. To explain why that is so, a poet has to stretch out and draw on all the sonic, figurative, and theological resources of lyric poetry. "Wonder" is ambitious.[31] Joyful love songs, even those that seem very simple, draw terms from familiar praise language. In their wake are histories of aspiration. Their concision, abbreviations, economies summon memories of lost moments and beliefs. How far is it from an "attitude of doin' right" to incarnational theology?

6. Hearts Are Fickle

Devotion is the master topos of love songs. Singular desire—
this woman or man, and no other—is where love song seems
to begin. Serial desire obstructs the current of representation,
if not of imagination. An array of literary, rhetorical, and institutional supports holds songs like Frankie Laine's "It Only
Happens Once" (1945) in popular memory.

> It only happened once.
> I'll never feel that thrill again.
> It only happens once.
> Why couldn't I have known it then?[1]

A slight variation from the first to the third line, the simple
past to the present indicative, moves from personal experience
to general claim. The truth proposed is that resistance to the
authority of monogamy may make one rue that day of error.
Songs of serial desire are often woe-tunes, exactly because life
is full of desires and shameful, heart-wounding lapses of faith.
The resilience of the heart, an embarrassment to all those who
recover erotic desire.

What would follow, if lovers and poets surrendered the ideal

One Love and frankly approved a series of loves? Would the gain in truth-telling about what life is like for many improve the songs?[2] The popular imagination treasures the artistic consequences of concupiscence, and not only in the blues. New springs and loves keep coming; nature is not to be refused. Cole Porter exults over the onset of a new love, as over a sunny day. "Onset" is the way to put it, because what he appreciates first is the otherness of a new love, just as monogamous desire is celebrated by Carmen McRae in "I Only Have Eyes for You" (1934): the glorious thing is that the lover does not *make* the love-changes; they have their own momentum. Hands off the wheel. A lover's agency is imagined (not only by Cole Porter) as barely relevant, and that is a familiar comfort: "something's happened to me." The lover receives not the beloved but Love itself, as formidable an agent as ever. A lover who chooses a beloved or constructs a love, will surely be asked—by him- or herself, if not by others—whether such love is wisely, prudently made, with a long view in mind. But such questions need not arise when love is thrust upon one. Sudden onset, its own sign of authenticity. Cole Porter, in "I'm in Love Again" (1925), declines to consider the difficulties of serial desire.

> Why am I
> Just as happy as a child?
> Why am I
> Like a racehorse running wild?
> Why am I
> In a state of ecstasy?
> The reason is 'cause
> Something's happened to me.[3]

Onset is a narrative kernel, not a theory, conjecture, prediction, or estimation. Repeat-lovers mean to be careful, even self-disciplined, aware that we fool ourselves into consolatory relationships. They claim to have analyzed, even understood, their situation. "The reason is . . ." the song says, as if abandon might have a rational basis.

> I'm in love again
> And the spring is comin',
> I'm in love again,
> Hear my heart strings strummin',
> I'm in love again
> And the hymn I'm hummin'
> Is the "Huddle Up, Cuddle Up Blues!"
> I'm in love again,
> And I can't rise above it,
> I'm in love again,
> And I love, love, love it:
> I'm in love again,
> And I'm darn glad of it,
> Good news!

A mind may resist love, as some sensibilities resist feeling, leaving one to wonder how strong or genuine is that feeling. "I can't rise above it," he says. *Cannot*: a lover wants to be constrained by a force beyond resistance. What might it mean to rise above love? What's up there, irony? This speaker puts irony behind him and wills innocence. There are no blues for cuddling; "rocks in my bed," yes, but no cuddling! Darkness has been dispelled. Bitter Eros, as Anne Carson calls him, be gone! Sweetness, all. That few words arise, even for Cole Porter, to express this feeling freshly suggests that the speaker means to be at the heart of ordinary life: "I love, love, love it."

Unashamed by enthusiasm, he starts and ends with nothing more than plain assertion, irreducible terms that no one can misunderstand. Courage is the thing: not just to love again—though that does take heart—but to love again and again, regardless of recriminations, as a horse runs free, pounding past rocks in the road.

Songs of *another* love affirm a present moment in the face of many other such moments: frank pleasure that one loves yet again. Almost no one wants to narrate the series; only *this* moment is golden with expectation. From Sappho's Hymn to Aphrodite until now, songs of serial love affirm an unwarranted optimism. The serial lover has repeatedly failed—that is a crucial ingredient of this sophisticated art—and nonetheless eagerly rushes in again, all hope and will, as if innocent of losses.

> Artfully adorned Aphrodite, deathless
> child of Zeus and weaver of wiles I beg you
> please don't hurt me, don't overcome my spirit,
>   goddess, with longing,
>
> but come here, if ever at other moments   5
> hearing these my words from afar you listened
> and responded: leaving your father's house, all
>   golden, you came then,
>
> hitching up your chariot: lovely sparrows
> drew you quickly over the dark earth, whirling   10
> on fine beating wings from the heights of heaven
>   down through the sky and
>
> instantly arrived—and then O my blessed

goddess with a smile on your deathless face you
asked me what the matter was *this* time, what I   15
   called you for this time,

what I now most wanted to happen in my
raving heart: "Whom *this* time should I persuade to
lead you back again to her love? Who *now*, oh
   Sappho, who wrongs you?   20

If she flees you now, she will soon pursue you;
if she won't accept what you give, she'll give it;
if she doesn't love you, she'll love you soon now,
   even unwilling."

Come to me again, and release me from this   25
want past bearing. All that my heart desires to
happen—make it happen. And stand beside me,
   goddess, my ally.[4]

Twice Aphrodite is said to be "deathless"—out of time. Yet she
is right on time when called, and teases Sappho for importu-
nate prayers, one after another, apparently all alike. The bane
of love songs is repetition. A love poet keeps repeating the
same poem, because one can get only so far with this subject.
"Since all alike my songs and praises be / To one, of one, still
such, and ever so," as Shakespeare complains in Sonnet 105.
   Yet the goddess of love describes for Sappho the utter instability of romance (ll. 21-24). Her assertion is not just that loves
fizzle and die, though they do, but that they also reignite; the
pursued ultimately come around, even repeatedly (l. 19). This
is simply the case, so long as Aphrodite intervenes in Sappho's
affairs. I have referred to what Aphrodite says and does as

if that were directly known. All that is known derives from Sappho's complex report: her direct praise and supplication of the goddess. This report is cast as a reminder of Aphrodite's former response to Sappho's prayers; the spectacle of the goddess in flight; and finally, Aphrodite's urbane speech to Sappho. The poet's recollection implies the justness of the goddess's chiding reassurance. There is no conflict between what the poet wants and what the goddess urges. Sappho's artful representation of the goddess's point of view conveys thorough self-awareness. One may think that serial lovers turn a blind eye to the past in order to give their hearts away *again*. The contrary may be the case, as Sappho suggests: this version of romance entails self-awareness without self-pity. All struggle is internal to the lover. Her praise of the goddess's appearance acknowledges that, in order to realize one's desires, the gods and life as it is constituted by them are to be accepted and wholeheartedly affirmed. Praise of the gods is but elaborate assent to life as it is, not as it should or might be. Such elegant assent in a state of anxious pining—that is mastery.

What Sappho fears is longing, or time when nothing happens to sate her appetite. She does not name or even characterize her beloved. She prays less for a person than for an event: "make it happen." What she wants is not to possess another's body or spirit but to re-experience an arc of romance— exactly what makes Cole Porter (and Bobby Short) want to sing. She makes no claim that *this* love is to be her last, or that this beloved is superior to her predecessors: comparison would be beside the point. Sappho wants to go on seducing women, as soldiers return to battle so long as they can. Intensity rather than patience is her virtue. For her, waiting is unbearable, as it is not for a poet of devotion. Her objective: immediate joy rather than enduring satisfaction, which is neither mentioned nor imagined. Her access to her ally protects her against ordinary temporality. Divine intervention speeds up seduction, so that Sappho may elude longueurs of courtship. She wants it now.

Intervention—help me!—is ordinarily summoned when an issue cannot be resolved with available resources. It may be desired by those who doubt their own agency, or by one who wants a quick and binding resolution. It may even be casually desired for facilitation of the inevitable—Aphrodite suggests this in her response to Sappho's prayer. That seduction leads eventually to fruition is a premise of song. For instance, there is a monogamous version of the plea for help that presents the matter simply and with charm. The Johnny Otis band performed "Cupid's Boogie" in 1950 with Mel Walker and Little Esther. The music and the lyric begin with a blunt imperative to intervene directly and immediately. Sappho's adornment of Aphrodite has no parallel here; "Mr. Cupid" is an ordinary fellow. Esther straightforwardly petitions for help without any suggestion that her need is anomalous: the lives of lovers are apparently always in the hands of others, whether Aphrodite or Cupid does not matter. These summonses all signify that lovers feel greater dependency than autonomy. Sappho beseeches Aphrodite, Esther beseeches Cupid, and Mel beseeches Esther (in the expectation that marriage will be as effectual for him as divine intervention seems to Esther).

> Hey, Mr. Cupid, step into my life.
> I met a fine cat and I just got to be his wife.
> Cupid, don't let me down this morning,
> Things will be ok,
> If you just help me get
> This fine, mellow man today.
> Pull down the shades, turn down the lights,

Make him sit here by my side and hold me tight.
Cupid, don't let me down this morning,
Things will be ok.
If you'll just help me get
This fine, mellow man today.

Well, pretty baby, I might as well confess:
Without you I can't find my happiness.
Baby, don't let me down this morning
Things will be ok.
Let's get the ring and tie the knot today.

I want a diamond ring, fine feathers that cling
A chicken shack and a Cadillac.
Oooeee. Take it easy, baby. Things will be ok.
Well, let's get the ring and tie the knot today.

Real early every morning
I want you on the spot.
Breakfast on the table
And coffee in the pot.

Uh, oh. I knew there was a catch to it.
But every thing will be ok.
Well, let's get the ring and tie the knot today.

One thing, baby: I've got to be the boss.
And don't you ever pull no double-cross.
There won't be no days like that.
I've got news for you.
I'm the captain of the ship
And you're just a member of the crew.
Aw, baby, don't be like that.

Are you kidding?
Let's get the ring and tie the knot today.[5]

The song's charm is that it imagines satisfaction as an immediately accessible, conventional arrangement: "tie the knot today." That much can be managed without divine intervention. Sappho's complaint is that her beloved is not yet even charmed by her. Aphrodite counsels patience, as this song does too in its central line, "Things will be OK." Every lover bound by frustration needs to hear such soothing advice. The apparently insoluble will soon be resolved. Mel Walker and Little Esther both want to wed, so the first issue—whether to wed—is easily settled. That Mel is a "fine, mellow man" suggests that this fancy guy may be callous and elusive, like Billie Holiday's in "Fine and Mellow"—not the marrying kind. But he is ready. No intervention is required by the situation. The terms of their union, though, are momentarily contested. Esther wants everything, "a chicken shack and a Cadillac"—which is to say: everything in between ordinary labor and luxury. Mel wants docility. "There won't be no days like that," he is told. But rather than call the whole thing off, they good-naturedly sing a chorus of mutual assent to the institution of marriage. Things will be OK. They have all the agency they need to consummate their arrangement. They know what they want, and it is within reach. Good humor is their lubricant.

Joni Mitchell's call for intervention is quite different. It draws out a rare element of seriality. Modern songs of serial love are often mournful—"Just One of Those Things," "Send Me Someone to Love," "My Foolish Heart," "Experiment," "I Have the Feeling I've Been Here Before," "I Fall in Love too Easily"—even when they are not plainly so. They inevitably sustain awareness of that one love that abides forever. Phantom monogamy orients singer and audience. Given that,

in this sense, songs of seriality acknowledge loss, or an ostensibly mature skepticism about one's "morning thoughts," what
is it they affirm? Knowledge, period. Serial lovers imagine
themselves self-aware, unconfused, if not always stable. Self-
approval is another matter. They do not look away from their
erotic migrations. Here is Joni Mitchell's "Help Me," from
Court and Spark (1974).[6]

> Help me
> I think I'm falling
> In love again
> When I get that crazy feeling, I know
> I'm in trouble again   5
> I'm in trouble
> 'Cause you're a rambler and a gambler
> And a sweet-talking ladies'-man
> And you love your lovin'
> But not like you love your freedom.   10

Her head is clear, and she has a name—"that crazy feeling"—
for a paradoxical concept. She should not love *this* man,
because he won't stay. But love is the crazy thing, and she's
falling for him anyway. He's a two- or three-woman man, a
type: Billie Holiday's beloved in "Fine and Mellow" and "My
Man."[7] This is the first version of her story: simple, conventionally gendered.

   Songs of serial desire seem almost always to derive from
experience—their access to pathos; the knowledge they articulate seems personal. What the lover claims to know, though,
goes beyond her own experience. That crazy feeling, bittersweet eros, is a general concept.[8] A serial lover needs to rise
well above any particular case. One might think that her call

for help in the first strophe is intended for some protectress of lovers, more Mother Superior than Aphrodite. One comes to see, though, even in the first strophe, that her summons, like the entire song, is addressed to her seducer, the "sweet-talking ladies'-man." She would not beseech him for protection *from* him. From him, she wants another kind of help: collaboration in love, as she says in the last strophe.

> Help me
> I think I'm falling
> In love too fast
> It's got me hoping for the future
> And worrying about the past   15
> 'Cause I've seen some hot hot blazes
> Come down to smoke and ash
> We love our lovin'
> But not like we love our freedom

The lover is an analyzer and explainer who grasps the immediate problem with sudden love. It has her stuck between an uncertain future and a painful past, not firmly situated in the present. No auditor needs an explanation of the future for which she hopes—a stable, enduring love. But she imagines that her beloved needs an account of the problems of the past, and she formulates that impersonally. Hot love burns out. An anonymous sixteenth century song has these cognate lines: "Love that is too hot and strong / Burneth soon to waste."[9] She may refer to a former love, or to an earlier beloved's love, or to both. But that is not how she puts the matter. She speaks as an interpreter who understands love's general features. The last two lines of this strophe dissolve the gender category invoked in the first one; women too love freedom (ll. 18-19).

The first-person plural usage opens her analysis to not only her beloved's but her own paradoxical nature—her appetite for love *and* autonomy. That "we" extends still more widely, experience shared with the beloved. She proposes an "or" as if one recollection or another might serve equally well, or as if the difference between a recollection and a hypothetical stipulation were immaterial (ll. 21-22).

> Didn't it feel good.   20
> We were sitting there talking
> Or lying there not talking
> Didn't it feel good
> You dance with the lady
> With the hole in her stocking   25
>
> Didn't it feel good
> Didn't it feel good

Three times she asks the song's kernel question. How good does it actually feel—romance without constraints? Her answer is close and definite. Its first element is intimacy, though not sexual intimacy: rather, that of two lovers who talk with one another or share silence easily, comfortably. The second is more surprising: general abandon—"general" because the singer is not the lady with the hole in her stocking. The singer infers that the beloved enjoyed dancing with another woman who kept on dancing regardless of a hole in her stocking. Abandon is contagious; it crosses from one person to the next. But universal joy is not all that it produces.

> Help me
> I think I'm falling

In love with you 30
Are you going to let me go there by myself
That's such a lonely thing to do
Both of us flirting around
Flirting and flirting
Hurting too 35
We love our lovin'
But not like we love our freedom[10]

The last strophe turns against the generalizing view of earlier strophes. Abandon produces particular pain as well as general exhilaration. The beloved's dance with the other woman is an assertion of just the free-ranging autonomy that the singer knows as her own. The lover's sense of a rival shows how the concept of seriality easily develops into plural loves not sequestered within temporal boundaries. The beloved's contradictions are hers too. Jealousy might justify not esteem for liberty and abandon but the familiar restraint of normative monogamy.

I have tracked the sentences grammatically to show where thematic complexities lie. On the page the lyrics seem plain, apparently slack rather than crafted; that is a common experience of printed lyrics. Once one has absorbed Joni's performance, though, the lyrics never again sit alone on a page: the music is bound to the words in memory, as when one hears instrumental versions of a familiar tune, the lyrics come to mind. In memory "help" is no longer a four-letter word. It takes about eight letters to signify orthographically the duration of its big, blasted *el* sound. This first word is sung by Joni and the back-up chorus; it comes forward, steadily and emphatically, like a controlled horn blast. And "freedom" too requires four *e*'s to represent the three syllables she makes of this six-second word. The bending of familiar words is a standard feature of song lyrics. Those open vowels that stretch out are the agents of change from prose to song. Against their displays the march of ordinary sentences holds the lyrics to a rhetorical contract to communicate the song's sense on a first hearing. Lines seven and eight come off the tongue quickly in a little dance of the stresses. The pacing of short syllables is conspicuous in these lines and just a little less so in lines twenty to twenty-five. Then comes a single word, stretched out to six seconds, to close each of the four stanzas: "freedom" and "good."

Release from monogamous constraints is no easy liberation for Joni and may rarely be for others. Are a lover's polyamorous pleasures sufficient to offset the spectacle of a beloved taking the same pleasure? Help me! The help sought is that of a beloved willing to collaborate in a difficult effort at symmetrical freedom. None is sought to constrain the beloved. *Good, freedom*, and *help*, the key terms, are meaningfully drawn out. They are elements of a transvaluation, from monogamous to serial desire, and then to polyamory; the distinction between seriality and polyamory comes down to "now" and "then." The play of vowels is at the heart of the poetry of the popular song, as is plainness of diction and syntax. It should be no criticism of song lyrics that they look inert on the page, because they are archived there only as a convenience. As art, they are properly preserved in performance, or as words across bars in a musical arrangement. Read literally, Joni is anticipating a pain that she knows, from experience, comes with plural desire in a life of serial romances. One momentarily thinks that prudence is making her anxious about a new romance; that she seeks help from some power greater than her will to resist eros. That is what she appears to say, but it is certainly not what the music says. Her phrasing and accompaniment indicate that she is with the power, and as glad to be so as Bobby Short ever was. The "help" she seeks is that of the beloved who should join her in brave, enthusiastic peace with eros. Sappho, Little Esther, and Joni Mitchell all summon assistance, which has a particular bearing on seriality. They admit no patience to let things run their course. A protracted courtship is not in view. Serial lovers move at a quickened pace, as if a horizon were dimming (though the talk is of blue skies).

Even Mel and Esther's celebration of mutual desire opens onto the issue of domination when Mel refers darkly to infidelity: "Don't you pull no double-cross." That is the shadow cast by a lover's praise. For a moment, Mel thinks that domination can hold off rivals. Praise poems awaken proverbial suspicion of the distinction between one love and many: "I'll bet you say that to all the girls." What praise truly honors a beloved? The blazon is a traditional form of praise that inventories a beloved's assets; it presents *evidence* of excellence, as if it were addressed to a doubter. John Freccero speaks of Laura's "component parts" as "scattered like the objects of fetish worship."[11] And other critics of the most devoted and influential love poet of all complain that Petrarch's image of Laura is a "composite of details," as Nancy Vickers puts it, not a "complete picture."[12] Patricia Parker connects the famous inventories with accounts of the New World, a desire for dominion, she argues.[13] Vickers and Parker explicate the political significance of a gendered claim to ownership of a female body. My interest is in the way that this trope expresses infidelity, of a love life made out of identifiable parts. Figures of plural women, in this context, inevitably entail a concept of polyamory—of the scoundrel. There are long-established means of asserting domination while pledging vassalage.

This sleight of pen is ancient. Here are the first two strophes of Bertran de Born's twelfth century *Rassa tan cries e monta e poja*, in Paul Blackburn's translation.

Rassa, I rise,
I prosper, I mount her
who is clean empty of deceit, whose sweet excellence
            insults all other women
                  by being so.
For there's no one has one quality so intense
or fine, it can subtract from hers one bit.
      Seeing her beauty convinces,
            wins to her service even those
who to their own detraction smart under it.
So she has the glory and profit from it, for
thus the most knowing and best maintain her
praise, proclaim her charm and valor forever.
As for integrity,
she would not take, or want, more than a single lover.

Rassa, the lady is sharp and clear,
comely and gay and a young devil:
                  auburn hair and white, white
                  in her body like a hawthorn blossom!
            Her neck is soft, the tits firm, with a back
            that feels like a rabbit under the hand.
Those who pretend to know me well
or well enough,
can guess with ease,
by the clear fresh color,
by the praise and price, incomparable as they are, toward
which part it is I incline—and adore.[14]

Before praising her hair, skin, neck, and breasts, he establishes
her exceptional moral character. If she is to be praised for
"integrity," in Blackburn's terms, she must be said to be faithful

and indifferent to the allure of wealth ("she disdains the rich," in the poem's next line). The difficulty is that even contrasts imply an index of the general value of women. Petrarch's critics rightly observe that his praise of Laura does not draw her virtues into one integral portrait; she is adored for her various parts, as Bertran's Bel Senher is too. Bertran states clearly that this beloved's parts rival those of other women; and that if another woman had one part superior to Bel Senher's, his estimation of his beloved might be adjusted downward (ll. 6-7). Devotion to one, who is all to the lover, as Thomas Hardy put it, is in constant tension with the attractions of others. In sixteenth century France, blazons were collected in an anthology preserving accounts of women's extraordinary parts, as if in heraldic representation.

Bertran's famous blazon, known as "The Borrowed Lady," sums the parts of other women into one artificial beloved. This hoax addresses the distinction between monogamous devotion and the sampling of a series. The former is at the heart of love-discourse, where Petrarch remains, but segmentation is familiar to ordinary mortals who, when lucky, must explain to a late-found One the insignificance of the predecessors. This is a moment for sophistry or shame, if one imagines these alternatives in terms of an ideal and a practicality. Bertran mischievously keeps the alternatives in close proximity, for his mistress's hearing. His blazon is a figure of substitution:

> And since I can find no one as good as you,
> none so beautiful and spirited,
> or her noble body so full of rejoicing,
> so graceful,
> or so courtly,
> or her proud fame so true,
> I shall go everywhere collecting

> from each lady one beautiful image,
> and so make one assembled lady
> until you are restored to me.[15]

Then he names the ladies and their parts that comprise his
dummy of the absent beloved. His mistress's cruel rejection
in this second strophe has him ranging among the beauties.
The syntax keeps in view a calculation about when to stick
and when to roam; he slyly combines praise of his mistress
with a threat to pursue the others. In later lines, designed for
his mistress, he explicitly praises the pulchritude of Mielhs
de-be and Bel Senher (ll. 48-50; 66-68). His inventory of eight
other beautiful women should provoke his mistress to restore
her favor: "my lady . . . will not then be foolish and mute" (ll.
29-30). The blazon's praise, in general, easily flips into recrimination. Each comparison identifies a lover's other options.
And his ability to wound a woman by displaying familiarity
with the feel of her breasts and so on is one of his resources. A
blazon, taken seriously, is anything but tribute.

Songs of devotion celebrate the discovered One; the surprise is that that involves the others come along too. The literary record indicates that there is no eluding the mobility of
desire. Donne begins "The Good-Morrow": "I wonder by my
troth, what thou, and I / Did, till we lov'd?" What attractions
did former intimates have, and what do they now mean to the
lovers? These are practical questions about late-chosen monogamy. Or more abstractly, in what manner does a series lead to
a singularity? The first stanza of "The Good-Morrow" closes
on a simple resolution: "If ever any beauty I did see, / Which
I desir'd, and got, t'was but a dreame of thee." Series may be
trials of imagination, efforts to envisage the One. This account
honors a lover's control and purpose against happenstance.

But any lover may be expected to feel, facing the ostensible
One, embarrassed recollection of many others. Artful lovers,
like Donne and Shakespeare, turn shame to gain. Sonnet 31
begins with a heraldic blazon; the parts, those of old lovers.

> Thy bosom is endearéd with all hearts
> Which I by lacking have supposéd dead;
> And there reigns love, and all love's loving parts,
> And all those friends which I thought buriéd.
> How many a holy and obsequious tear   5
> Hath dear religious love stol'n from mine eye,
> As interest of the dead, which now appear
> But things removed that hidden in thee lie!
> Thou art the grave where buried love doth live,
> Hung with the trophies of my lovers gone,   10
> Who all their parts of me to thee did give;
> That due of many now is thine alone.
> Their images I loved I view in thee,
> And thou, all they, hast all the all of me.

His has been a life of "loving parts" (l. 3). Old beloveds
were as dead to him, and this is said not merely to placate
his current beloved. The surprising claim is that his current
beloved has inherited his heart's investments in them. The old
ones are termed "hearts" (l. 1), then "parts" (l. 3), "friends" (l.
4), and midway "things removed that hidden in thee lie" (l. 8).
Their former meaning has been effectively transmitted to his
new beloved by his former beloveds (l. 11), and that is their
current value. He could not have conveyed that value, because
he lacked those loving parts (l. 2). Their names do not matter
because their particular significance has been entirely absorbed
by the new beloved—an encumbered gentleman (l. 12). A

less surprising poem would claim that the latest includes all the value that the former beloveds had *and more*. The last line rather insists on a definite sum: "all they." Those two words, in the nominative, mean: "thou who art effectively all they," neither more nor less; exact equivalence. The lover has assembled a new beloved, as Bertran made his Borrowed Lady. How audacious to say: "Thou art the grave where buried love doth live, / Hung with the trophies of my lovers gone." The ordinary objective would be to convince the beloved that the lover has given *him* all, but lines nine and ten, frank and grim, show little concern for the feelings of another. Helen Vendler says the poem is "as much a *Liebestod* as a love-poem." She observes that there is "a burial in each of its three quatrains." "Inside this complimentary sonnet lies a powerful metaphysical one . . . trying to get out."[16]

The imprisoned poem is a self-correction; the tone is cool insofar as the sustained figure concerns payments, transactions, not embarrassment about former loves. The two conspicuously polysyllabic terms in the second quatrain, "religious" and "obsequious," are ironic, playful concerning Mediterranean fin'amor. (The diction is predominately Germanic: bosom, heart, dead, friend, bury, tear, eye, thing, grave.) He erroneously conceived of his former loves as forever gone from his life, dead. With their apparent departure went parts of his heart—costly severances. The speaker grants the proverbial notion that serial lovers' ability to love erodes over time; that segmentation is deadening. However, Barbara Correll observes that in a gift economy, like that described by Bataille, a point of intensity arrives when losses are inverted.[17] That turning point has arrived. Correll's claim is that early modern lyric, in particular Sonnet 31, imagines an alternative to general economy, the lover made again whole. The second quatrain is anomalous, Vendler observes, because it does not include the key-term "all." It figures the religiosity of romance as a regime of pain and subordination. Erotic seriality, like potlatch—giving the heart away without exchange—is meant to displace the religion of love. Its objective is to enable lovers like Joni ("I fall in love too easily, I fall in love too fast")[18] to put behind them their many losses, to move forward in hope of a restoration to come. The final One makes "all" not dismissible but recoverable.

The same topos—all loves past fulfilled in the One—is given still more complicated expression in Donne's "Aire and Angels": "Twice or thrice," it begins, invoking multiplicity when leading a beloved to believe that she is the One. A beseeching lover ought instead connect a present moment to an attractive future: be mine now and we will enter a new world. Instead he explains, as if questioned, how past loves have led to this one. Critics note that the poem consists of two inverted Petrarchan sonnets: sestet, then octave. (I'll analyze only the first.) The inversions are thematic too: the decisive event is not the lovemaking to come, but a spirit-presence in the past. Normally, Charis Charalampous notes, "the sonnet tradition followed the standard Neoplatonic progress of love from body to spirit." But here is the counter-traffic.[19] In his past, the lover once felt an indefinite, uncanny presence of his beloved who is now observably present. A notion of destiny is implied: the future was vaguely foreshadowed by a voice heard and an uncertain desire felt as a flickering flame (lines 1-6). She was then insubstantial, not yet a person. The lover concedes other loves, fleshly ones. Who were they, and what did they have? They were the beloved in disguise, of course. The poem's real delight is its metaphysics shaped to a sensual situation in which exactness is everything.

Twice or thrice had I loved thee,

Before I knew thy face or name,
So in a voice, so in a shapelesse flame,
Angells affect us oft, and worship'd bee;
   Still when, to where thou wert, I came,   5
Some lovely glorious nothing I did see.
   But since my soule, whose child love is,
Takes limmes of flesh, and else could nothing doe,
   More subtile then the parent is,
Love must not be, but take a body too,   10
   And therefore what thou wert, and who,
      I bid Love aske, and now
That it assume thy body, I allow,
And fixe it selfe in thy lip, eye, and brow.[20]

The poem is an elaborately reconstructed sonnet. Prosody describes the arrangement of stresses and rhymes; half of these lines are iambic pentameter (3, 4, 6, 8, 10, 13 and 14), six are tetrameter (1, 2, 5, 7, 9 and 11), and line twelve is trimeter. The arrangement corresponds to a complex pattern of alternation. The rhyme scheme unifies the sestet (ABBABA). The octave as rhymed (CDCDDEEE) makes a cinquain and a tercet. Syntax governs the sequence of words in a sentence: the first sentence runs through the opening six lines, making a syntactic sestet; the second, making an octave, completes the poem. And the felt form of a poem—its sequence of statements, the ease or difficulty of transitions from one to the next—has a direct bearing on its credibility. The felt form is composed and dignified. Transitions are rational and cued by conjunctions. As statement, the poem is well made, secure without strain. The sestet divides into three syntactic couplets. The first, on predecessor loves. The second draws an analogy to spirit-messengers, an apparent flourish, or accessory, to the meaning of the sestet. But actually angels are an implied cause of the intervention described in the third couplet. The first two lines assert that love does not derive from knowledge. He says nearly nothing of her qualities in these fourteen lines. Love is rather experienced, vaguely, intangibly, derived from some elsewhere. The third couplet begins with the conjunction "Still," as in repeatedly, pointing back to the first couplet. The poet's hand is firmly in place, indicating the logical structure of the sestet. Line six is oddly and surprisingly poised between praise and offense. "Lovely" and "glorious" must refer to the beloved, in her insubstantial presence, but who is to be characterized as "nothing"? Insofar as she was physically absent from the site of his visitation, the term is accurate. Nonetheless this is a cheeky epithet with which to conclude the sestet, as the first line too audaciously invokes multiplicity in face of the One.

The poem has a teasing, rakish undertone. Line seven starts with an adversative as explicit about direction as "Still." Lines seven and eight are syntactically different but both are bisected by a medial pause. Line nine begins a parenthesis that continues with an explicit sign of transition, toward the mid-point of line ten. The syntax of this parenthesis is firmly resolved as a couplet at the end of line ten, though a parenthesis without orthographical markers is tricky for readers, let alone listeners. The syntax of lines seven through ten is obviously intricate, unlike that of the more direct sestet. The poet displays in the octave his mastery of the poem's grammar. And the sequence of the last four lines is especially peculiar. In lines eleven and twelve he requests that Love ask concerning the identity of the beloved whom he once knew as a premonition. (Whom might Love ask? Love is imagined as a part of a metaphysical order that it does not govern. In lines thirteen and fourteen Love is twice identified as "it.") The consequence of this lover's request is that he acknowledges ("I allow") in line thirteen that Love has taken the beloved's body, with the lover's permission, as its own. How strange then is the syntax of the last line, which skips over his acknowledgment to return with an apposition to Love's assumption of the beloved's body.

One must attend closely to the syntax in order to make coherent sense of this upside-down sonnet. The lines make a reader eventually *feel* a difficult passage from clause to clause, as a serial lover feels turns and reversals in passing from one partner to another. "There is hardly a word in this poem," Judith Scherer Herz remarks, "that cannot be read upside down or inside out."[21] To get this back-and-forth effect, Donne has built a structure that is far from song. Readers will assess the significance of the stanza's uncertain movement. The assurance expressed by the lover is not reinforced by the poem's form, and that complicates the stanza. The prosodic form is intricate in that the lengths of lines vary according to a pattern that is not closely aligned with syntax. The first two lines of tetrameter are followed by two lines of pentameter; the symmetry of this quatrain is aligned with the sense of the statements. The shorter lines recall experiences; the longer ones generalize the phenomena recalled. A sequence of three oscillations of single lines of tetrameter followed by a line of pentameter follows, but without any particular correspondence of the short to the long lines; the lines simply vary between two prescribed lengths. The cinquain of lines seven through eleven has no particular coherence of sense. This is to say that the rhyme pattern presents opportunities for points of closure that are foregone. The couplet of lines ten and eleven is strongly enjambed to line twelve.

One recognizes, as the poem progresses, an arbitrariness of form. The poem concerns surprising conjunctures of past and present moments; of apparent circumstance and actual significance. It does not demonstrate a collision or rivalry of form and content; it rather reveals that simply *different* orders prevail simultaneously. That which one does not notice sometimes determines one's future. The first foot of the poem is a catalectic iamb: a syllable (unstressed) is missing at the start of the poem, a common variant in iambic verse.

The logic of Donne's argument is implicit in the figure of the blazon: a trope by which the One is confirmed by her predecessors. ("So all their praises are but prophecies / Of this our time, all you prefiguring," as Shakespeare has it in Sonnet 106.) Her (or his) parts may be segregated in time and space, a series of reminders of the One. Donne sees that the figure works in the reverse direction too: the lips, eyes and brows of the now absent beloveds may be recalled as fragments of the true One now before him. The lover is one person, abiding in time, who loved serially in the past but pledges to love singly in the future, not because he is a different person, but because the beloved is metaphysically continuous with his earlier life. She does not negate, but instead, on this account, completes his former life. He sought her always. Shakespeare claims that all his former loves are dead to him but remembered still. His One is the sum of the series. One recognizes Sonnet 31 and "Aire and Angels" as rhetorically driven, efforts to manage a beloved's skepticism. But they are intellectual explorations too. They construct a metaphysical base to support a late or subsequent love.

"Aire and Angels" draws from the blazon a thematic not perfectly explicit in Donne's poem, though it is explicit in Sonnet 106. Serial love songs are always in dialogue with monogamy, as songs of monogamous devotion need to confront the variety of the heart, if only by full-throated denial. Seriality and monogamy need each other. When a lover discovers the One, he or she must, intellectually, relate the One to the Many. In the history of the love song, this does not change. The popular Rodgers and Hart song "Where or When" (1937) has been variously performed by Sinatra, Johnny Hartman, Dion and the Belmonts, Rod Stewart, and the Kinks, as if it were easy for generation after generation to believe what it says, though in fact that is not at all easy. It begins with a tendentious proem about temporality and mind (ll.1-9) that few performers retain. This song, like "Aire and Angels," constructs metaphysical continuity in a love-life that is shifting from seriality to singularity.

> When you're awake, the things you think
> Come from the dream you dream.
> Thought has wings, and lots of things
> Are seldom what they seem.
> Sometimes you think you've lived before   5
>
> All that you live today.
> Things you do come back to you,
> As though they knew the way.
>
> Oh, the tricks the mind can play.

Thought originates in dream—all thought, not just some thoughts (ll. 1-2). Although the first line refers to the literal sense of "dream" as sleeping, the sentence indicates that thought originates in desire and moves swiftly over great distances (ll. 3-4). "Wingèd thought" is archaic, Homeric. The song coordinates these claims with déjà vu and the charm of discovery.

> It seems we stood and talked like this, before.   10

We looked at each other in the same way then,
But I can't remember where or when.
The clothes you are wearing you were wearing then.
The smile you are smiling you were smiling then.
But I can't remember where or when.   15
Some things that happen for the first time
Seem to be happening again
And so it seems that we have met before,
And laughed before, and loved before.
But who knows where or when?   20

Mind's echo may be a sign that, in terms of the song's initial claims, one's very dreams are fulfilled by a particular person (ll. 13-15), or a way of being with another (ll. 10-11, 18-19). Recurrence, or even a momentary, illusory sense of recurrence, confirms a path in life. A surrender of responsibility in the face of such recurrence may feel deeply right. "Things you do come back to you, / As though they knew the way." Are one's acts then one's own? Agency may be mysteriously qualified by acts that determine themselves, like a horse returning to a stable. Augustine puzzles over this question in relation to his desire to know God: "Where, then, or when have I experienced a life of blessedness? How is it that I can recall it and love it and long for it? This is not true of me alone; nor me and a few others; everyone wishes to be blessed; and did we not know it with such sure knowledge, we would not will it with such sure will."[22] His claim is that the love of God is universal, and it is known with such certainty that one imagines a former life, from which it is remembered. Lorenz Hart is writing about the certain knowledge of being in love. That conviction rests on what seems a memory of a former life.

In just so far as devotion is profound, seriality appears

shallow. "Change partners and dance . . ."[23] To think from
the perspective of a *subsequent* love encourages melancholy.
One love after another like beads on the string of one's mere
years; that's the structure behind Carmen McRae's 1975 version of "I Have the Feeling I've Been Here Before" by Roger
Kellaway and Alan and Marilyn Bergman. Carmen stresses
the syllables evenly across the melody to accentuate the dull-
ness of the series. One may reasonably come to the end of
one's tolerance for loss, as in Christina Rossetti's "Mirage" and
Haven Johnson's "My Last Affair." But Shakespeare and Donne
instead imagine metaphysical continuity in the series. That
is an intellectual advance; or more accurately the absence of
that continuity constitutes a loss poets (and lovers) bear in the
modern era.

The big issue for serial lovers is the burden of memory.
One recalls old loves, then questions the depth and authority
of another one. Or one's new beloved asks whether the new
love on offer is not, for the lover, a passing infatuation. Some
poets avoid this issue by focusing, as Cole Porter does, on
the exhilaration of a new beloved. The deepest of these serial
poems meet this topic head on, as Sappho, Shakespeare, and
Donne do. The intellectual challenge is to integrate one's loves
in an ongoing life. None of the poems here attempts to discuss
the meeting of two lovers' memories. Just one party's record
is tough enough. Richard Strier observed that the differences
between Renaissance and modern love songs are not great:
modern lyricists just do without neo-Platonism, and the loss
seems to him bearable. Modern songs express cognate structures of feeling and thought, but with less learning, and less
confidence in the available consolation. Renaissance poems
are often arch, proud, witty. Modern lyricists take comfort
in the powerful notion that love is not chosen, not made,

but experienced or received; they draw on notions familiar from medieval love songs, and then Dante's *Vita Nuova*. If one's loves were metaphysically continuous, one might confidently conceive of desire as recurrent, even abiding, rather than serial. One's loves might merge into one figure of hope. The abstractness of the term "the beloved" has this sense that the blazon arrays: former and present lovers contribute to one perfect summation of one's aspirations, or capacity for love. The assemblage of parts may substitute for a lost beloved, or for that which has not cohered in one organic person. That is a display of ardor: a grand imagination that wants some of them all.

7. Money Can't Buy Love

One says "not for love or money," meaning by the logic of contraries that nothing could induce one to do that thing in question. Or one asks if someone married "for love or money," as though those opposed motives cover a known terrain. The distinction refers to the role of instrumental reasoning in the choice of a partner; the deliberate *use* of intimacy is commonly thought dishonorable. The motive of love signifies the suspension, however temporary, of ordinary instrumental reasoning. In talk of romance, "money" more than "hate" is a presumed antonym to "love." The meaningful connection between these terms is exchange—of affection, care, trust, vows, and then reparations. This economy underlies approved forms of reproduction and the transfer of property. To exchange cash for a simulacrum of love is anathema to those who esteem families as units of social organization. Poems about prostitution rest on an assumption that monogamous desire expires and conventional families fail. These poems imagine an economy in which goods other than trust and vows are exchanged. They are thought experiments, particularly relevant to societies that give marriages a less than 50/50 chance of surviving the duration of paired lives. Poems about money suggest what might be missing from monogamy. One asks what values are proposed by those who sing of love *and* money. Who would we be if we admittedly exchanged goods other than trust and vows? That other existence, its ethos, is what this chapter explores.

If money doesn't buy love, it does, in poems, generate fortitude, physical and spiritual, adaptability, and the resources to be had from articulateness. (I begin with the sunniest analyses of love and money, then on into the dark.) The first thing to acknowledge is that, as Joe Williams and Shirley Horn sing, "love without money isn't funny."[1] In 1953 the Drifters had a hit with Jesse Stone's tune "Money Honey," which outrageously asserts that there is no separating the two.

> I've learned a lesson, and now I know,
> The sun may shine, and the winds may blow.
> Women may come and women may go.
> But before I tell 'em that I love 'em so,
>
> I want money, honey; oh, money, honey; oh, money,
>   honey;
> If you want to get along with me.[2]

Cash circulates through some basic transactions of life among landlords, tenants, and lovers. Romance, in this novelty lyric, is a name for a single sector of cash flow. The lesson that surprises the singer is that, like all his women, he too is replaceable; but money is indispensable. He quickly makes his adjustment to this fact of life—as Gascoigne's lover had done—and proceeds without further difficulty. Insofar as the song has any point of advocacy, it's just: Get real! If one complies, all is well. The point is less the low-down significance of cash than the human capacity to adjust to the conditions of

existence, once those make themselves felt. Malleability, that
is, not unyielding devotion—that, which sounds like faithlessness, is the wisdom this song imparts—with good cheer, as if
adjustments were not costly.

A love that changes easily in response to circumstances:
who else sings that? Cavafy does, admirably, in Stratis Haviaris'
translation of "Two Young Men, 23 to 24 Years Old." To what
end, one may wonder. Stone and Cavafy have something serious to say on behalf of what is commonly regarded as shallow. They assert a just esteem for the material conditions of
romance.

> He'd been in the café since ten-thirty,
> expecting him to appear at any moment.
> Midnight passed, and still he waited for him.
> The café, by one-thirty, was nearly deserted.
> He'd grown tired of reading the newspapers
> without really reading. Of his last three shillings
> just one remained: he had waited so long that
> he'd spent the other two on coffee and brandy.
> And by then he'd smoked all his cigarettes.
> Waiting for him had exhausted him. For in that
> he'd been alone for so long, he'd fallen
> prey to disagreeable notions
> about the decadent life he'd been living.
>
> But when he saw his friend come in—the tedium,
> the weariness, the unpleasant thoughts disappeared.
>
> His friend brought him some surprising news:
> he'd just won sixty pounds in a card game.

Their lovely faces, their gracious youth,
the passionate love they felt for one another
were invigorated, revitalized, emboldened
by the sixty pounds from the gambling-house.

Then full of joy and vitality, all beauty and emotion,
they set off—not for the homes of their virtuous
     families
(where, besides, they were no longer welcome),
but to a house of their acquaintance, a very special
house of wantonness, where they asked for a room
and expensive drinks; and they drank still more.

And when the expensive drinks were finished,
and as it was nearly four o'clock in the morning,
they happily surrendered themselves to fervent love.[3]

What is fervent love? Another translator refers to bliss. Several say simply "love." The suggestion is that their love is finally without hesitation or qualification. They find their way, at evening's end, to an immoderate love. And how did they get there? Loveliness, grace, and passion enter the poem with a little windfall of cash. The means are superficial, one sees, but they serve well. Cavafy expresses no censure of the lovers' pursuit of pleasure. Their families' disapproval of their sons' activities seems unnecessary, unappreciative of the young men's joy—small, familiar, intolerant. Just how far one can go on the surfaces of life is the issue throughout the poem. The lover who waited for three hours in the café may have been stood up, but they may not have had an appointment, and the waiting lover never reproaches his beloved with tardiness. The lover may simply have expected the beloved, whose custom may have been to arrive at the café soon after 10:30. This is not a reliable way to arrange a meeting, but the two deliberately avoid pressing hard on what presents itself to them. The windfall seems to head off conflict about the arriving beloved's delay. They rather accept circumstances without interrogation, as if on the other side of this practice lay trouble. The lover, for instance, had "been alone for so long, he'd fallen / prey to disagreeable notions / about the decadent life he'd been living." The opening lines instruct one to make do with what is given, to work with one's reasonable presumptions. The loose use of pronouns is not to be resisted. Who are these young men? Enough to know their approximate age. Whose shillings, cigarettes does not really matter.

The poem is largely about patience. The first man waits for three hours. More revealing is the fact that they wait another couple of hours before making love. Sex is not urgent for them. They enjoy each other's company and the extravagance of costly cocktails. They are civilized. Waiting makes everything better: no waiting, no poem. They make a night of delay. Money does not buy love, but it transforms delay from a cause of anxiety to one of anticipation. The poem records details about pocket change, drinks, and cigarettes, the passing hours, but the metaphysical issues that define the lives of these two young men are rather named than analyzed ("the tedium, / the weariness, the unpleasant thoughts disappeared"). The style oscillates between concrete details, worried over for their significance, and large-scale abstractions (joy, vitality, beauty, emotion) accepted as they come, like so many old friends. (Frank O'Hara must have known his Cavafy.) The style encourages acceptance, not analysis: In what ways were their faces lovely? What did they do to make themselves unwelcome at their familial homes? A reader knows that more might be said—but only in a different style.

The ethos of this style is gentle and generous—and patient. The poet tells his story directly in simple, familiar language. Like the lovers, he avoids pressing hard on any one term. The poet accepts these lovers as adequate, they accept the unfolding of their evening, as one might generally accept one's days, without worry about the endurance of devotion, or the aptness of superlatives.

Of all the ways in which wealth affects intimacy, prostitution is the most obvious; bluntness is rarely a poetic resource, except that it does affirm frankness. Poems uttered by prostitutes constitute a minor wisdom literature: theirs, an authoritative counsel of prudence.[4] Here is a translation of an ancient Chinese courtesan poem by Yü Hsüan-chi, "Advice to a Neighbor Girl," that presents a scene of giving counsel. The speaker, a mature woman, offers a young courtesan strategies for surviving well in a faithless environment. Poems on money and intimacy are inevitably didactic.

> Afraid of the sunlight,
> You cover your face with your silk sleeves.
> Tired out with Spring melancholy,
> You neglect your makeup.
> It is easier to get priceless jewels   5
> Than to find a man with a true heart.
> Why wet your pillow with secret tears?
> Why hide your heartbreak in the flowers?
> Go, seek a handsome famous man like Sung Yü.
> Don't long for someone who will never come back.[5] 10

Working girls have knowledge from the far side of a social boundary. The poem's authority derives partly from its conformity to a (syntactic) couplet form, but more obviously from

the presumed experience of the speaker. Her values are implicitly presented in reproaches of the young courtesan. The girl
misuses her resources. She fears not the dark but sunlight; her
springtime is joyless. The older courtesan speaks on behalf of
nature's cycles. Put your pillow to better use, the girl is told; to
pine for the return of one particular lover is silly. "Advice" has
five pairs of syntactically matched lines (here I am obviously
analyzing a modern English translation by Kenneth Rexroth
and Ling Chung, not an ancient Chinese poem), and at its
center, this proverb: "It is easier to get priceless jewels / Than to
find a man with a true heart." Or, to put it plainly: get paid up
front. The poem reveals its formal principle with two pairs at
the start that directly repeat a single syntactic pattern (ll. 1-4).
Thereafter the pairs vary from one to the next, but readers have
already learned to read *pairs* of lines. The central pair is the
didactic kernel, its hypogram, in Riffaterre's terms. Couplets
as packages for the delivery of wisdom are thoroughly familiar to readers of English. The translators put "hide" in second
position in line eight, and "seek" in the same position in line
nine. The girl needs to play, but she has the wrong game for a
courtesan. The point of her work is availability. Waiting is for
lovers, not for courtesans or their clients.

The couplets summon her to display, not conceal, herself;
exhibition is in harmony with the seasons, but also with the
ways of men as they in fact are—faithless, yes, but famous
too, and presumably monied. The interesting thing here is
that no question is raised concerning the realistic possibility
of a young courtesan living a sound, healthy, and naturally
attuned life. Prostitution does not close off access to natural
order. What obstructs that access is the immodesty of romantic love, according to which a woman pines for a particular
suitor. The *idée reçu* that a prostitute's body degenerates under

the pressure of exploitation plays no role here. Yü Hsuan-chi (or Rexroth and Ling Chung) writes simply of a young girl providing wisely for herself. Youth is also Cavafy's concern. His critical perspective on his two young men is marked by a single preposition ("to") in the title. This narrative belongs, that is, to a single phase of life, a very brief, recognizable one, when one may skate successfully over the deeps. Whereas the Drifters advocate an adult realization that romance too runs on money, Cavafy celebrates youthful innocence, vigorous, bold love, but with an awareness that very little, only time and money, protect the young from the familiar unpleasantness of frustration. Both poems reveal benign truths about the heart that are commonly concealed by a strict opposition of money and love. This translation advocates proper management of one's resources; the capacity to cope is the one resource affirmed by all three poems.

The darkness of prostitution is almost too familiar for song; one wants to push back against that gloom, to figure another story. Coping is that story. These songs promote resilience, after disappointment. The very alacrity of the kernel exchange—money for sex—is a wonder to all who have waited for romance. Cavafy begins with the hours: from 10:30 P.M. until 1:30 A.M. the lover anticipated a meeting with his particular beloved. The poem's report ends at 4 A.M. Time is the issue, durations of expectation, not moments. Love-in-time is Cavafy's subject. Money does not replace, it facilitates love. The best is money that arrives, like love, by chance. Cavafy's young lover is worn down by just three hours in a café. Money helps one to accept losses, setbacks. A prostitute in a poem has found a way to cope with financial adversity. The topic is readily fascinating, and that is hazardous for the art. In a traditional sense a prostitute should not be described because the office of the poet is, as Allen Grossman has argued, to preserve figures of honor. A hooker, imagined accessible to all, is just what Petrarch's Laura is not: cash inverts the value of the beloved, and desire itself. For ignition of the flame is a crucial subject for poetry since Sappho, and that vanishes where cash displaces natural desire.

Cole Porter's "Love for Sale" (1930) is the best-known popular song about prostitution. It has been variously censored and raced since its first performance. It was recorded by Billie Holiday in 1952 and by Ella Fitzgerald in 1956.

> When the only sound in the empty street
> Is the heavy tread of the heavy feet
> That belong to a lonesome cop,
> I open shop.
>
> When the moon so long has been gazing down
> On the wayward ways of this wayward town
> That her smile becomes a smirk,
> I go to work.
>
> Love for sale,
> Appetizing young love for sale.
> Love that's fresh and still unspoiled,
> Love that's only slightly soiled,
> Love for sale.
>
> Who will buy?
> Who would like to sample my supply?
> Who's prepared to pay the price
> For a trip to Paradise?
> Love for sale.

Let the poets pipe of love
In their childish way,
I know ev'ry type of love
Better far than they.

If you want the thrill of love,
I've been thru the mill of love,
Old love, new love,
Ev'ry love but true love.

Love for sale,
Appetizing young love for sale.
If you want to buy my wares
Follow me and climb the stairs,
Love for sale.[6]

Loneliness is the horizon of the scene—the streetwalker's loneliness, but that of the unrepresented john too. Cavafy and Cole
Porter begin with waiting, the late hours. Porter's prostitute
sells substitutes to those who know, at the end of the evening,
that no beloved is coming their way. They have no reason to
wait longer for the One. She speaks of her "wares," her "sup-
ply," "types" of love, for a cold version of a serial love life. Hers
is a grim solicitation, but a compelling account of the cor-
ruptions of sexual liaison. Nowhere more so than when Cole
Porter claims to have written what the poets won't say: namely,
just how degrading the pursuit of romance and pleasure can
be. "I know every type of love / Better far than they. / If you
want the thrill of love, / I've been through the mill of love."
Who knows as well as a streetwalker the extent of sexual appetite, the range of erotic imagination? That people buy and sell
sex is well known, but the song refers to "the wayward ways of

this wayward town." She knows what the illusion of normalcy conceals. She works nightly on the far side of monogamy and repression. "Wayward" often means "perverse," but it is a particularly native term, from the fourteenth century. It also indicates stubborn resistance, as in "refractory" (*OED*, 1A). Cole Porter's song is uncharacteristically moralizing, though beautiful and delicate too. He does not approve of the hypocrisy of the wayward town, because that is what drives the sex trade into the late-night streets. The song acknowledges the pathos of the young prostitute.

What Ella Fitzgerald's performance reveals is the fortitude of the singer who copes with her adversity. There is little suggestion of a remedy here. Look at the line "I've been through the mill of love." It rejuvenates a cliché by locating a profound truth in an overused turn of phrase; this is a subtle artistic function. "Call me Flower/Flour; I've been through the mill." That's the conventional expression (maid as flower) that turns on a homonym. One who's been through the mill has been fully processed, from kernel to powder. What might that mean from the mouth of a streetwalker? Hard-won knowledge, self-acceptance, skepticism of pretension. A merely moralizing poem by a streetwalker would include complaint against the forces that drive women to prostitution—bad men, drugs, poverty—but that topic isn't broached here.[7] Prostitution isn't going anywhere; Cole Porter gives an account of the state of things, as the ancient Chinese poems do, not of causes. Nightlife reveals the immemorial diversity of creation.

To which gender is crucial. When a shepherd solicits, it's a lovesong; but when a woman does, it's a work-song. Her auditors may be thinking this is forced labor among the rough elements. They are meant to be saddened and superficially shamed: a woman should not have to sell herself, least of all on the street . . . and so on. But the performing character demonstrates control of language, even though she has compromised control of her body. The first two stanzas sound heavy handed, as anapestic verse often does. The first and second lines are alternating anapests and iambs, two of each. The third line of the first stanza breaks that emphatic rhythm with two anapests followed by a single iamb; the third line of the second stanza has only one anapest followed by two iambs. The final line of both stanzas is comprised of two iambs. The hooker's mastery is heard in the opening quatrain, in the thudding array of five trochaic modifiers (only, empty, heavy, heavy, lonesome) that render a leaden scene. Billie heard in the song that sense of a load to carry. She left the first two stanzas for someone else to perform. Her version bears a spirit-crushing weight in every line. Yet she manages. That is known to her auditors only because her expression is artful. Words and rhythms are her character.

Her artfulness—and of course Porter's—has to do with achieving richness of representation and understanding within the limits of a song that began its life on the stage. Again and again one sees that the simplicity of love songs is only apparent. They invoke commonplaces only to qualify, challenge, or dismiss them with terse ironies. The phrase "slightly soiled" seems simple: an understatement. These two words close the rhyme with "still unspoiled." Just that combination of words invokes a concept of degree and reminds listeners that some matters do not admit easily of such measurement. A spot on a garment can usually be cleaned and removed. But the experience of prostitution may be harder to expunge from memory, the phrase implies. Chastity or one's sense of one's chasteness may be hard to recover after nights of streetwalking. "Let the poets pipe of love, in their childish way," the singer asserts. One may recall that William Blake begins Songs of Innocence with these trochaic quatrains:

Piping down the valleys wild
Piping songs of pleasant glee
On a cloud I saw a child
And he laughing said to me

Pipe a song about a Lamb;
So I piped with merry chear,
Piper pipe that song again—
So I piped, he wept to hear.

Porter may well have had Blake's songs in mind as he wrote "Love for Sale," particularly the last quatrain of "London":

But most thro' midnight streets I hear
How the youthful harlot's curse
Blasts the new-born Infants tear
And blights with plagues the Marriage hearse.

Blake wrote in "London" of the systematic organization of poverty and oppression. The streets and the river are all "chartered": nothing undetermined. "Slightly soiled" is an apparently simple but laconic phrase; it exposes the violation of a young woman as no simple matter. She is capable of reproduction, but her "marriage" will not be completed by a carriage ride. No social advantage can offset the apparently simple phrase that ends the poem, "Marriage hearse." A whole way of life is lost by some violations. Simple phrases, "slightly soiled" and "Marriage hearse," make that point economically, memorably. Blake's judgment is fierce.

And yet Ella Fitzgerald heard triumph in Porter's lyric and extracted that from the dramatic setting. What is on display is not flesh but resourceful management. There is an implicit contrast between this control and the misrepresentations of sexual capitalism. Admire the song and you feel the strength of the character's language. Hear, she says, what words do for those out in the cold. Hooker-songs are about language. Ella's version of the tune expresses (as she so often does) a lightness of spirit. One might think that the darkest moment in the tune derives from the loneliness of the cop on his beat. Her voice rises when she sings: "I open shop" and "I go to work." The syntax of those periodic sentences of the first two quatrains is resolved by short declarative clauses; the satisfying pleasure of grammatical closure is audible in her delivery. Grammar matters, because so much thematic stress falls on the speaker's effective agency. The ethical issue of Robert Hass' "Ezra Pound's Proposition" and Langston Hughes' "Listen Here Blues"—namely, who bears responsibility for prostitution?—is answered easily here: the speaker makes her own decisions; grammar makes that point stick—contra Blake, Hass, Hughes, and everyone's wish to make the sex trade go away.

Ella's performance is an affirmation rather than complaint. That's a surprise. She is not a blues singer, and it's a bluesy lyric. For the dramatic sense of the song, for the experience of a streetwalker, she cares little, though the song was written for the Broadway stage, and censors were aroused by the presence of a prostitute there. The last stanza is dark in semantic terms: buy her wares; climb the stairs. But Ella's lines swing. However rough the life of a prostitute, however accessible a streetwalker is said to be, Ella is untouchable, beyond damage, protected by art. Her aplomb takes the song beyond the street-drama. She has something deeply right that many other versions miss. In ethical terms, the realistic sense of the lyric is unavoidable. Ella's aesthetic affirmation is ultimately brought to bear on the dramatic situation. The prostitute understands the actual orders of her life and her town, and she's not looking for change. She awaits no protector, no reformer. Ella's musical performance is beautiful, and that validates her authority. Form affirms, as Merrill says.

Compassionate citizens *should* ask how a woman comes to prostitution, as Robert Hass and Langston Hughes explicitly do. Behind that question, though, is hope of some correction or protection, an expectation of eventual social progress—non-issues for Baudelaire and Cole Porter. Baudelaire was attracted by the gruesomeness of the trade, so much so that his own writerly description shamed him, as is clear in "Le Jeu." The character of no one prostitute engages him, and pulchritude is only a memory; milieu interests him.

> Dans des fauteuils fanés des courtisanes vieilles,
> Pâles, le sourcil peint, l'oeil câlin et fatal,
> Minaudant, et faisant de leurs maigres oreilles
> Tomber un cliquetis de pierre et de métal;
>
> Autour des verts tapis des visages sans lèvre,   5
> Des lèvres sans couleur, des mâchoires sans dent,
> Et des doigts convulsés d'une infernale fièvre,
> Fouillant la poche vide ou le sein palpitant;
>
> Sous de sales plafonds un rang de pâles lustres
> Et d'énormes quinquets projetant leurs lueurs   10
> Sur des fronts ténébreux de poètes illustres
> Qui viennent gaspiller leurs sanglantes sueurs;
>
> Voilà le noir tableau qu'en un rêve nocturne
> Je vis se dérouler sous mon oeil clairvoyant.
> Moi-même, dans un coin de l'antre taciturne,   15
> Je me vis accoudé, froid, muet, enviant,

Enviant de ces gens la passion tenace,
De ces vieilles putains la funèbre gaieté,
Et tous gaillardement trafiquant à ma face,
L'un de son vieil honneur, l'autre de sa beauté!   20

Et mon coeur s'effraya d'envier maint pauvre homme
Courant avec ferveur à l'abîme béant,
Et qui, soûl de son sang, préférerait en somme
La douleur à la mort et l'enfer au néant!

In Richard Howard's blank-verse quatrains:

They sit in shabby armchairs, ancient whores
with eyebrows painted over pitiless eyes,
simpering so that the garish gems they wear
jiggle at their withered powdered ears.

Around the green felt, lipless faces loom
or colorless lips and toothless jaws, above
feverish fingers that cannot lie still
but fumble in empty pockets, trembling breasts;

under the dirty ceilings and a row
of dusty chandeliers, the low-hung lamps
sway over famous poets' shadowed brows,
the sweat of which they come to squander here;

this hideous pageant passed before my eyes
as if a nightmare picked out each detail:
I saw myself in a corner of that hushed den
watching it all, cold, mute—and envious!

envying the stubborn passion of such men,
the deadly gaiety of those old whores—
all blithely trafficking, as I looked on,
in honor or beauty—whatever they could sell!

Horrible, that I should envy these
who rush so recklessly into the pit,
each in his frenzy ravenous to prefer
pain to death, and hell to nothingness![8]

    This is brilliant description: their earrings' grim rattle. Prosody counts for a lot: the syllables line up neatly in this site of supposed abandon. The words register sonically and fit exactly the scheme of the quatrain, each detail destined for its one place. The anatomies in the second stanza allude darkly to the blazons of sunnier love poems. The large point made by this craft is that the players are wholly absorbed in a material environment, at one with it, which is why terms of placement initiate the first five quatrains. As the walls and furnishings decline in time, so do the habitués. This smudged, eroded setting is without hope of regeneration; the art of pretended passion is not forever. All that craft has rendered stylish is obviously mortal: "l'oeil câlin et fatal," the eye arch and deadly, he writes in the second line. The habitués are visible and audible (though they do not speak), because their lives are reduced to matter. Human interaction is confined to a silent card game. The one sound, from those earrings, "un cliquetis de pierre et de metal." Only that remains of the conventional glitter of casinos. The observing poet is struck mute by the scene, he says, though the poem is notable evidence to the contrary. His mastery of sound—his craft—sets him entirely apart from the mute ones, as a voyeur is removed from his object.

Little is predicated of these professional mimics of eros. The subject settles into a tableau, and every reader, like the poet, is a spectator. He feeds a familiar appetite for the demi-monde moralisé: the degeneration of whoredom and so on—exactly what one does not find in the ancient Chinese poem. He is explicit about his own complicity. His first three quatrains lead to a sudden vision of famous poets and then of impotence. He connects his art to this scene of mortal gamble and suggests that the craft of stylish representation is squandered here, by poets as by whores; that the proper end of illustrious art is to rise above materiality, money, honors, bordellos, and description. His Dantesque poem proceeds under a judgment: "In the sweat of thy face shalt thou eat bread, till thou return unto the ground" (Gen. 3:19). Labor and damnation.. "Working girls," we say.

Of the seven deadly sins, one reasonably expects to find lust in a bordello; money too, exploitation, sad resolve. But these topics do not move Baudelaire. The poem has two distinct parts that diverge on a single repeated term, "enviant," envying, wishing oneself another. How remarkable that envy should play any role. In the last two quatrains he names the basis of his envy of the habitués: tenacity. Despite age, infirmity, and diminished allure, they refuse to surrender the lives they made in pursuit of pleasure and advantage. They are in the game still, though nothing desirable remains on the table. His courage is as nothing compared to theirs. His heart shows fear at the very presence of his own envy ("mon coeur s'effraya d'envier")—never mind fear of death and nothingness, the real adversaries. Eliot appreciated in Baudelaire a recognition of good and evil; his critical observation bears exactly on this single poem.[9] The habitués show admirable, conservative tenacity in the face of a modernity in which death and nothingness

supplant pain and retribution. The master-describer and the
habitués are all one in their refusal of capitalist production.
They are avatars of slow labor. Gambling is an industry that
produces not growth but loss. Nonetheless they all hold to an
old way. In fact, the poem depicts no whoring, no acts at all,
only being. Prostitution generates a milieu in which matter
represents desire. Desire is dried and preserved in matter, a
kind of taxidermy, until the acts it usually spurs disappear
altogether.

The aged, wizened prostitutes fascinate Baudelaire: "vieilles"
twice characterizes the women (ll. 1 and 18) and "vieil" once
modifies "honneur" (l. 20). Cavafy, Porter, and Yü Hsüan-chi
all speak of the young whom one expects to be discouraged
after selling themselves but who, on the contrary, manage
money and sex well enough. Baudelaire's old ones seem to be
in the wrong place: how can their wrinkled flesh attract clients?
With years they have grown tough, shameless, and certain of
their interests. They have adjusted to their milieu, its furniture
and ornaments. They have had lots of time to reconsider their
choices and are no one's victims. What attracts Baudelaire is
their resolve to stay with the game long after it ceases to pay.
His objection to prostitution is that it induces a materialism
not to be explained by capitalist economics; it distracts even
poets whose vocation is to look at life deeply and widely. Of
his own poor judgment and bad taste, he expresses shame.
Given enough time and conducive surroundings, poets too
settle into a papery art.

Why is materiality so meaningful to Baudelaire? Eliot, as
a Christian, would understand spirit as the contrary to matter, but there is nothing in the poem to designate a sense of
spirit beyond what is spoken of as "character." Nor is there
any sense of damnation here. The poem does not address

Christian belief. One is commonly told that prostitutes age poorly because the tempo of their trade ruins their physical health: too many, too fast. This mundane aspect of materiality—distant far from Eliot's concerns—does relate directly to "Le Jeu." Here is a translation, by Rexroth and Ling Chung, of an anonymous ancient Chinese (non-Christian) poem, all about tarting up.

> After kicking on the swing,
> Lasciviously, I get up and rouge my palms.
> Thick dew on a frail flower,
> Perspiration soaks my thin dress.
> A new guest enters.
> My stockings come down
> And my hairpins fall out.
> Embarrassed, I run away,
> And lean flirtatiously against the door,
> Tasting a green plum.[10]

"Le Jeu" is concerned not with sexual acts in a bordello but with the lives of habitués aside from their sexual transactions, as if one asked what one does after sex. "Is that all there is?" Peggy Lee famously asked.[11] The answer, for Baudelaire, is that one returns to mere material existence in time. One ages into decrepitude. The Chinese courtesan is young, ageless, in the poem, but she too returns to the *matter* of life. She welcomes the next gent in line. One client, one romance after another: seriality and prostitution share an abstract structural opposition to monogamy. "Who is it *this* time?" Aphrodite urbanely asks Sappho. Movement from one lover to the next is hard on the spirit, and the difficulty worsens as the tempo picks up. Aphrodite's response to Sappho, remember, is that *soon enough* Sappho's resistant beloved will be entirely willing. The cycles of resistance and desire do not need to be sped up. In line one, this courtesan is "kicking on the swing," an "obvious cliché for sexual intercourse," according to the translators Kenneth Rexroth and Ling Chung. The poem depicts the work of arousal through figures. Four lines after the kicking, "A new guest enters." In between she grows sweaty. As soon as the new client arrives, she begins to perform her disrobing. One is struck by the physical demands of prostitution. There are no refreshing pauses, but she is not complaining. Instead she works the role of insatiable femme. She bites into the plum, just for one taste. A spectacle of fatigue, or of appetite, ignites desire in others and enhances a courtesan's control. Baudelaire was ashamed to be an observer in a bordello, evidently drawn there by his art. (The plural "poètes illustres" has some generalizing force, as if *of course* poets want to observe bordellos [l. 11].) Poetry too manages others' desires. Its syllables click; its figures are paint. He constructed a scene, an illusion of physicality. The term "trick," for a client, or a sexual transaction, gets at the link between prostitution and misrepresentation. It's all theater.

Seriality usually indicates a chain of misses, as in chapter six, but it also refers to the resilience of desire; the courtesan disguises her physical resilience as intensity. Of her sweaty labor she makes a scene of apparent craving. The details rendered are convincingly specific, as Baudelaire's are too. Hers is genuine labor, but she is master of the spectacle of even her disarray. Her rouged palms are meant to suggest to an eager client that she is flushed, hot; ladies rouge their lips, the title reminds one. How she came to be a courtesan was not what interested an audience for ancient Chinese courtesan poetry. How she manages her appearance, her traffic, and her stamina—all that was of interest. The poem examines her duplicity with curiosity, rather than judgment. For Blake, prostitution is evidence of moral corruption caused by economic forces. The state enforces a regime of repression and hypocrisy. Cole Porter recognized too the force of civil law in stigmatizing the sex trade, but he speaks only of waywardness. The distinction between romance and prostitution seems obvious, firm in the abstract. One explains it in terms of autonomy and instrumentality. But one's autonomous deliberation easily declines into strategies. One might, after due consideration, resolve to please oneself and benefit from another's need or desire.

Autonomy and instrumentality are often intertwined. Andrew B. Horwitt's lyrics for "Gentleman Friend" get at the complications of compensated sex outside of prostitution. For years I naïvely enjoyed Sarah Vaughan's version as sung by a woman glad to have a courteous lover after a long dry spell. (What was I thinking?) A "gentleman friend" is one who can pay. The song tells of a relationship that renders a controversial economy rational.

> I got myself a hat with cherries
> And a brand new yellow dress
> It isn't very hard to guess
> That the answer will be yes
> I'm ridin' high
> And I approve of the trend
> Look what I've found me
> I got myself a gentleman friend.[12]

The word "approve" explicitly acknowledges an ethical judgment met; implicitly it suggests a mutual arrangement. (The cherries on her hat, a traditional hymenal figure.)

His kind of kissin' suits me to a T
What I was missin'
In the used to be
I'm getting frequently

"Getting any?" men ask each other in vulgar jest. The phrase
is rendered more inclusive here: yes, kisses and sex; but money
and gifts too. Her one qualm is heard in a single, final word
of the last line of the fifth stanza: "Wanna laugh and sing and
cry." That last term, a non-sequitur, identifies some sacrifice
accompanying this arrangement. In performance Sarah makes
nothing at all of the difference between laughing and crying.
Once made, her judgment is forever, like a church wedding:
"Gonna love him till I die." Their exchange of money and sex
is like a marriage, a condition of a life chosen. The cry could
express regret that her romance requires willfulness.

The poems discussed concern elective prostitution. They
admit no claims of coercion. There is no apparent misdeed
because the subjects seem able to deliberate their options,
however limited those may be. The poems barely mention
conventional sexual morality. One cannot say they are for-
giving where no offense is on the horizon. Is one's body one's
own to give to others as one wishes, at whatever risk and for
whatever benefit? Cole Porter's "Love for Sale" is uttered by
one who has broken a taboo and claimed control over the use
of her body. Her "wares" are her own, an asset to be used for
one purpose today and another tomorrow, or for one purpose
in one house, and another next door. This is the significance
of the pseudo-prostitutes in love songs ("I Wanna Know"
and "Gentleman Friend"). Taking compensation for sex or
affection and being a prostitute are distinguishable. One may
engage in prostitution without being for all one's days defined

by that transaction. Cavafy conveys regard for pleasure in liberty worn lightly. Consider his "Days of 1909, '10 and '11":

> He was the son of a much-tormented, destitute
> seaman (from one of the Aegean islands).
> He worked for a blacksmith. He wore shabby clothes.
> His working shoes were torn and shoddy.
> His hands were grimed with rust and oil.
>
> In the evenings, when they closed shop,
> if there was something he fancied a lot,
> a rather expensive tie,
> a tie to be worn on Sundays,
> or if he'd seen in a shop window and yearned
> for a nice lavender shirt,
> he would sell his body for a few shillings.
>
> I wonder whether in times of old,
> glorious Alexandria could boast of a lovelier youth,
> a lad more exquisite than he—who went to waste:
> needless to say, no statue or painting of him was ever
>   made;
> thrown into a blacksmith's run-down shop,
> he quickly wore himself out
> with strenuous labour and cheap, wretched
>   debauchery.[13]

This too is a prudential tale, though more obviously a praise poem for one of the flowers of the anonymous poor. It begins with the question of a praise-poem: Who was he? The poet's first concern is to honor this young man; a counsel of prudence comes second. Cavafy is more particularly sensitive to

the economics than to the ethics of prostitution. He begins
with the young man's class origins, because that explains why
the young man was precipitously apprenticed to a blacksmith
without consideration of more suitable alternatives. The poem's
main point is not the familiar one that economic pressure on
the poor led this young man to prostitution. Rather, a recognizable taste for ornaments to a grimy existence led him to sell
his body—and apparently without incurring any great difficulty with that transaction. Prostitution did not have him in
its grip. He sold his body when he wanted some luxury and
didn't when he didn't. The beauty of the young man is that he
is without ambition or real self-regard. And without remorse.
His wants are simple, sometimes costly, but easily satisfied.
Debauchery itself is not the problem. Had he not sold his
body, the speaker might not have known him at all. A more
remunerative sort of debauchery, however, might have been
less debilitating. What offends Cavafy is the fact that low-
priced debauchery inappropriately led this young man to waste
his beauty on many mute acts of the street-trade. Cavafy's
point is aesthetic: not *this* fellow for the street. To the young
man's wish to sell his body, Cavafy expresses no objection.
The poet respects the young man's desire for mobility. Son
of a seaman, assistant to a blacksmith, male prostitute. These
identities are his, but only partially, temporarily, more or less
fitting at one moment or another.

I want to conclude with a last prostitute's monologue,
again a solicitation-scene. Joni Mitchell's wonderful "Raised
on Robbery" will stand up to comparison to "Love for Sale,"
though the tone of this song is bright by comparison. I press
the point that these work-songs are about fortitude, and that
this is the dominant theme of songs about money and love.

He was sitting in the lounge of the Empire Hotel
He was drinking for diversion
He was thinking of himself

A little money riding on the Maple Leafs
Along comes a lady in lacy sleeves
She says . . .
"Let me sit down here
Drinking alone's a shame
It's a shame, it's a crying shame
Look at those jokers
Glued to that damn hockey game
Hey honey—you've got lots of cash
Bring us round a bottle
And we'll have some laughs
Gin's what I'm drinking
I was raised on robbery

I'm a pretty good cook
I'm sitting on my groceries
Come up to my kitchen
I'll show you my best recipe

I try and I try but I can't save a cent
I'm up after midnight, cooking
Trying to make my rent
I'm rough but I'm pleasin'
I was raised on robbery
We had a little money once

They were pushing through a four lane highway
Government gave us three thousand dollars
You should have seen it fly away
First he bought a '57 Biscayne
He put it in the ditch
He drunk up all the rest
That son of a bitch
His blood's bad whiskey
I was raised on robbery

You know you ain't bad looking
I like the way you hold your drinks
Come home with me honey
I ain't asking for no full length mink
Hey, where you going . . .
Don't go yet . . .

Your glass ain't empty and we just met
You're mean when your loaded—
I was raised on robbery."[14]

This tight, driven, and comic narrative scares off the john. Talk is the thing. Marlowe's passionate shepherd may as well be alone: his nymph was a cipher until Ralegh gave her a voice. Joni has to represent the man, but he gets no voice. The poem begins with him, his mood, his type. Their types don't match up, so he runs off; that is all the drama there is. The apparently delicate lady in lacy sleeves is way too quick and tough for him. In poems written by men to women, there is often no drama because there is only one character, a fluent wooer. Songs of articulate women ("Cupid's Boogie" is another instance) test the staying power of delicate creatures.

Some phrases communicate little information; others,

a great deal. Conventionality factors into that distinction. Marlowe's phrase "pretty lambs," for instance, provides no new information. But the line "I like the way you hold your drinks" is definite about the circumstance of the utterance: it's not easy to express admiration of a stranger, because one knows too little. If admiration must be expressed, as here, one may grasp at something superficial. Insofar as it is an honest observation about the guy, it indicates how much is foregone in seeking intimacy with strangers. The line also clarifies the character of the speaker: she doesn't wish to lie, even for money. (Possibly Joni means to acknowledge Ira Gershwin's "They Can't Take That away from Me": "The way you wear your hat, / The way you sip your tea.") The speaker's candor is there to stay. Writerly craft has condensed this character into four bright strophes. A verbal display of a striking character is the pleasure offered by the poem—as by Browning's monologues.

Her fluency is frightening. A single line is enough to show that she hears sounds at a level well below ordinary speech: "His blood's bad whiskey." The lines beginning with "First he bought a '57 Biscayne" and continuing to the refrain are quick, musical, condensed, a whole little story there in six lines. Joni is a real writer; the poem, a made thing. This is not to say that every line is new to the English language. Some phrasing is conventional. "I'm sitting on my groceries" presents a clever figure: she sells her ass, and thus survives. From there she offers her "best recipe," a nice euphemism. But the figure has already circulated in a vernacular region not amply represented in poetry. Part of the song is attributable to a flamboyant hooker, part to the vernacular. This is no qualification of Joni's genius, only a description of her resources. There is good reason to celebrate the verbal abilities of prostitutes; men and women seldom approach sexual liaisons with confidence in their terminology. Prostitutes who sing masterful songs are

implausible objects of pity. They insist that listeners credit
them with self-control. They are the ones loved by writers.

I made the obvious point that poems *about* prostitution
(Baudelaire's "Le Jeu," Porter's "Love for Sale," Joni Mitchell's
"Raised on Robbery") praise strength. Cavafy turns that proposition inside-out: a prostitute's virtue, in the sense of power,
may be mobility where others are rigid, fixed. He observes
that those who use sex to raise extra money for stimulation
or immediate pleasures are light spirited, unconcerned with
the discipline of devotion. This is not a new or strange idea.
Charles Cotton wrote of the delicacy of the prostitute M.H.
in seventeenth-century London.

> As soft, and snowy, as that down
> Adorns the blow-ball's frizzled crown;
> As straight and slender as the crest
> Or antlet of the one-beam'd beast;
> Pleasant as the odorous month of May:
> As glorious and as light as day.

They are not all tough broads, and strength is just one issue
raised by money. Everyone pays for love, intimacy, and trust—
with heart and being, as Shakespeare says. One risks oneself
on a sense of another. When that transaction proves ill-ad-
vised, the losses are as costly as can be. "Who's prepared to pay
the price / For a trip to Paradise?" From Cavafy's perspective,
Porter's "paradise" need not be ironic. A streetwalker asks a
pittance. Her own liability (and that of her clients) is sharply
limited: defenses, in order. These are poems about imitation or
artfulness. Concerning love, they say only that intimacy is not
metaphysical, and does not take anyone beyond rationality.
They speak of makers, fakers, and calculators—ordinary folks.

Baudelaire's prostitutes endured because they excelled at deception and held by their choices. Vernacular songs are efforts at realism, an extension of the representation of social life, but more meaningfully songs of fantasy, of *imagined* strength. Imagine a man or woman so obviously strong he or she asked nothing more of one than the bills in one's pocket. That might be felt as relief. If one could name the price, in bills, of a trip to paradise, or effectively limit liability, that would be a considerable strength. Money buys not love, but autonomy.

8. Love Abides

"Hello, young lovers, wherever you are. / Be kind, be faithful and true." Singers address young lovers; the old ones, not so much. Love-talk, not for the wrinkled. Observing young lovers is a major industry. The old ones sell only recliners and time-shares. Alain Badiou observes: "The literature on love contains very little in terms of the experience of its endurance over time . . . Important works . . . are often built around the impossibility of love, its being put to the test, its tragedy, its waning, its separation, end, etc. But there is very little on it lasting positively. We could even say married life has hardly produced a great work."[1] However, from being knocked off one's feet, when young, one learns prudence, probably not more. "Who is it *this* time?" Aphrodite asks Sappho. Now and then one wisely listens to the old who may actually *know* something: imagine, understanding eros. What species of romantic love endures? An answer could help lovers fulfill the pledges they routinely make and break; that would be progress.

Love is lovelier
The second time around.

Just as wonderful with both feet on the ground.[2]

Love poems are always about the passage of time. The promise to love forever refers to an alternative life. Badiou says, "Love invents a different way of lasting in life . . . It is the desire for an unknown duration."[3] The poems of old lovers report how well or ill they have fulfilled their promises. They give testimony about the feasibility of the most common dreads of changing life. Can one *make* a life, or is it inevitably the sum of circumstances in time?

One remembers complaints of love abandoning the aged. And songs that recommend alternatives to young love. Ralegh's "Walsingham" is a ballad-complaint of an aged lover, set aside. Here are the last five of its eleven anapestic quatrains.

> "I have loved her all my youth,   25
>   but now, old, as you see;
> Love likes not the falling fruit
>   from the withered tree.
>
> "Know that love is a careless child
>   and forgets promise past;   30
> He is blind, he is deaf when he list
>   and in faith never fast.
>
> "His desire is a dureless content
>   And a trustless joy;
> He is won with a world of despair   35
>   And is lost with a toy.
>
> "Of womenkind such indeed is the love,
>   (or the word 'love' abused)
> Under which many childish desires
>   and conceits are excused.   40

"But Love is a durable fire
in the mind ever burning—
Never sick, never old, never dead,
from itself never turning."[4]

The first three quatrains here spell out an unsurprising critique of love as insensitive not only to the charms of mature
persons but to those goods that require duration (promises,
faith, trust) for fulfillment (ll. 30, 32, 34). Experiencing age
and betrayal are the same here. The second and third quatrains in particular dismiss young love as inconsiderable. The
fourth distinguishes between love and the term "love" and
(with conventional misogyny) attributes to women abuse of
language. None of this is freshly conceived. It renders memorable, though, aged lovers' resentment. The last quatrain is
a glorious affirmation of a fierce love that endures beyond
erotic experience. It endures (hence "ever," "never," "never,"
and "never") because it is an *idea*; experienced only insofar as
the life of the mind is experienced. A prisoner feels the force of
this distinction. (Elizabeth I incarcerated Ralegh, her favorite
courtier, when she learned that he had secretly wed one of her
ladies-in-waiting.) An aged lover is a figure for a faithful mate.
The poem's power comes from the effort to understand something abstract and difficult—against a background of ordinary faithlessness. The aged lover defines the nature of love
exactly without abusing language, as Edwin Muir also does
four hundred years later, in "In Love for Long." The turn to
language-use in the fourth of these stanzas and to definition
in the last brings the poem to a conclusive affirmation of the
survival of love among many others in the future. The objective of this faux ballad is neither dialogue nor complaint but
instead the preservation of wisdom.

Later poets poignantly describe the distinction of mature love as gentleness, though they claim less for that love than Ralegh and Muir do. The tone of old lovers' song derives characteristically from loss and reduction, and that narrows their emotional range. Nabokov's translation of Fyodor Tyutchev's "Last Love" is a good example:

> Love at the closing of our days
> is apprehensive and very tender.
> Glow brighter, brighter, farewell rays
> of one last love in its evening splendor.
>
> Blue shade takes half the world away:
> through western clouds alone some light is slanted.
> O tarry, O tarry, declining day,
> enchantment, let me stay enchanted.
>
> The blood runs thinner, yet the heart
> remains as ever deep and tender.
> O last belated love, thou art
> a blend of joy and of hopeless surrender.[5]

Mortality makes eros seem small. Comparison of Ralegh's and Nabokov's lines makes one suspect that a tender tone concedes too much. Mature lovers sense approaching terror, and love in fear of loving no more, do so tenderly in order not to inflict on others what they have felt themselves. No assurance is offered that love's pains are ever offset or warranted. No beloved is addressed or described. Late love is a comfort in a diminished state, a desperate, impersonal stay against mortality and skepticism. The late lover does not ask to learn anything new, only to renew enchantment. Another old one, Stanley Kunitz, asks

rather for more sensuality, in the masterful, apparently effortless, trimeter of "Touch Me." And this is a big ask, as we say,
because sensuality is the least likely element of romance to
survive the years. However love may abide, surely it is not as
sensuality.

> *Summer is late, my heart.*
> Words plucked out of the air
> some forty years ago
> when I was wild with love
> and torn almost in two   5
> scatter like leaves this night
> of whistling wind and rain.
> It is my heart that's late,
> it is my song that's flown.
> Outdoors all afternoon   10
> under a gunmetal sky
> staking my garden down,
> I kneeled to the crickets trilling
> underfoot as if about
> to burst from their crusty shells;   15
> and like a child again
> marveled to hear so clear
> and brave a music pour
> from such a small machine.
> What makes the engine go?   20
> Desire, desire, desire.
> The longing for the dance
> stirs in the buried life.
> One season only,
>   and it's done.
> So let the battered old willow   25
> thrash against the windowpanes

and the house timbers crack.
Darling, do you remember   30
the man you married? Touch me,
remind me who I am.[6]

Kunitz remembers an old love-time and grieves for his losses—
of love and life. He remembers other poems, as well. The
conventional figure: "the falling leaves drift by my window,"
Nat King Cole sings in "Autumn Leaves." One imagines that
"Touch Me" is addressed to a still-living wife of forty years
or so. He married his third wife, Elise Asher, in 1958, and
published the poem a little short of forty years later. In lines
six and seven, though, he is thinking in particular of Thomas
Hardy's devastating elegy "During Wind and Rain," written
after the death in 1912 of Emma Gifford Hardy, his first (and
divorced) wife. Hardy looks back on her family home, recall-
ing their music-making there when they were happy together.
The first stanza ends:

> Ah, no; the years O,
> How the sick leaves reel down in throngs!

The poem expresses grief for Emma and her family and
estrangement from that former life. Kunitz thinks in line
twenty-four of Matthew Arnold's "The Buried Life," about
love benumbed by ordinary repression: "Alas! Is even love too
weak / To unlock the heart, and let it speak? / Are even lovers
powerless to reveal / To one another what indeed they feel?"
Kunitz wants to recover vigor: the sensuality of young love,
obviously, but also the clarity and courage of the crickets trying
to shed their crusts, as he could be rid of his own. He is now
bereft of his art (l. 10). Desire, he says, drives the life cycle on.
And he frankly asks his beloved for an arousing touch, to help

him feel once again like a lover. This poem is close to common understanding of the effect of years on an erotic body. It is poignant, but surprising only in its candor. Modest, in that sense. The imperative voice comes easily to Tyutchev and Kunitz, who remain in proximity to commonplaces, not out on an edge. They are doing their best to assert their remaining strength, as they register time's reductions. Celebrations of old love, however enthusiastic, veer toward elegy.

But aged love is an ideal prized not only by old people. Pledges of love habitually insist on longevity as a practical measure of ardor. "I will love you always." "Do you take this woman [man] to be your lawfully wedded wife [husband] until death do you part?" A mate who will not leave, regardless of circumstance, or of the cooling of passion, is rare; pledged partners leave for innumerable reasons. An aged lover is a persistent, reliable partner—not necessarily an old man, not necessarily an ardent lover. For "old lover" read "faithful lover," and the poems gain significance. Love songs of the aged assess the validity of monogamous desire; they should be weighty, golden, dense with promises fulfilled. Ralegh had this right; tenderness is for the wounded.

In the land of Wish, yes, love abides and conquers all, as in Ira Gershwin's "Love Is Here to Stay":

> It's very clear,
> Our love is here to stay,
> Not for a year
> But ever and a day.
>
> The radio and the telephone
> and the movies that we know
> May all be passing fancies,
> And in time may go.

But oh, my dear,
Our love is here to stay.

Together we're going a long, long way.
In time the Rockies may crumble,
Gibraltar may tumble.
(They're only made of clay.)
But our love is here to stay.[7]

How fine to know, or just to say, "our love is here to stay,"
not because it is true. The claim is justly appreciated only by
those who recognize its implausibility. Nothing is less predictable than a love's longevity. Legions of the divorced know
this, and for them this song was written. This is a paradoxical,
Petrarchan discourse: young lovers who wish to be old ones.
"The Rockies may crumble, Gibraltar may tumble; / They're
only made of clay." *We* are proverbially made of clay, fallible,
malleable, and mortal. Mountains constantly crumble, and
epochal technologies are set aside. But a sure love is a four-leaf
clover, a sweet wish and reminder of what we were "when our
love was new, and each kiss an inspiration." Robert Hass says,
in "Against Botticelli,"

The myth they chose was the constant lovers.
The theme was richness over time.
It is a difficult story and the wise never choose it
because it requires a long performance
and because there is nothing, by definition, between
the acts.[8]

Their story is nearly impossible to tell because it has no conflict,
or drama. Ongoing love is material for song more than narrative, and even in song it is usually prospective. Temporality

has a distinctive look in maturity. The idea of plural loves too looks different as one nears the end of the series. Notions of fullness are harder to justify at the far end. Does love fulfill, or only consume, one's life? Completeness is what poets seek in sound and sense, even when they only imagine themselves old.

Endurance proves that love is metaphysical: crepe skin and circumstances have not killed it. Old lovers, the survivors, have precious authority, because they have succeeded where many have failed. Even a lonesome lover, like Petrarch, a long-lived aspirant, has credibility. Yeats borrows authority from an *imagined* past, which complicates the matter. He wants the piquancy of *lost* love, the earnestness of one who has lived long with injury, and accepted failure as his end. That speaker is to be believed because he has little to gain from misrepresentation. But he speaks only of what might have been. The loss of the hypothetical is what he wants his beloved to feel in the future. Yeats was twenty-six, eager for retrospection, when he wrote "When You Are Old" (1893), an imitation of a Ronsard poem.[9] In a twist of the carpe diem topos, he tells the beloved to remember one day what she lost by rejecting him.

> When you are old and grey and full of sleep,
> And nodding by the fire, take down this book,
> And slowly read, and dream of the soft look
> Your eyes had once, and of their shadows deep;
>
> How many loved your moments of glad grace,   5
> And loved your beauty with love false or true,
> But one man loved the pilgrim soul in you,
> And loved the sorrows of your changing face;
>
> And bending down beside the glowing bars,
> Murmur, a little sadly, how Love fled   10

> And paced upon the mountains overhead
> And hid his face amid a crowd of stars.[10]

Yeats writes as a forsaken young lover imagining his beloved as aged. This is a poem of constructed longevity, edgy even in the first stanza, when he refers to the "shadows deep" in her eyes. Her thoughts are dark but scrutable to him, where others see only a glad young beauty. The punishment he wishes her is to realize in old age that she lost a great love. Age will clarify their relationship by certifying his exceptionality. The expression of romantic devotion is easily attractive; recrimination, less so. Her only offense in this poem is that she did not give herself exclusively to the poet. Yeats wields the moral authority of constancy against a wayward beloved: the outcome is a great poem, but not because the speaker is admirable. He is too self-approving. In order to speak forcefully to her while young, he mortgages the future, even though there is no question of kindling a flame. Robert Lowell later did the same, "Don't fool yourself. / You'll not be loved like that." Both poets exploit a dark future for no purpose greater than their present authority—a purpose, it must be said, that enabled the writing of two great love poems!

Old lovers step back for distance on their fussing. In the second quatrain Yeats says that others loved her "beauty with love false or true." Who loved her truly and who falsely is not worth inquiry. The dichotomy that does interest him is that between the many and the one (ll. 5 & 7). She was inconstant, a person of moments. Only one—he—loved her flashes of grace and what disappointments did to her face. Many admired her, but only he loved her steadily. Age, even faked age, is conducive to abstraction. Through personification he renders love a figure with agency, as Dante and Rossetti had too (l. 10). Love "fled," as if across a tapestry.

This is a beautiful, archaic way to characterize the end of a romance. It would be merely ordinary to reproach her directly for his pain. Love fled into the mountains, and then buried his face in the stars. What a gorgeous way to refuse to blame. Love has been absorbed into the many stars. A crowd of others has won its way. A cosmic shift ended their affair. He takes no responsibility for their failure, and with the final figure he lightens her responsibility. His greater concern is to establish his love as one for the long run. The young Yeats imagines maturity as self-satisfied, and that is a limitation of the poem. This poem makes one realize more generally that the topic of abiding love entails a dubious claim to knowingness concerning lovers' obscure acts and feelings.

Old lovers should display some sanity in the face of love; stunning onset, crashing heartbreak, not their song. Have they still access to joyfulness? "Joy" is a word that recurs often in songs of mature love, as if poets all knew that the great high of sudden onset is taken from the old ones. Swift's "Stella's Birthday March 13, 1727" indicates that romance grows contorted in time. Joy looks unfamiliar among the aged. Swift no more slept with Stella than Petrarch did with Laura.[11] His love of Stella is described in terms of exceptional friendship, a Horatian virtue. After decades, one sees that the woman one loves above all others is one's partner at cards. Swift was devastated by Esther Johnson's illness and greatly feared her death. What is known as her birthday poem was written to arouse a recovery.

> This day, whate'er the Fates decree,
> Shall still be kept with joy by me:
> This day then let us not be told,
> That you are sick, and I grown old;
> Nor think on our approaching ills,   5

And talk of spectacles and pills.
To-morrow will be time enough
To hear such mortifying stuff.[12]

Eros was not a religion for him; Christianity was. Rossetti,
Yeats, Pound, and Robert Duncan—another story. Swift's
poem is an epistle, well-considered, speech-like verse to a close
companion. Cole Porter claimed in 1934 that anything goes;
one would not say that now, especially in regard to the elderly.
A strong sense of decorum prevails among the progressive.
Lyric transport is for the young. Swift's poem is uncharacteristically earnest. "Accept for once some serious lines," he writes,
"From not the gravest of divines." The theme of maturity has
him out of his usual element, after a short humorous introduction. He argues closely that Stella ought to adhere more
firmly to reason. And the poem is designed to display its own
reasonableness on its surface. Nothing rash.

The issue is whether recollection of one's achievements sustains one in adversity. He urges Stella to approve of her life of
serving well the needs of others.

Although we now can form no more   15
Long schemes of life, as heretofore;
Yet you, while time is running fast,
Can look with joy on what is past.

Approval is my term, joy is his. He does not bother to argue
that virtuous deeds take one to heaven. He esteems a joy one
can feel in an idea, or a memory; from this point of view, joy is
all around. He feels just that in celebrating her birthday (l. 2).
The ordinary understanding of joy as momentary, immediate
is of no use to him. Sudden joy, not for an old lover.

Virtuous action survives in memory and fortifies one

against the losses of old age—not a point easily taken. The next
sentence stretches over sixteen grammatically challenging lines.
One may accept the claim but nonetheless doubt his account of
the range of feeling that accompanies good behavior. Joy seems
too exuberant; satisfaction, peace, complacency, or (as he later
says) contentment seem more plausible. Joy may be apt if one
believes eternal damnation the consequence of bad behavior,
and lives with a sense of the close proximity of evil, of temp-
tations. But those Christian beliefs are not expressed, however
familiar they were to Swift. His interest instead is in the secular
quality of social lives. He asks Stella to grant, hypothetically, that
an afterlife is a mere human fiction. Even so, he argues, it is hard
to think that virtuous deeds leave no record, if only in the feelings of virtuous agents. Of such deeds pleasing God, he says
nothing at all (ll. 25-30). He speaks of pleasing the minds of
virtuous agents, for that is where the lives of such people occur.
The key values of the poem are pleasure, joy, and reason, three
terms derived from French. He asks her in lines thirty-five and
thirty-six whether she does not actually feel content in looking
back. This is what Socrates asks at the outset of the *Republic*:
whether virtuous action produces happiness.

> Say, Stella, feel you no content,   35
> Reflecting on a life well spent?

He lists the qualities that have enabled her to help her
friends: boldness, courage, detestation of vice, and patience (ll.
43-50). These are qualities one wants in a lieutenant or coun-
selor. Of pulchritude or passion nothing is said. The admirable
features of a mature beloved have little to do with gender. Aged
lovers survive passion and social conventions. And do these
abstract qualities not have some abiding substance? Are they

"empty shadows," or mere words "that fly and leave no marks behind"? (ll. 51-54) Are such notions just ink on paper? This is a genuine question. One infers from his writerly difficulties in the lines that follow how seriously he took these questions (ll. 55-72). He draws an analogy to the consumption of food which is hazardous in a poem meant to praise: food is to the body as virtue is to the mind. Virtue keeps the mind going, as food does the body. "Does not the body thrive and grow / By food of twenty years ago?" (ll. 55-56) The thought of old food in the body is distracting, and the inquiry gets worse when he asks, "Then who with reason can maintain / That no effects of food remain?" The effects of consuming food are familiar, but they provide little support for the thesis that virtuous deeds enjoy longevity.

The final paragraph of this epistle is especially touching. Swift repeats from line 1 the fact that her life is in jeopardy (l. 79). One is reminded too of the particular quality of her illness: paranoia (ll. 81-82). Even in these circumstances, he addresses her in a challenging epistle; his confidence in her intellectuality is deep.

> O then, whatever Heaven intends,
> Take pity on your pitying friends;   80
> Nor let your ills affect your mind,
> To fancy they can be unkind.
> Me, surely me, you ought to spare,
> Who gladly would your sufferings share;
> Or give my scrap of life to you,   85
> And think it far beneath your due;
> You, to whose care so oft I owe
> That I'm alive to tell you so.

Swift's poem is admirable because he argues feelingly and reasonably too for an understanding of human relationships based on justice and balance. Obligations derive from benefits received from others—not from religion, nor from kinship. Friendship is constructed and maintained by deliberate care. She should trust Swift because he acknowledges a great debt to her. Reciprocity underlies a system of proprieties and responsibilities. He explains his love of her and her responsibilities to others in terms of rational social relations. His plain-style advocacy demonstrates the control of mind that he urges her to exercise. This is obviously different from "only-you" songs of devotion. Affection for her friends is plural without any difficulty. This is when one learns that Stella is ill, and that in her illness she has come to mistrust her friends. The value of this poem cannot depend on the argumentation about food and virtue, but these last lines demonstrate control over words and syntax far beyond that on display in the earlier passages. The conclusion is celebratory in its reference to his own utterance. One has no reason to doubt his sincerity in saying that he would give his life for her. In face of a threat to her sanity, Swift, who would go mad, reasons forthrightly with her, confident that he can reach her. He cannot do otherwise than help her to hold firm to mind and identity. She is the one who expertly cares for others and saves him.

Love-play requires two. The open threat behind this poem is that dementia or mortality is about to take one. Temporality is not to be toyed with, as it is in many carpe diem poems. The sincerity of an aging writer may lead to straining, awkwardness. Williams's "Asphodel" is flawed by inelegances and banality. But there is great seriousness in these poems that push beyond rhetoric, or authorial mastery. An aged lover rightly speaks of what abides: character. Rational pleasure derives from ethical behavior, according to the poet, and this joy is sustaining, indispensable. The familiar pleasures that lovers typically celebrate have nothing to offer aged love.

One thinks of old lovers as settled into social place. Stella was twelve years Swift's junior; she became his tutee at age eight. She and her mother, at Swift's suggestion, moved their household from London to Dublin when Stella was 21. She remained close to him until her death at age 46, though it is said that they were never alone together. The poem articulates values generally affirmed in the daylight of their social circle. Given time, loves gather legitimacy. But a suppressed love—not consummated, not avowed—may endure partly because it remains private. Covertness, masked as coolness, serves love well. Wyatt did not write as an aged lover, but he was drawn to the idea of love's longevity. His version of Petrarch's Rime 140—"The Long Love that in My Thought Doth Harbor"—examines privacy. His beloved urges him to hide his love from view, so that he may appear not to love at all. Repression is service given to the beloved. With this sonnet, an English imagination enters medieval Provence—two centuries after the fact. Its values, retro and foreign in fourteenth century Italy, were archaic in sixteenth century England, but they nonetheless have something for us still.

> The long love that in my thought doth harbour,
> And in mine heart doth keep his residence
> Into my face presseth with bold pretence
> And therein campeth, spreading his banner.
> She that me learneth to love and suffer   5
> And will that my trust and lust's negligence
> Be reined by reason, shame, and reverence,
> With his hardiness taketh displeasure.

Wherewithal unto the heart's forest he fleeth,
Leaving his enterprise with pain and cry,   10
And there him hideth and not appeareth.
What may I do when my master feareth,
But in the field with him to live and die?
For good is the life ending faithfully.[13]

Marriage promotes social stability: capital formation and preservation, the security of families. However, fidelity entails deprivation. And secrecy is at odds with the social institution that still purports to represent love fulfilled. The standard reason for secrecy is that illicit lovers are not free to marry. Fine love was a hedge against the authority of arranged marriage. Songs are written for the forbidden women, the elevated or the married ones. Wyatt's poem recommends repression unto death without stipulating why love is better unacknowledged. The beloved can presume that the lover recognizes the risks of romance, because they both maneuver within a court society.

From the Lord of Love, the beloved has taken over the role of domination. His "enterprise" (l. 10) is under her supervision; this term did not take on its commercial sense until the nineteenth century. Here it indicates the bold undertaking of bringing together the lover and the beloved. Petrarch's Rime 140 is explicit about the education of the lover: the beloved instructs him how to live with love; with signs of disfavor, she disciplines him for behavior that exposes his love to view. She wills (a strong verb) that his "trust" be constrained by "reason, shame and reverence" (ll. 6-7). Her prudent counsel is not what a lover wishes to hear from a beloved. And trust of whom? Surely not of the beloved herself. The pertinent trust must be that of acquaintances permitted to see the lover's heart in his face. The beloved is aroused by fear of exposure; the lover may be trusting that such exposure is not harmful. Surrey's translation of the same poem has a "doubtful hope" that should be shadowed, where Wyatt refers to trust to be reined in. Surrey's is the more direct interpretation, but Wyatt's term indicates the paradoxical aspect of his beloved's judgment: she seeks to restrain the construction of trust, an achievement of the spirit. She wants invisible devotion. Her advocacy of obscurity is registered formally by the departure of sentence structure from stanzaic structure in the sestet. The poem promotes a strenuously private love. That, the poem suggests, is conducive to a "long love." Which is a claim worth considering, not only in a courtly context.

Wyatt's phrasing, his insistence on large-order terms, reveals a sense that restraint is appropriate. The octave presents an abstract account of the subjective operations of love. Long love, my thought, mine heart, pretense, my trust, lust's negligence, reason, shame, reverence: these are all impersonal, inclusive terms. Of these, one needs to know more. "Lust's negligence" is particularly difficult: does it indicate negligence of desire or negligence driven by desire? These are contraries. And what ought the lover better revere? The beloved's privacy? A concept of *fin'amor*? The social order? I easily list possibilities because the poem is so terse and thereby abstract. The felt consequence of this diction is a reader's sense that constraints are being urged on the speaker; in which case reason seems unwisely invoked. (Reason is said to urge repression. Two hundred years later, reason is invoked by Swift to pull his beloved out of the darkness.) The sestet is altogether different in style: the diction is simpler, and the manner, narrative rather than discursive. The poem makes a brief for submission in the form of flight, or retirement. The lover's only option is to live out his days in seclusion. That, not understanding, is what faithfulness requires of the lover. For this reason, the poem is remote from the intellectual traditions of English poetry—a necessary translation, from Wyatt's viewpoint.

One prefers to think of love ripening with age, of marriage gathering richness over time. J. V. Cunningham was a hoarse-voiced, wiry man who spoke of love grown leaner, tougher, truer over time. In 1958 he wrote two unforgettable poems on aged love. Here is "To My Wife."

> And does the heart grow old? You know
> In the indiscriminate green
> Of summer or in earliest snow
> A landscape is another scene,
>
> Inchoate and anonymous,   5
> And every rock and bush and drift
> As our affections alter us
> Will alter with the season's shift.
>
> So love by love we come at last,
> As through the exclusions of a rhyme,   10
> Or the exactions of a past,
> To the simplicity of time,
>
> The antiquity of grace, where yet
> We live in terror and delight
> With love as quiet as regret   15
> And love like anger in the night.[14]

The first line asks how love endures, and then answers: "You know," as if the matter could rest there. The passage of time entails movement from love to love, here a process of subtraction, not accrual. What we have made eventually stands revealed at the end of a series. Cunningham used the phrase "the exclusions of rhyme" as title to his collected poems. The British poet Charles Tomlinson wrote of the "chances of rhyme." Cunningham regards his words as decisions, alternatives forgone, women left behind. So lives are made too: the past, a record of what has been excluded. To exact means to drive out. Simplicity is achieved by exactions: the inchoate and anonymous richness of summer and winter is reduced by choices, acts. The shapeliness of his lines expresses intensification. Charles Olson said,

>   people
> don't change. They only stand more
> revealed. I,
> likewise.[15]

In time we become emphatically ourselves, accompanied by faintly voiced regrets, and the silent anger of our mates.

One conspicuous feature of Cunningham's poem is the lexical familiarity of lines one and six. Another is a distinctive selection of analytical terms: "indiscriminate" (l. 2), "exactions," "exclusions" (l. 10-11). These terms require choices of a reader: where to discriminate, exact, and exclude. Then come the plainly abstract modifiers seeming to evolve toward substantives. "Inchoate and anonymous," "in terror and delight": Cunningham's art assigns names to qualities. And lexical positions matter. The opening line is monosyllabic, as is the second, with one exception: "indiscriminate." Those two lines instruct one how to attend to this poem. Three- and four-syllable terms are prominent throughout the poem as approximations of what has been forgone. A poem's task is to fix in words and memory not only the feel but the meaning of experience. Cunningham, like Wyatt, loves weighty terms, dense with deliberation. "Our affections" (l. 7), for instance, distinguishes carefully between loves and lesser bonds, maybe directly tied to the senses.

"The antiquity of grace" reveals Cunningham's Roman aspiration to permanence; he is a perfect poet for old love. That phrase is the fourth term in something like a quatrain overlapping the last two quatrains (ll. 10-13). Lines ten and eleven draw two phrases into apposition: "exclusions of a rhyme" and "exactions of a past." The next two lines do the same for the phrases that complete the syntax of the sentence: "simplicity of time" and "antiquity of grace." The aesthetic that leads the poet to an old form overlaps with the excisions one makes moving through time. "Alter" is less grand than "change," as in Alterations Done Here. One gets trimmed to actual proportions by losses that, with luck, come gradually. "Terror and delight" (l. 14) are more. The poet has not leaned on them. Responsibility for their sense rests with readers alone. One comes from leaves and snow to these inclusive terms in short order—just four tetrameter quatrains. Leaps are taken. The poem moves through twos and fours, pairs of terms and quatrains. For all the relevance of discrimination, or choices, one still has pairs at the end. There is no one thing of old love. Instead: terror and delight, quiet and anger, abrupt reversals—even in abiding love.

Songs of mature love express a drive beyond physicality—for obvious reasons. Edwin Muir's "In Love for Long" makes an extreme case for love's metaphysicality: a constant love, he argues, one person alone may realize, because constant means enduring not faithful; but then one realizes that he is writing of a fidelity of spirit, a manner of being that is properly considered a consequence of faith. Love may be a quality of existence rather than an attachment to an identifiable person. When we speak of someone as a loving person, we mean something of this diffuse sort, as if that person could be expected to meet the world generally with love.

I've been in love for long
With what I cannot tell
And will contrive a song
For the intangible
That has no mould or shape,   5
From which there's no escape.

It is not even a name,
Yet is all constancy;
Tried or untried, the same,
It cannot part from me;   10
A breath, yet as still
As the established hill.

It is not any thing,
And yet all being is;
Being, being, being,   15
Its burden and its bliss.
How can I ever prove
What it is I love?
This happy happy love
Is sieged with crying sorrows,   20
Crushed beneath and above
Between todays and morrows;
A little paradise
Held in the world's vice.

And there it is content   25
And careless as a child,
And in imprisonment
Flourishes sweet and wild;
In wrong, beyond wrong,
All the world's a day long.   30

This love a moment known
For what I do not know
And in a moment gone
Is like the happy doe
That keeps its perfect laws   35
Between the tiger's paws
And vindicates its cause.[16]

Celebrations of new love seem to come easily; this is about one older than any beloved. Most lovers are clear about the identity of their beloved, even if his or her name will not be disclosed; that the beloved is the one-and-only is commonly the point. The riddling oddity here is that this lover cannot identify the object of his love. The will to metaphysicality draws his diction to schoolish and impersonal terms—too abstract for even a beloved. Nor does he claim to come by his expression naturally or inevitably; he did not look into his heart to write, as Sydney advised. He instead *contrives* a song.

Love poems often relate a moment of experience—often joyful; they are anecdotal, as if bits of life adequately or wondrously reveal the meaning of one's long duration. This poem, on the contrary, describes love as all the grander for being steadily itself, a constant resistance to the familiar judgments misapplied to it (ll. 1-18). Its revelatory moment is its surrender of existence to force (ll. 19-37). Halfway through the poem, he resets the question of definition: "How can I prove," he asks, "What it is I love?" Personal report is beside the point: the opening stanzas (the first through the third) develop a notion of impersonal, constant love of all being. "Prove" (l. 17) has the sense of demonstrate, or render evident, or establish as fact. This is a question he asks after sixteen lines of abstract reasoning of object, being, constancy, intangibility, and shapelessness—all intellectual terms concerning categorical distinctions. In stanza four he turns to the felt qualities of love in the face of adversity, and to a poem Muir remembers by a poet famous for discouraging the irritable reaching after fact. The figures on the Grecian urn enjoy a "more happy, happy love" because temporality does not disturb them. Love is consumed by the rapacious orders of ordinary life. Yes. And yet lovers have a moment.

Love thrives in the present, like a child, briefly immune to ordinariness. Routine consequences mean little to new lovers. The term "careless" (l. 26) indicates negligence, imprudence, recklessness but also, simply and exactly, without care. Eventually the doe is torn apart and consumed. The verb to "vindicate" commonly means "clear from censure, criticism, suspicion, or doubt, by means of demonstration; to justify or uphold by evidence or argument" (*OED*, 3). The poem is haunted by calls for demonstration: "tried or untried" (l. 9), "established" (l. 12), "prove" (l. 17). The love poet feels challenged to make an intellectual case for the existence of love, especially for its too little regarded features, and to do so in the face of worldly skepticism. His anxiety is that he cannot adequately establish its existence, particularly in the face of skepticism. The first thing to test, after time has passed, is the existence of actual love.

Muir invokes the primary sense of inventing with ingenuity,

not the secondary one of deceiving, but in using "contrive" so deliberately he recalls its seventeenth-century currency. The Metaphysical poets are his models. However, the ABABCC trimeter stanzas are unfriendly to ratiocination: the short lines are conducive to assertion, not qualification. The concluding couplets nonetheless call for a memorable point—six times in this thirty-seven-line poem (the final couplet is rendered a tercet). Muir writes a riddling exposition. Love is presented as enigmatic, as a quality of being already in place, even in excess. The poem's imperfect form (one line too many) is bicameral: not-this-but-that. He does not have to contrive it; only its explanation is contrived. Love is there like the landscape. "Old as the hills," we say.

Endurance, like naturalness, is a master-figure used to end inquiry by presenting an illusion of arrival at a given. It obscures historical changes.[17] Choices alter circumstances. Nature determines less than literary representations routinely suggest. That which endures is considered more a given than a product of choice and will; what is transient pales by definition. The losses generated by such thinking are many, because life is always passing. Stendhal expressed a sense of something surprising gained by old lovers: "When love loses its intensity—which is to say, loses its fears—it acquires the new charm of absolute abandon, of unlimited trust. Then it becomes a sweet routine that tempers life's troubles and lends its pleasures an entirely new interest."[18] The fears to which he refers begin with transience. One fears loss, an empty pocket, an empty bed. An intimacy comes of sharing losses, particularly when endurance is no longer the issue.

Those who want to go on loving to the end wonder how well maturity can support that aspiration. One hears that love grows subtler, that passion fades but tenderness abides.

Many great love poems are simple and direct (and songs often seem so: "Sweet Lorraine," "Cheek to Cheek"), but others are guarded, dark—and indispensable. I would not have them otherwise. These canonical poems resist commonplaces with bold but sweet toughness. Rochester's "A Song of a Young Lady" is one example. Shakespeare's Sonnet 138 is another:

> When my love swears that she is made of truth,
> I do believe her though I know she lies,
> That she might think me some untutored youth,
> Unlearnèd in the world's false subtleties.
> Thus vainly thinking that she thinks me young,   5
> Although she knows my days are past the best,
> Simply I credit her false-speaking tongue:
> On both sides thus is simple truth suppressed.
> But wherefore says she not she is unjust?
> And wherefore say not I that I am old?   10
> O love's best habit is in seeming trust,
> And age in love loves not to have years told.
> Therefore I lie with her, and she with me,
> And in our faults by lies we flattered be.[19]

The dominant figure is barter (ll. 7-8). Love for sale, not far from thought. Carnal well-being is there well before the thirteenth line. The couplet affirms flattery, but first sexual congress. The poem is designed to achieve that conclusion. The first line cites what could be a plausible response to a claim that her concern is mere flesh.[20] No, "truth," she is said to have said. The poem is strikingly monosyllabic, as if it concerned a "simple truth," and all one's questions had definite answers. Shakespeare's sentences suggest something of that sort—maybe as an indication of a contrary indefiniteness. The first two

clauses are direct, without hesitation, but the third adds a paradoxical twist essential to the poem's movement—and sense.
The fourth clause (ll. 3-4) expresses a motive much modified
as the sentence approaches its close with a distinction between
true and false subtleties. That the world has true subtleties, as
does this sentence, is the basis of the statement, and an implicit
cue to readers. The chief subtlety of the first quatrain, and of
the poem generally, is that one chooses what to believe, even
in the face of knowledge. Reason, intuition, be gone.

How does that go? Line two may mean that the lover
believes his beloved's particular statement (that she is made
of truth) even though he knows that now and then she lies, as
everyone does. That is not a hard challenge to a lover's credibility. Or the line may mean that he believes her statement
even though he knows that it is false; that is the hard one. In
what sense can one believe that which one knows to be false?
One may know that a statement is literally false but believe it
to be figuratively true. Which is only to say that a false statement in one context is true in some other. This would be a
true and worldly subtlety. The young may not discriminate
well between true and false subtleties. But an aged lover spots
subtleties that elude truth altogether. The octave ends with two
lines about simplicity; that is the poem's core. Helen Vendler
identifies another subtlety when she observes the asymmetry
of "unjust" and "old" in lines nine and ten.[21] This observation
takes one back to barter, a transaction between two parties
with unlike assets. They recognize their differences and seek an
equation based on compensation for each. This bears a relation
to the poem's many puns: double entendre identifies a more or
less unapparent correspondence between two unlike senses of
a single term. Stephen Booth remarks, "every assertion in the
poem is demonstrably true and also a lie."[22] "Lies" is the poem's

favorite pun. The early version of this poem has "forgeries" where the later one has "subtleties" (l. 4). ("Fake forgeries" is comical or redundant.) One who mistakes a forgery for true is an injured party, as is someone who suffers an injustice. But this poem is about lovers who know their beloveds' infidelities and nonetheless credit the beloveds as true. Their minds are wide open. They are satisfied, not injured. "Therefore," the couplet begins, as if to insist on the necessity of this exchange of untruths; the transaction entails obligations to be met.

That makes the poem seem a general account of aged love. It is rather a report on two lovers who survive duration. No remedies are proposed for cooling passion, reduced libido, residual recriminations. It comes at mature love modestly by stating what one pair does to go on loving, or just continue as sexual partners, after too-full knowledge of each other's limitations. It's a frank poem about dissembling. With each pun ("lies," "simple," "habit") the point is made that words and all they enable are doubled. The duplicity of his relationship corresponds to communication generally; the puns are familiar, not recondite. Nor are they mean-spirited. The one on "lies" asserts that these lovers gladly sleep with one another; that validates their bond (l. 13). The pun on "told" as counted as well as narrated is simple but exactly right. A mature lover does not wish to circulate narratives of his or her former loves. Critics speak of the poem as "depressing," "small-spirited," and "tawdry"; "slight and superficial."[23] Booth says the tone is "downright smug," and that may be accurate in reference to Shakespeare's manner of elaborating his statements. An announcement of paradoxes is conducive to knowingness. But in the history of romance the account of this love can be no cause of pride. In comparison to the avowals of earlier European love-sonnets, it is obviously debased. But neither is there much room for pathos. The tone rests on a sense of realism: so this, then, is what maturity requires. It is nothing to hide or to do without: he is glad to have her and wishes for no other terms between them. Mature lovers are entitled to illusions, especially if they recognize them for what they are. It's the speaker's willfulness that one admires. He sees the contradiction between knowing and believing, and pushes right past it with assertion. Vendler is right that he says "unjust" less with the beloved than with himself in mind, and right too about his coyness in matching unjustness with ageing. The artistry is in phrasing those two lines to expose that bit of self-protectiveness. He accepts his own limits quietly, and hers too, less quietly. He accepts the limits within which they love; his deliberateness is honorable, and all about self-understanding. One may wish to do without this poem in hope of grander things. But it puts the issue of candor up for a pragmatic test. The pair continues to sleep together; that, more than metaphysics, is the outcome desired, if it comes to a choice.

Poems of enduring love of course stress mind: no blazons. Narratives of the body end poorly. The concept of endurance is difficult to dissociate from that of love itself. Pledges of eternal devotion rest on a belief that love is metaphysical and enables one to do that which is otherwise unlikely, even unnatural. If it were never to endure, those pledges might be met with ridicule. Insofar as it endures but changes over time, its nature must be reconceived. Remember the collaboration of Duke Ellington and Bob Russell, "Do Nothing 'til You Hear from Me." Sexual fidelity over time does not concern Russell or Muir. If lovers avow their love as their clocks wind down, one concept of love as solidarity survives. Swift argues that the work of the will characterizes mature love: kindness toward another, fortitude, and perseverance. Some joy is the objective of Ralegh, Tyutchev, and Swift. Muir's term is "bliss." Lovers are in the cruel hands of a greater force. Muir has a "happy doe" caught between the tiger's paws. And there is nothing to be done. Love is subject to a greater force, mortality, to which all surrender. Kunitz similarly says, "let the battered old willow / thrash against the windowpanes / and the house timbers crack." Being subject to a greater power matters less to an aged lover than it did to Dante. Tenderness, after many years, is consolation enough.

"Be greeting in our Lord's name, which is love." That is from the first quatrain of Rossetti's translation of Dante's first sonnet in the *Vita Nuova*. A name for intense yet indefinite feelings that are governed by a power greater than one's will. The name refers to both eros and the redemptive God. That love cools with betrayals and the sag of flesh, is a dark report. Accounts of its endurance are spotted with shadows. But imagine what is said only very rarely: This, this at last is what is called love? (Peggy Lee had a memorable hit in 1969 with "Is That All There Is?") The poets cited here—with the exception of Swift—nonetheless acknowledge a fit between the expectations aroused by the term and an experience of decades. However protean, the term identifies a range of feelings that have remained communicable not just for decades, as in the lives of particular lovers, but for centuries. Nearly all my poets match their aspiration to this one word. (A banal point: of course they do, they're love poets.) This is the most ambiguous and consequential word in the language. Mallarmé, Eliot, and Pound claimed that poets rid important terms of haziness. Yet one wants the word plump with the senses that have moved others. That archaism about lordliness refers to a wish to believe that love is not the sum of what one wants or does. That lord is its mover, lovers themselves are pawns. A single syllable summons one to praise with legions a value that transforms lives. With authority it says, "Du muss dein Leben aendern." (You must change your life.) And you do.

Conclusion

Poems and songs both give pleasure. One often falls for a song on first hearing, before its lyrics are entirely clear, and then listens again, with increasing pleasure, as the words register, maybe only after several hearings. Intuition urges one to persist at least until one has those words. How different is it with a poem? Paraphrasable sense is not a prerequisite to appreciation, though a semantic justification of one's attention is good, and good too that critics reveal deferred, unapparent pleasures. However, insofar as readers and students infer from critics that the pleasure poems offer is predominately cerebral and difficult of access, something has gone wrong. From poems, as from songs, one wants an appeal more immediate than a promise of enlightenment. My movement back and forth between poems and songs should encourage readers to ask of poems some of the pleasures obviously had from songs; to remind them to attend to the sounds of poems and the feel of words in the mouth and throat. Immediate pleasures are not everything, but neither are they trivial.

The poets of the *Norton Anthology* and the Tin Pan Alley songwriters who reinvented the popular song for the twentieth century engaged in one project: rendering analytical and memorable a romantic code that structured the aspirations, at the very least, of their contemporaries. Canonical English poets influenced US songwriters and versifiers in ways not evident in imitations of single poems. Their collaboration is well dispersed: legible in conventions of diction and figuration certainly, but more importantly in their concentration on a small set of commonplaces. One would expect that the extraordinary generation of US poets born in the 1880s would have directly affected the songwriters born in the following three decades, but that was not the case. The songwriters were most affected by the poems they had read in the anthologies of their youth, and then too by the light verse of their contemporaries. It would be decades again before Stevens, Pound, Eliot, Moore, and Williams attained that form of canonicity. There is a verse culture, more or less fecund in different periods, that includes all three kinds of writing. Songwriters complete the work of canonical poets. They write late sequels to poems of an earlier era. The point is not that poetry, light verse, and the popular song always collaborate with one another effectively, only that they did so in the US in the twentieth century, an especially distinguished period for poetry in the English language—and for the popular song. Songwriters and poets know that audiences are often reached by familiar topics. Those topics render some songs and poems recognizable and, therefore, approachable by many. It would be splendid if this dynamic between poetry and song prevailed constantly, but that is too much to expect.

I began with poetry and songfulness and now approach romantic experience, which commonplaces simplify. Journalists and attorneys debate the justness of rival representations of romance. The genres of poetry conserve, for poets, ways of making poems; for readers, "ways of feeling," as Empson said.[1] Formal devices facilitate recollection of representations,

propositions, and feelings—all that words convey. And love
poetry is especially conservative. I have stressed the conformity of poets and songwriters but also their thematic invention. This last comes from two contrary directions: the appeals
of realism and of an ideal. As a critic, one wants to describe
the features of a text but also the value of a poem or song,
or even of *a type* of poem or song. One wants to consider
what should be made of the differences among texts. When
a thought aligns well with the forms of a poem or song, one
registers the validity that comes with handsome expression,
endurance. "Validity" usually refers to truth, but as well to
health and survival—to what is left standing. Love's lessons are
valid in the sense of remaining in view. My chapter headings
express proverbial versions of a code of romance, but poems
and songs elaborate a truer, more various account of heterogeneous values, beliefs, doubts, anxieties, and misgivings rendered memorable for readers and auditors.

Two notoriously incompatible models of desire structure
this book. Monogamous desire is commonly said to promote
emotional and spiritual depth, even stability. Chapters one to
five explicate this line of thought. My students expect to find
a single soulmate to whom they can feel devoted. Chapters
six to eight analyze the relations of liberty and eros in lives
of multiple romances. When pressed, students acknowledge
their concerns about prosperity and break-ups. But this is the
B-side, entirely secular, imperfectly understood, whose poems
and songs seek less to fortify a tradition than to reveal alternatives to family values. The sunny side is a pseudo-religion
of romance, and a beloved above all others. The shadowy one
presents desire as serial and repeatable, and beloveds as plural. The first is fulfilled, as Poe said, in death; the second, in
longevity, survival. The second is worldly, pragmatic and, in

view of the first, base and shameful. Many live some version
of the second and imagine their lives fallen away from the
first. The first is commonly approved and has the support of
the courts. Pledges of unwavering devotion express a willed
proclivity toward simplification, which is to say sentimentality.
The songs and poems of chapters six to eight, on the contrary,
seek peace with cupidity and adversity. The collisions of these
models produce feelings of betrayal, despondence, and shame.

A Book of Love is a brief for governance. The monogamous
model rules by exclusion. But one may adhere in imagination
to both models, navigating now by magnetism and then by
fixed stars. The most intellectually ambitious of the popular
songs are those that, after Shakespeare's Sonnets 31 and 106,
and Donne's "Aire and Angels," reconcile these rival models
more or less plausibly: Rodgers and Hart's "Where or When"
and Joni Mitchell's "Help Me." I admire Duke Ellington and
Bob Russell's "Do Nothing 'til You Hear from Me" for proposing avowal, rather than abstinence, as a medium of commitment. Like Gascoigne's "And If I Did What Then?" it defends
polyamory. Intellectual reconciliation of these two models has
a long way to go, but these exceptional poems and songs indicate how wide-open love's lessons are. One may think that
the claims of chapters one to five constitute a former line of
thought and those of chapters six to eight, a future within view.
But the poems analyzed here do not conform to a chronologi-
cal sequence, as my readers have doubtless noticed.

Some songs and poems revise commonplaces by acknowl-
edging the pressure of serial desire. Theirs is a counter-idealiza-
tion, like Neal Hefti and Jon Hendricks' "Li'l Darlin." For the
duration of a reading or listening, one understands a song or
poem dramatically, and thereafter tests its idealizations against
personal experience. The writers discussed in chapters six to

eight, with an eye to money, promiscuity, and age, imagine alternatives to the pseudo-religion. No single alternative to the romance of monogamy has been established, but that is the direction in which these writers have taken the love song. They are explorers; you've got to love them. Poems and songs that pull away from the expected require interpretation, because they reveal something fresh or peculiar about the mobility of desire. For a didact like myself, they have particular appeal. But aren't they generally deserving in a society committed to second chances?

Many love songs pledge exclusive and eternal devotion in the first breath. Adults know that, however seductive in poems and songs, in life those claims lead to woe. How worldly is the pleasure one takes from love songs? There is a period when one desires only the beloved, and that commonly ends. A pledge of unwavering love is understood as something other than a plausible prediction of behavior. However, the related phrase "love of my life" is often used without irony. It suggests two possibilities: that one loves one beloved more intensely than one ever loves any other; or that one could never love another at all after that signal love. Only the latter conforms to monogamous desire, and that is understood to be an unhealthy state of the heart. The former is more commonly taken as plausible. Which leads me to conclude that love poems and songs are generally received with mild irony, that they are widely understood as idealizations of romance rather than reports on experience. Romantic commonplaces describe what one *wants* love to be; great songs glorify an ideal. Romance traditions of both sorts urge one to *remember ardor*—and to consider well what might in time replace it, or what deference that memory deserves.

I have assessed love poems and songs in terms of their

thematic relation to commonplaces, and referred to a romance ideology, by which I mean a reasonably coherent set of beliefs and propositions—not just reports and recollections—that seeks currency. Three questions have guided my exposition. What is repeatedly said of love? How is this contested? And what is retained over time? Not all that people think and say constitutes advocacy; rather, what poems and songs have summoned for preservation—that is, what is *already known* to readers and listeners—is their equipment for living. Poems and songs that depart distinctively and intelligently from familiar notions are the ones I most esteem. But eloquence is also pertinent. Poems that speak about as well as one can imagine speaking deserve admiration. We speak of living in a time and place, the sites of experience, but much experience concerns concepts, ideas, and values more than matter in time and space. We live largely in language and wish to do so well and memorably. When a poem or song achieves what seems superlative expression, the validity of concepts, ideas, and values is affirmed. This is a grand achievement, easy to underestimate, because we have at hand many terms that refer to failed eloquence, "grandiloquence," for instance. Allen Grossman wrote of poems as instantiations of ways of being fully human; eloquence is a part of that. A critic examines diction, syntax, prosody, and figure in order to demonstrate the eloquence of poems one by one. Of songs one should do the same, but there is a further level of analysis that the eloquence of songs deserves: the matching of words to musical forms. My skills do not allow me to do this last job adequately. I leave that to musicians and musicologists, and acknowledge here my awareness of another level of analysis required by the texts I have singled out for attention.

With effort, I can imagine a reader doubtful of my general

claims about love poetry and song because they rest on a distinctive selection of texts. A different selection would yield a different account of love's lessons. A more idealistic critic than I might bring to one's attention poems and songs that have been overlooked by other critics and musicians, lesser-known texts. One might then argue that, had these texts received the attention they deserve, other and better ideas of romance would have been kept in view. My selection is deliberately canonical in that the poems discussed have circulated through anthologies and later poets; many readers and writers have recognized their power. The songs, too, have been memorized out of affection by millions of listeners and reinterpreted by generations of admiring performers. These texts have already circulated widely, and still do. Their circulation validates the idealizations I have described. The idealizations that count most are expressed in memorable art whose lessons have been taken by large audiences in diverse settings. It is hard to imagine a very different selection of US songs of the last century that could command the authority that mine has. But the future is open.

Acknowledgments

I want to acknowledge enlightenment I've taken from the writing, conversation, or music of the following individuals: J. Vincent Adams, Danielle Allen, Kelly Austin, Patricia Barber, Charles Bernstein, Edith Brinkel, Stephanie Burt, Bradin Cormack, Darlene Dente, Helen Deutsch, Jeff Dolven, Kurt Elling, Robert Faggen, John Farrell, Ken Fields, Rudy Gintel, Susan Hahn, Elizabeth Helsinger, Jon Hendricks, Travis Jackson, Eddie Jefferson, Joshua Kotin, Erin McGinnity, Nate Mackey, Sarah Nooter, Marjorie Perloff, Haun Saussy, Joshua Scodel, Hank Scotch, Dustin Simpson, Nigel Smith, Richard Strier, Richard von Hallberg.

I am grateful as well for research support from the University of Chicago and Claremont McKenna College.

An early version of chapter two appeared in *TriQuarterly*, published by Northwestern University Press.

Notes

INTRODUCTION

[1] Philip Furia is the great exception. See his pioneering study of American Songbook lyrics: *The Poets of Tin Pan Alley* (New York: Oxford University Press, 1990).

[2] David Lehman makes this point in his wonderfully informative and spirited volume, *A Fine Romance: Jewish Songwriters, American Songs* (New York: Schocken, 2009).

[3] The historical scholarship on the relations of poetry and song is extensive. The following two volumes are excellent and include instructive bibliographies: John Hollander, *The Untuning of the Sky: Ideas of Music in English Poetry, 1500-1700* (Princeton: Princeton University Press, 1961) and H. T. Kirby-Smith, *Celestial Twins: Poetry and Music through the Ages* (Amherst: University of Massachusetts Press, 1999). See too John Hollander, *Vision and Resonance* (New York: Oxford University Press, 1975) for brilliant analyses of formal interaction of poetry and song. The history of love song itself has been ambitiously and admirably constructed by Ted Gioia in *Love Songs: The Hidden History* (New York: Oxford University Press, 2015).

[4] C. S. Lewis, in *The Allegory of Love* (New York: Oxford University Press, 1936), wrote an influential book that brought this continental tradition into relation with medieval English literature. Much later he reflected on the tendency of eroticism to imitate religion: "Years ago when I wrote about medieval love-poetry and described its strange, half make-believe, 'religion of love,' I was blind enough to treat this as an almost purely

literary phenomenon. I know better now. Eros by his nature invites it. Of all loves he is, at his height, most god-like; therefore most prone to demand our worship. Of himself he always tends to turn 'being in love' into a sort of religion" (C. S. Lewis, *The Four Loves* [New York: Harcourt Brace, 1988], 110-11).

[5] Philip Furia made the case for the influence of light-verse models in his *Poets of Tin Pan Alley*, 7-8, 39-40, 99, 127.

[6] Allen Grossman wrote at length of poetry articulating an image of the fully human: "a successful poem seems to me a picture of a successful person. I mean to say, a good person in a given context" (*The Sighted Singer* [Baltimore: Johns Hopkins University Press, 1992], 197; see also 274).

[7] Stephanie Burt argues for this point and cites Hans Ulrich Gumbrecht, *Production of Presence* (Stanford: Stanford University Press, 2004), 109, in support of the claim. ("Are Song Lyrics Poems or Not? And Why Do We Keep Asking?" [paper delivered at Lyricology conference, "Situating Lyric," Boston University, June 7-11, 2017]).

[8] Max Wilk, *They're Playing Our Song* (New York: Da Capo, 1991), 133.

[9] Wilk reports that hour after hour Hammerstein "would stand at his desk, agonizing over the choice of the exact word, the perfect choice for the thought he wished to communicate" (Wilk, 81). See too Philip Furia, *Ira Gershwin: The Art of the Lyricist* (New York: Oxford University Press, 1996), 4.

[10] Wilk, 56. Milton spoke of poetry as "simple, sensuous, and passionate," as distinguished from the subtlety of grammar and logic.

[11] Elizabeth K. Helsinger, *Poetry and the Thought of Song* (Charlottesville: University of Virginia Press, 2015), 4.

[12] D. A. Miller, *Place for Us* (Cambridge MA: Harvard University Press, 1998), 1.

[13] Critics commonly speak of poems *unsettling* their readers. The poet Brad Leithauser recently reported that "over many years, I've spent dozens, maybe hundreds of hours listening to [Irving] Berlin, who by turns has cheered, amused, enlivened, saddened and consoled me. But unsettled? Rarely. Why even seek to unsettle? Berlin's breezy working credo was 'the mob is always right.' He wasn't out to challenge or convert but to feed the

public's taste—the broadest public, in its global tastes" (*Wall Street Journal*, December 20, 2019).

[14] Wilk, 230. Philip Furia tells the story of Harburg and Ira Gershwin's apprenticeship in light verse. He explains that Ira built up a library of 200 volumes of verse, including anthologies of light verse. In these books the two aspiring songwriters, Furia explains, "found their literary antecedents—Lewis Carroll and Austin Dobson, James Russell Lowell and Thomas Hood, as well as a distinguished poetic lineage that reached back through Dryden and Lovelace, Suckling and Herrick, to Jonson, Raleigh, and even Shakespeare" (Furia, *Ira Gershwin: The Art of the Lyricist*, 12; and ch. 1 *passim*). In *Irving Berlin: A Life in Song* (New York: Schirmer, 1998), Furia explains that in 1935 Irving Berlin "turned more of his attention to collecting works of art, and to purchasing rare volumes of Shakespeare and other classic writers." "I'm trying" Berlin remarked, "to get at least a bowing acquaintance with the world's best literature." (pp. 68-9) Furia notes that two decades earlier Berlin had followed with interest the Imagist poetry that then appeared in little magazines. He also observes that Pope was among his favorite poets (pp. 74, 96). Oscar Hammerstein II was also a reader of poetry. Robert Russell Bennett said that in 1941 Hammerstein was discouraged about his career. He wanted to get a small place in France where he could live modestly with his wife and write poetry. Then came the idea of re-writing Bizet's Carmen, and his dream of a literary retreat left him (reported in Wilk, 83).

[15] David Yaffe, *Reckless Daughter: A Portrait of Joni Mitchell* (New York: Farrar, Straus and Giroux, 2017), 266.

[16] "Ohne Musik waere das Leben ein Irrthum" (Friedrich Nietzsche, *Saemtliche Werke*, eds. Giorgio Colli and Mazzino Montinari [Berlin: de Gruyter, 1980], VI, 64).

[17] A good example is the 1960 recording of "Cloudburst" on the fourth album by the vocalese group *Lambert, Hendricks, and Ross*, released by Columbia.

[18] As quoted by Maurice Valency, *In Praise of Love* (New York: Macmillan, 1958), 110-11. Paolo Cherchi makes the point that the discourse of courtly love departs from conventions of linear progression: "The main point is that the world of a courtly lover finds the key to its existence in repetition"

(*Andreas and the Ambiguity of Courtly Love* [Toronto: University of Toronto Press, 1994], 77).

¹⁹ Michael Field and Newt Oliphant wrote "The Same Old Story."

²⁰ Pierre Hadot, *The Veil of Isis* (Cambridge MA: Harvard University Press, 2006), xiii.

²¹ *Literary Essays of Ezra Pound*, ed. T. S. Eliot (Norfolk CT: New Directions, 1954), 21.

²² Quoted by Sharon Cameron, *Lyric Time* (Baltimore: Johns Hopkins University Press, 1979), 29.

²³ *The Poems of Emily Dickinson*, ed. R. W. Franklin (Cambridge, MA: Harvard University Press, 1999), poem 781; *The Cantos of Ezra Pound* (New York: New Directions, 1970), 229.

²⁴ Michael Riffaterre, *Semiotics of Poetry* (Bloomington: Indiana University Press, 1978), 19, 13.

²⁵ Ibid., 19, 31.

²⁶ Ibid., 42.

²⁷ Ibid., 1.

²⁸ Wilfred Sheed, *The House That George Built* (New York: Random House, 2007), 15.

²⁹ Wilk, 232.

³⁰ Lawrence Kramer, *Musical Meaning* (Berkeley: University of California Press, 2002), 66.

³¹ Ezra Pound, *Literary Essays*, 51.

³² One knows too that a bond between words and sounds has staying power. Once one takes a lyric into memory, an instrumental version of the melody often brings the words to mind without effort. I recommend Gene Ammons' charismatic version of "My Romance" as an instance of this phenomenon.

³³ J. H. Prynne argues that the limits of what Wordsworth is able to know derive principally from class. See Prynne's remarkable self-published analysis, *Field Notes: "The Solitary Reaper" and Others* (Cambridge, 2007).

³⁴ Kramer, *Musical Meaning*, 63.

³⁵ See Susan Wolfson, "Wordsworth's Craft," in *The Cambridge Companion*

to Wordsworth, ed. Stephen Gill (Cambridge: Cambridge University Press, 2003), 108-24.

[36] Hoagy Carmichael wrote the melody in 1927. Mitchell Parrish wrote the lyrics in 1929. Nat King Cole recorded it in 1957, long after the song had become a standard, for his *Love Is the Thing* album. For a history of performances of the song, see Will Friedwald, *Stardust Melodies* (New York: Pantheon, 2002), ch. 1.

[37] Ted Gioia traces the history of love song so far back that the origins of particular features of love songs can only be imagined; see his indispensable *Love Songs: The Hidden History*, particularly ch. 2. Marisa Galvez recovers in troubadour lyrics the roots of modern ideas of songbooks and anthologies. Her analysis reveals a tradition of continuity between performed songs and written poems; she demonstrates as well various ways in which medieval lyrics were designed to respond to didactic interpretation (Galvez, *Songbook: How Lyrics Became Poetry in Medieval Europe* [Chicago: University of Chicago Press, 2012], esp. 3, 11, 24, 27).

[38] *Sappho: A Garland*, trans. Jim Powell (New York: Farrar, Straus and Giroux, 1993), 23-24.

[39] Valency, 2.

[40] L. T. Topsfield, *Troubadors and Love* (Cambridge: Cambridge University Press, 1975), 71.

[41] For an analysis of *fin 'amor* see Moshe Lazar, in *A Handbook of the Troubadours*, eds. F. R. P. Akehurst and Judith M. Davis (Berkeley: University of California Press, 1995), ch. 3.

[42] Moshe Lazar argues that the secularity of the land-owning classes was driving the development of fine love poems; he cites in particular the development of social life outside the churches in the later-eleventh century (ibid. 61ff.). For an analysis of the literature on the origins of fin 'amor, see Gerald A. Bond, "Origins," in *Handbook of the Troubadours*, ch. 9.

[43] On *mesura*, see Cherchi, *Andreas and the Ambiguity of Courtly Love*, 42-80.

[44] Galvez shows convincingly that the martial virtues of loyalty and commitment-despite-exile (now still understood as essential to literary romance) were established by poems written in response to the crusades

of the eleventh and twelfth centuries. Subsequent love-songs and poems by lonely and true lovers describing painful departures and longing over distance derive their topoi from experiences of much earlier pilgrim- and warrior-poets. She is interested in the transmission of conventions from one century to the next, though she speaks more generally of the afterlife of "anachronistic forms," and it is just these resemblances over many centuries that I find so striking (Galvez, *The Subject of Crusade: Lyric, Romance and Materials, 1150-1500* (Chicago: University of Chicago Press, 2020), 10-11, 153.

[45] Valency, 35.

[46] Ibid., 86.

[47] Zumthor, "An Overview: Why the Troubadours?" in *A Handbook*, 14. On the composition of the fighting forces of Occitan, see Linda M. Paterson, *The World of the Troubadours* (Cambridge: Cambridge University Press, 1993), chs. 3 & 4.

[48] Topsfield, 24.

[49] Ibid., 26.

[50] The club that folk-rock musicians of the 1960s played was Doug Weston's Troubadour in West Hollywood.

[51] Valency, 5.

[52] See Michael R. G. Spiller, *The Development of the Sonnet* (London: Routledge, 1992), ch. 2.

[53] Dante Alighieri, *The New Life*, trans. Dante Gabriel Rossetti (New York: New York Review, 2002), 7.

[54] Jessica Benjamin, *The Bonds of Love* (New York: Pantheon, 1988), 3-5.

[55] Alain Badiou [with Nicholas Truong], *In Praise of Love*, trans. Peter Bush (London: Serpent's Tail, 2011), 16-17.

[56] Valency, 160.

[57] Ibid., 174.

[58] Cherchi, *Andreas and the Ambiguity of Courtly Love*, 57.

[59] Zumthor, in *A Handbook*, 15.

[60] Elisabeth Schulze-Busacker, "Topoi," in *A Handbook*, 421-22.

[61] Valency, 210.

[62] *The Poems of Andrew Marvell*, ed. Nigel Smith (London: Pearson, Longman, 2003), 108.

[63] William Empson brilliantly analyzes Donne's interpretation of the possibility of multiple "worlds." See Empson, *Essays on Renaissance Literature*, ed. John Haffenden, vol. 1 (Cambridge: Cambridge University Press, 1993), ch. 2.

[64] *Poems of Andrew Marvell*, 109-111.

[65] See Frank Kermode, "Institutional Control of Interpretation," *Salmagundi* 43 (Winter 1979), 72-86.

NOTES TO CHAPTER 1

[1] *Petrarch's Lyric Poems*, trans. Robert M. Durling (Cambridge, MA: Harvard University Press, 1976), poem 118.

[2] *The Poems of Catullus*, trans. Charles Martin (Baltimore: Johns Hopkins University Press, 1990), poem 70.

[3] *Petrarch's Lyric Poems*, poem 112.

[4] "Only You" was written by Buck Ram, who managed the Platters. The original group recorded it in 1954, but their label, Federal, would not release it. In 1955, with Tony Williams as the lead, the Platters re-recorded it, and released it on the Mercury label. It was the first top ten hit for the group. One account of the stammer in Williams' rendition has it that they were rehearsing the song in a car that swerved and Williams was alarmed; another has it that his voice just gave out in a recording session. Either way, they liked what they heard.

[5] Troy Jollimore, *Love's Vision* (Princeton: Princeton University Press, 2011), 93: "What is required, in ordinary circumstances at least, is not just that one's beloved's interests win the contest but also that there be *no contest*." Laura Kipnis understands ordinary expectations similarly: "A 'happy' state of monogamy would be defined as a state you don't have to *work* at maintaining" (*Against Love* [New York: Pantheon, 2003],17).

[6] Carmen McRae released "Only You" on her *When You're Away* album with Verve in 1959. The Flamingos had a big hit with this tune the same year: *Flamingo Serenade* on the End label.

[7] Here is the full text of the Harry Warren/Al Dubin song "I Only Have Eyes for You," though wisely no one sings lines three and four.

> My love must be a kind of blind love;
> I can't see anyone but you.
> And dear, I wonder if you find love
> An optical illusion too.
>
> Are the stars out tonight?
> I don't know if it's cloudy or bright
> 'Cause I only have eyes for you, dear.
> The moon may be high
> But I can't see a thing in the sky,
> 'Cause I only have eyes for you.
> I don't know if we're in a garden,
> Or on a crowded avenue.
> You are here, and so am I.
> Maybe millions of people go by,
> But they all disappear from view,
> And I only have eyes for you.

Arnaut Daniel, in Paolo Cherchi's translation, says: "I am blind to seeing other women and deaf to hearing them, because I see and hear and contemplate only her" (Cherchi, 16).

[8] Neal Hefti composed "L'il Darlin'" in 1957 and Count Basie's band recorded it that year. The Roulette label released the track on *The Atomic Mr. Basie* in 1958. Jon Hendricks wrote lyrics for the tune that year and recorded it with Lambert, Hendricks and Ross; that was released on *Sing along with Basie*, on the Roulette label in 1958. Mark Murphy recorded the vocal version for *Rah*, released on the Riverside label in 1961. Kurt Elling recorded it in 2001, and released it then on *Flirting with Twilight*, on the Blue Note label.

[9] This song was originally written for the Broadway musical *Whoopee!* Nat King Cole recorded a version in 1949, and Nina Simone made a stunning one in 1957.

[10] Frank Bidart, "Luggage," in *Star Dust* (New York: Farrar, Straus and Giroux, 2005), 16.

[11] *John Coltrane and Johnny Hartman* was released on the Impulse label in 1963.

[12] *Petrarch's Lyric Poems*, poem 124.

[13] Sir Thomas Wyatt, *Complete Poems*, ed. R. A. Rebholz (London: Penguin, 1978), 82.

[14] *Petrarch's Lyric Poems*, poem 124.

[15] *The Poetry of Petrarch*, trans. David Young (New York: Farrar, Straus and Giroux, 2004), poem 124. Here is Robert Durling's prose translation:

> Love, Fortune, and my mind, which avoids what it sees and turns back to the past, afflict me so that I sometimes envy those who are on the other shore. Love torments my heart, Fortune deprives it of every comfort, and so my foolish mind is troubled and weeps; and thus I must always live struggling in much sorrow. Nor do I hope that the sweet days will come back, but rather expect that what is left will go from bad to worse; and I have already passed the middle of my course. Alas, I see all hope fall from my hands, made not of diamond but even of glass, and I see all my thoughts break in half. (p. 238)

[16] *Petrarch's Lyric Poems*, poem 309.

[17] *The Poetry of Petrarch*, poem 309. Here is Durling's prose translation:

> The high new miracle that in our days appeared in the world and did not wish to stay in it, that Heaven merely showed to us and then took back to adorn its starry cloisters, Love, who first set free my tongue, wishes me to depict and show her to whoever did not see her, and therefore a thousand times he has vainly put to work wit, time, pens, paper, inks. Poetry has not yet reached the summit, I know it in myself and anyone knows it who up to now has spoken or written of Love; he who knows how to think, let him esteem the silent truth which surpasses every style, and then let him sigh: "Therefore blessed the eyes that saw her alive!" (p. 408)

[18] Durling, poem 366.

[19] Ibid.

[20] *W. B. Yeats, Collected Poems* (Toronto: Macmillan, 1956), 79.

[21] Frank Bidart, *Star Dust*, 28-29.

[22] Wyatt, *Complete Poems*, 140.

[23] "Why Did I Choose You," by Michael Leonard and Herbert Martin, was first performed by Barbra Streisand in 1965.

[24] Peter Murphy, in *The Long Public Life of a Short Private Poem* (Stanford: Stanford University Press, 2019), argues that Wyatt may have advanced his political career by writing and circulating "They Flee from Me": "Henry would . . . see Wyatt's talent for indirection, for veiled threat, for elegant language and sharp discernment: the skills of a diplomat. . . . He would see Wyatt's delight in simultaneous subservience and mastery" (p. 25). However, those skills are deployed against the honor of a woman Henry went to trouble to marry. Murphy's representation of Wyatt's self-interest is implausible unless one thinks, as Murphy does, that the poem presents "a fantasy of intimacy" (p. 11).

[25] On the mutuality of shame and shamelessness, see John Limon, "The Shame of Abu Ghraib," *Critical Inquiry*, XXXIII, 3 (Spring 2007), 43-72.

[26] The poet Jim Powell has argued that Wyatt's actual corpus is much smaller than Ron Rebholz wants it. Powell claims that many of the poems Rebholz attributes to Wyatt could not have been written by a poet of Wyatt's prosodic expertise. This argument has left me uncertain of the authorship of "When first mine eye," though Kenneth Muir also attributes it to Wyatt. In 24 lines of iambic tetrameter, there are only two variations: lines two and three.

[27] See, e.g., Yvor Winters, "Poetic Style in Shakespeare's Sonnets," in *Discussions of Shakespeare's Sonnets*, ed. Barbara Herrnstein Smith (Boston: D. C. Heath, 1965), who disapproves of Shakespeare's "servile weakness" in relation to the young man addressed (p. 107).

[28] Trans. Reginald Mainwaring Hewitt, *A Book of Love Poetry*, ed. Jon Stallworthy (New York: Oxford University Press, 1973), 68.

[29] Robert Lowell, "Will Not Come Back," *History* (New York: Farrar, Straus and Giroux, 1973), 117.

[30] *Poems of Catullus*, Martin, poem 8.

[31] Martin, poem 8; *Poems of Catullus*, trans. Peter Green (Berkeley: University of California Press, 2005), poem 8.

[32] *Poems of Catullus*, Green, poem 87.

[33] *Poems of Catullus*, Martin, poem 87.

[34] *Poems of Catullus*, Green, poem 87.

[35] A shallow reading of the song has the lover asserting that nothing sexual occurred between her and the new interest, that gossips are maligning her. But the song's profundity is metaphysical. Gladys Knight's 2006 performance rests on the shallow reading. She adds these lines at the end: "Don't believe what they say / Cause I didn't do it. / Take my word that it's you I love, / Hold on to it." Nothing more than a hug and a kiss was involved, on this view, and that isn't infidelity: "I didn't do it." A deeper reading acknowledges the incoherence between her concession of intimacy with the new interest and her avowal of devotion. The music was composed by Duke Ellington. Ted Gioia says that it "started out [in 1940] as a big band instrumental, with words added after the fact. 'Concerto for Cootie,' as the piece was originally named, was quite self-sufficient without all the guile and evasions of the lyrics [contributed by Bob Russell in 1943]." Gioia calls it "an anthem for cheatin' lovers" (*The Jazz Standards* [New York: Oxford University Press, 2012], 83).

NOTES TO CHAPTER 2

[1] Will Friedwald, *Sinatra! The Song Is You* (New York: Scribner, 1995), 24.

[2] Anthony Summers & Robbyn Swan, *Sinatra: The Life* (New York: Random House, 2005), 31.

[3] Friedwald, 127.

[4] Evidently Sinatra's press agent had coached a corps of young women to scream on cue, and they were able to provoke a large crowd response (Summers & Swan, 84).

[5] Friedwald, 69.

[6] Ibid., 85.

[7] Ibid., 93.

[8] I. A. Richards, *Practical Criticism* (1929; New York: Harcourt, Brace, 1967), 247.

[9] T. S. Eliot, *Selected Essays* (New York: Harcourt, Brace, 1960), 248.

[10] Cleanth Brooks, *Modern Poetry and the Tradition* (1939; New York: Oxford University Press, 1965), 37.

[11] Ibid., 51.

[12] John Crowe Ransom, *The World's Body* (New York: Scribner's, 1938), 76-110.

[13] T. S. Eliot, *The Sacred Wood* (1920; London: Methuen, 1960), 64-65.

[14] Eliot, *Selected Essays*, 247.

[15] Pete Hamill, *Why Sinatra Matters* (Boston: Little, Brown, 1998), 127; see also Summers & Swan, 222.

[16] Hamill, 26-27.

[17] Summers & Swan, 93.

[18] The critique of male sentiment, in particular, the notion that it is a shallow indulgence, is ancient. Socrates reminds Glaucon of the hypocrisy of appreciating poetic representations of lamentation and breast-beating and yet priding oneself on resisting such womanish expression in actual experience. Is it right, Socrates asks, to praise in poetry what is reprehensible in fact? (*Republic*, 605d-606a). Sentimentality, from this viewpoint, is insincere; a poet asks one to take pleasure in values by which one is unwilling to live. One should not enjoy in art the pleasure of expressing overwhelming grief, so long as one means to move stoically past one's losses in life: this is supposedly what distinguishes sentimentality from honorable male comportment.

[19] Summers & Swan, 225.

[20] Hamill, 96.

[21] I am aware of two premises that I want to express plainly here. My interest is chiefly in lyric poetry. I presume, first, that a poet achieves a lyric by finding a music in the materiality of words and the intervals of clauses, not by ending the line before the right margin. No musicality, no lyric. This genre of poetry is closely related to accompanied song. But popular songwriters try instead to find the words in a particular piece of instrumental

music. I wonder what is to be learned about lyric poetry from an analysis of its obverse art. Second, I presume too that one's critical observations of poems gain validity to the degree that they correspond to the best poems within a class or kind. The songs I have selected for analysis are the best I know of their kind—here, the sob ballad. Insofar as my assessments are off, I acknowledge, the validity of my observations is in jeopardy.

[22] Philip Fisher, *Hard Facts* (New York: Oxford University Press, 1985), 105.

[23] Fred Kaplan, *Sacred Tears: Sentimentality in Victorian Literature* (Princeton: Princeton University Press, 1987), 3.

[24] See Robert Pinsky, ed., *The Handbook of Heartbreak* (New York: William Morrow, 1998).

[25] Matthew Arnold, "Preface to First Edition of *Poems* (1853)," (Arnold is surely alluding to Johnson in *Rasselas*: "Human life is a state in which much is to be endured and little to be enjoyed.")

[26] Ransom discusses sentimentality and gender in two essays, "The Poet as Woman" and "Sentimental Exercise," in *The World's Body*, see esp. 76-78, 216, 220, and 231-32.

[27] George Gershwin wrote the music and Ira Gershwin, the lyrics to "Someone to Watch over Me" for the musical *Oh, Kay!* (1926). The show opened in Philadelphia before coming to Broadway, where it was very successful.

[28] The song of a chastised lover is a sub-type of the forsaken-lover's song. See, e.g., The Five Royales, "Help Me, Somebody," for a doo-wop expression of the theme. I read sob-ballads as abbreviated narratives that invite skeptical interpretation.

[29] Harold Arlen wrote the music and Ira Gershwin, the lyrics for "The Man that Got Away." The song was written for Judy Garland to perform in the 1954 film *A Star Is Born*. Sinatra, Tony Bennett, and other male vocalists later performed it as "The Gal that Got Away."

[30] Philip Furia interprets the breakdown of the second-person address as a sign of the forlorn state of the lover (*Ira Gershwin* [New York: Oxford University Press, 1996], 216). He considers the song an expression of "innocent longing," whereas it seems darker to me (219).

[31] David Mann wrote the music and Bob Hilliard, the lyrics for "In the Wee Small Hours" (1955). Sinatra performed it on the album of that title in 1955. Johnny Hartman recorded it on his album *I Just Dropped by to Say Hello* (1963).

[32] Will Friedwald speaks of it as "one of the most subtle torch songs ever written," and credits Sinatra with its revival (Friedwald 154).

[33] Ibid., 33.

[34] Ibid., front matter.

[35] Summers & Swan, 234.

[36] Jack Strachey (1894-1972) wrote the music and Holt Marvell (Eric Maschwitz [1901-69]), the lyrics for "These Foolish Things." The song was intended in 1935 for a late-night BBC revue broadcast. Billie Holiday recorded it in 1936. McPhatter adds lines 1-3 and 22-24 to Maschwitz's text. Maschwitz wrote an initial verse and three refrains. Most vocalists (Billie Holiday, Johnny Hartman, Nat King Cole) skip the initial verse and begin with the first refrain ("A cigarette . . ."). Ella Fitzgerald, however, sings the entire song; Nat King Cole sings the first and second refrains; Johnny Hartman sings the first and part of the second refrain. Like McPhatter, Hartman adds a short initial verse: "Candle lights on corner tables remind me of you. / Perfume and silk stockings / make me think of you."

[37] Paul Fussell, "Sentimentality," in *The New Princeton Encyclopedia of Poetry and Poetics*, eds. Alex Preminger, T. V. F. Brogan et al. (Princeton: Princeton University Press, 1993), 1145.

[38] "These Foolish Things," is sung from the perspective of a lover forsaken only because the beloved is dead. Thematically one might compare this tune with Thomas Hardy's *Poems 1912-1913*. Maschwitz's beloved is truly a ghost. His lyric begins with Hardyesque lines that neither Sinatra nor McPhatter sings: "Oh! will you never let me be? / Oh! will you never set me free?" Lines 1-3 and 22-24 (the frame of the McPhatter version) were not written by Maschwitz.

[39] Philip Furia, *The Poets of Tin Pan Alley*, 153.

[40] Ibid., 156.

[41] Deborah Grace Winer, *On the Sunny Side of the Street* (New York: Schirmer, 1997), 99. Fields wrote the lyric in early 1936 for the George

Stevens film *Swing Time*, with Fred Astaire and Ginger Rogers.

42 Ibid., 101.

43 Ibid., 100.

44 David Lehman, *A Fine Romance*, 85.

NOTES TO CHAPTER 3

1 Wyatt, *Complete Poems*, 116-17.

2 Anne Ferry makes the point that Tottel's title, "The lover sheweth how he is forsaken of such as he sometime enjoyed," emphasizes the fact that the poem is "not a complaint or a description, but more exactly a demonstration or proof" (Ferry, *Tradition and the Individual Poem* [Stanford: Stanford University Press, 2001], 91).

3 Wyatt, *Complete Poems*, 107-08.

4 It may be objected that I read Wyatt too romantically, as if his utterances derived from his own actual thought and feeling. Samuel Johnson argued that sincerity is essential to love poetry: "he that professes love ought to feel its power" (*The Lives of the Poets*, ed. Roger Lonsdale [Oxford: Clarendon, 2006], I, 193). This judgment presents a problem because love poems are so obviously based on commonplaces, conventions of expression. Donald M. Friedman argues that Wyatt characteristically writes in a more dramatic mode than is commonly recognized. He states that "They Flee from Me" is a "dramatization of the mind of an imagined figure, in this case of a courtly lover attempting to deal with the experience of faithlessness" ("The Mind in the Poem: Wyatt's 'They Fle From Me,'" *SEL* [Winter 1967], 3). From his point of view, many interpretations of the poem, are unduly romantic analyses of a "curious phantasm" (p. 3). Peter Murphy develops this sense of Wyatt as dramatic lyricist. The poem, on his view, presents a "staged, coherent overhearing, an overhearing of private thought adapted and shaped so it makes sense and then dramatized—turned into a story—so it feels like the sudden outpouring of feeling" (*The Long Public Life of a Short Private Poem*, 38). This leads Murphy to speak mechanically of the poet's intention and the poem's effect: "The feeling and thought in the poem are packaged in a carefully made semitraditional box so someone else can make it theirs" (p. 34). He argues further that this poem would have served Wyatt well as an

ambitious, aspiring diplomat in the Tudor court (p. 25). However, Wyatt's evident mastery of sly recrimination may have had a contrary effect; as a performance, the poem might have been more costly than advantageous for Wyatt. I negotiate between sincerity and commonplace in each poem, because usually neither pole of this dichotomy is adequate by itself.

[5] George Gascoigne, "And If I Did What Then?" in *Norton Anthology of Poetry*, 3rd ed., 100.

[6] Billy Strayhorn, "Lush Life," in *Reading Lyrics*, ed. Robert Gottlieb and Robert Kimball (New York: Pantheon, 2000), 504-05.

[7] See David Hajdu, *Lush Life: A Biography of Billy Strayhorn* (New York: Farrar, Straus and Giroux, 1996), 34-36, 98, 110-111.

[8] Roger Kellaway (b. 1939) wrote the music, and Marilyn (b. 1929) and Alan Bergman (b. 1925) the lyrics for "I Have the Feeling I've Been Here Before." Carmen McRae had the first recording of the song in 1975 on her Blue Note LP *I Am Music*.

[9] Lorenz Hart, "It Never Entered My Mind," in *Reading Lyrics*, 202. Richard Rodgers wrote the music and Lorenz Hart the lyrics for the musical *Higher and Higher* (1940).

[10] I owe the suggestive notion of sobriety to Klas Molde.

[11] Martha C. Nussbaum, *Love's Knowledge* (New York : Oxford University Press, 1990), Ch. 11.

[12] When he was working on the staging of the Broadway production of *Higher and Higher*, feeling doubts about the entire show, Hart agreed with others to add a performing seal to the show. Frederick Nolan tells an anecdote about the opening night on April 4, 1940. As the crowd was moving up the center aisle after the performance, a French woman was heard to say to her husband: "'I deed not say zee *show* was good—I shuzz say see *fuck* was good—zee *fuck*, and oh, how I loved zat *fuck*," By this time the whole aisle was laughing.'" Nolan explains that the French word for seal is *phoque* (Frederick Nolan, *Lorenz Hart: A Poet on Broadway* [New York: Oxford University Press, 1994], 270). Hart had written his song about that pun three years earlier.

[13] Lloyd Schwartz, "One Art: The Poetry of Elizabeth Bishop, 1971-76," in *Elizabeth Bishop and Her Art*, eds. Schwartz and Sybil P. Estes (Ann Arbor:

University of Michigan Press, 1983), 150.

14 Megan Marshall, *Elizabeth Bishop: A Miracle for Breakfast* (Boston: Houghton, Mifflin, 2017), 270-74.

15 Elizabeth Bishop, *The Complete Poems: 1927-1979* (New York: Farrar, Straus and Giroux, 1983), 178.

16 Susan McCabe, *Elizabeth Bishop: Her Poetics of Loss* (University Park: Pennsylvania State University Press, 1994), 27.

17 Brett Millier, *Elizabeth Bishop: Life and the Memory of It* (Berkeley: University of California Press, 1993), 512.

18 See Gary Fountain and Peter Brazeau, *Remembering Elizabeth Bishop* (Amherst: University of Massachusetts Press, 1994), 332-36.

19 Christina Rossetti, *Poems and Prose*, ed. Jan Marsh (London: Dent, 1994), 75.

20 Haven Johnson wrote "This Is My Last Affair" for the Broadway musical *New Faces of 1936*. Ella Fitzgerald recorded it that year on Decca. Billie Holiday recorded her version in 1937 on Brunswick with the Teddy Wilson Orchestra.

21 A Preface to First Edition of *Poems* (1853), *Poetry and Criticism of Matthew Arnold*, ed. A. Dwight Culler (Boston: Houghton Mifflin, 1961), 204.

NOTES TO CHAPTER 4

1 *Norton Anthology of Poetry*, 5th ed., 152.

2 *Norton Anthology of Poetry*, 3rd ed., 270.

3 *Norton Anthology of Poetry*, 5th ed., 279.

4 *Ben Jonson and the Cavalier Poets*, ed. Hugh Maclean (New York: Norton, 1974), 187.

5 Jim Powell, *It Was Fever That Made the World* (Chicago: University of Chicago Press, 1989), 26.

6 Harold Arlen wrote the music and Johnny Mercer, the lyrics to "That Old Black Magic" in 1942. The song was included in the film *Star Spangled Rhythm* (1943). Mercer wrote the words with his lover Judy Garland in mind. She was the first to record it in 1943. Louis Prima and Keely Smith

recorded a single of the song for Capitol in 1958. In 1961 they performed it at the inaugural for JFK.

[7] Johnny Mercer, *The Life, Times and Song Lyrics of Our Huckleberry Friend*, eds. Bob Bach and Ginger Mercer (Secaucus, NJ: Lyle Stuart, 1982), 173. Sonny Burke, Lionel Hampton, and Johnny Mercer wrote "Midnight Sun" in 1947. Sarah Vaughan recorded her version in 1965.

[8] *The Poems of Andrew Marvell*, ed. Nigel Smith, rev. ed. (Harlow: Longman, 2007), 81- 84.

[9] J. B. Leishman, *The Art of Marvell's Poetry* (London: Hutchinson, 1968), 77-78.

[10] Lew Spence wrote the music, and Marilyn and Alan Bergman, the lyrics to "Nice 'n' Easy Does it" in 1958. In 1961 it was the last-minute substitution for "The Nearness of You" on Frank Sinatra's hit album entitled *Nice 'n Easy*.

[11] Laura Kipnis, *Against Love*, 153.

NOTES TO CHAPTER 5

[1] Kipnis, *Against Love*, 60.

[2] Percy Bysshe Shelley, "Mutability," in *The Norton Anthology of Poetry*, 5th edition, 864.

[3] In 1919 Jerome Kern (1885-1945) wrote the music and Buddy DeSylva the lyrics to "Look for the Silver Lining" for a musical, *Zip, Goes a Million*. The song was first recorded in 1920, and then several times by Judy Garland, and by others, including Bing Crosby and Aretha Franklin.

[4] Mercer, *The Life, Times and Song Lyrics of Our Huckleberry Friend*, 128. Harold Arlen wrote the music and Johnny Mercer, the lyrics for "Accentuate the Positive" in 1944. They wrote it for a film, *Here Come the Waves* (1944), starring Bing Crosby and Betty Hutton. Mercer recorded it with the Pied Pipers that year. It has been covered by many performers: Dinah Washington, Ella Fitzgerald, Connie Francis, Dr. John, and Stephen Colbert and Julie Andrews. Mercer's idea for the lyric came from a report he heard about a sermon by Father Divine who said, "you got to accentuate the positive and eliminate the negative." Mercer's 1944 recording was featured in the film *L.A. Confidential* (1997), quite deservedly.

[5] Irving Berlin, *The Complete Lyrics*, ed. Robert Kimball and Linda Emmet (New York: Knopf, 2001), 231. The song was introduced in the musical *Betsy* by the singer Belle Baker in 1926. The score for the production was otherwise written by Rodgers and Hart. Al Jolson sang the song in the first talking picture *The Jazz Singer* (1927). The song has been recorded by Bing Crosby in a film called *Blue Skies* (1946) and by Willie Nelson in 1978.

[6] See Alain Badiou, *In Praise of Love*: "To an extent, every love states that it is eternal: it is assumed within the declaration. . . . Because, basically, that is what love is: a declaration of eternity to be fulfilled or unfurled as best it can be within time" (47). And C. S. Lewis, *The Four Loves*: "To be in love is both to intend and to promise lifelong fidelity. Love makes vows unasked; can't be deterred from making them. 'I will be ever true,' are almost the first words he utters. Not hypocritically but sincerely. No experience will cure him of the delusion" (113).

[7] *Norton Anthology of Poetry*, 5th ed., 801.

[8] Ibid., 260.

[9] Helen Vendler, *The Art of Shakespeare's Sonnets* (Cambridge, MA: Harvard University Press, 1997), 162.

[10] It matters that the corrective to self-regard comes with heightened grammaticality, for grammar underwrites rational analysis governed by familiar rules. The pleasure of grammatical structure has this comforting significance in the Sonnets that becomes rarer in 19th century poetry (Wordsworth, however grammatical, does not fondle grammatical structures) and thereafter, as the objective of a transparent or speech-like style gained currency.

[11] Troy Jollimore, *Love's Vision* (Princeton: Princeton University Press, 2011), 1.

[12] Cole Porter, *The Complete Lyrics*, ed. Robert Kimball (New York: Da Capo, 1992), 102. Porter wrote this first of his list-songs in 1928 for the musical *Paris* of that year. Billie Holiday recorded the original lyrics in 1941 on the Okeh label owned by Columbia.

[13] Irving Berlin wrote "Cheek to Cheek" for the film *Top Hat* (1935), in which Fred Astaire sings the song to Ginger Rogers as they dance. Louis Armstrong, Billie Holiday, Rod Stewart, Tony Bennett and Lady Gaga,

and many others have also recorded the song.

[14] Jimmy Harris and Leroy Kirkland wrote "Cloudburst," which Lambert, Hendricks, and Ross recorded in 1960 on their album, *The Hottest New Group in Jazz* for Columbia.

[15] In 1928 Cliff Burwell wrote the music and Mitchell Parrish, the lyrics for "Sweet Lorraine." Nat King Cole recorded the vocal version in 1956 for the Capitol album *After Midnight* (1957). He had earlier recorded an instrumental version with his trio.

[16] Jonathan Culler, *The Pursuit of Signs* (Ithaca, NY: Cornell University Press, 1981), 140, 142.

[17] Czeslaw Milosz, "On Angels," in *Selected Poems*, rev. ed. (New York: Ecco, 1980), 112; Milosz himself translated this poem into English.

[18] Allen Tate, *Essays of Four Decades* (New York: William Morrow, 1970), 422.

[19] See Robert Hass, "Privilege of Being," in *Human Wishes* (New York: Ecco, 1989), 69-70.

[20] Robert Frost, "Never Again Would Birds' Song Be the Same," in *The Norton Anthology of Poetry*, 5th ed., 1242-43.

[21] Robert Pinsky includes the poem in *Handbook of Heartbreak* (New York: William Morrow, 1998), 3.

[22] Thomas Traherne, "Wonder," *The Works of Thomas Traherne*, ed. Jan Ross (Rochester NY: Roydell Brewer, 2014), VI. M 4-6.

[23] Culler's analysis of this reciprocity: "one who successfully invokes nature is one to whom nature might, in its turn, speak. He makes himself poet, visionary. Thus, invocation is a figure of vocation" (*Pursuit*, 142).

[24] The notion of things talking is often focused directly on what things say. In 1940 Louis Zukofsky published "A"-9 (First Half), a canzone in which commodities are made to talk: they explain Marx's theory of surplus value. In 1974 Ry Cooder recorded "If Things Could Talk":

> If shoes could tell where they've been
> when you say you've been
> visiting a friend,
> Ain't you glad that things don't talk?

. . .

What a world of trouble there'd be
if things ever told on me.
My whole life would be through,
'cause I'm guilty, how about you?
If things ever talked that way
no telling what they might say.

[25] See William Empson, *The Structure of Complex Words* (1951; Cambridge MA: Harvard University Press, 1989), for a brilliant philological analysis of "sense" and "sensibility," chs.12-15.

[26] Barbara Kiefer Lewalski, *Protestant Poetics and the Seventeenth-Century Religious Lyric* (Princeton: Princeton University Press, 1979), 387.

[27] Christopher Ricks and James McCue have an enlightening note on Eliot's phrase "waning dusk" in *Little Gidding*. Eliot worked in fascinating fashion on this phrase for the first glimmers of dawn. *The Poems of T. S. Eliot*, ed. Ricks & McCue (Baltimore: Johns Hopkins University Press, 2015), I, 1009-11.

[28] Kenneth Rexroth, *Poems from the Greek Anthology* (Ann Arbor: University of Michigan Press, 1999), 83.

[29] Lawrence Lipking, *Samuel Johnson: The Life of an Author* (Cambridge MA: Harvard University Press, 1998), 294.

[30] "Review of A Free Enquiry into the Nature and Origin of Evil," in *Johnson: Prose and Poetry*, ed. Mona Wilson (Cambridge MA: Harvard University Press, 1967), 366.

[31] Critics have tended to underestimate the poem. Anthony Low characterizes it as "passive." (Low, *Love's Architecture* [New York: New York University Press, 1978], 268.)

NOTES TO CHAPTER 6

[1] "It Only Happens Once" was written by Frankie Laine, and first recorded by the Nat King Cole Trio in 1945. Frankie Laine recorded it in 1949.

[2] Among Americans between the ages of 18 and 24, 38.1% report having had between two and four sexual partners in the past five years; 28.5%

report having had five or more partners; 21.5% report having had just one partner during that time. Between the ages of 25 and 29 the figures begin to even out: 36.6% report having had between two and four partners in the preceding five years; 21% report five or more partners; 38% report having had only one partner. Between the ages of 30 and 34 the figures change significantly: 28.9% report having had between two and four partners in the past five years; only 12.8% report having had five or more partners; 53.2% report having had a single partner. These figures are derived from the National Opinion Research Center study conducted in 1992. Edward O. Laumann, John H. Gagnon, Robert T. Michael, and Stuart Michaels, *The Social Organization of Sexuality* (Chicago: University of Chicago Press, 1994), 178.

[3] Cole Porter, *The Complete Lyrics*, 88.

[4] *The Poetry of Sappho*, trans. Jim Powell, expanded edition (New York: Oxford University Press, 2019), 3-4.

[5] Little Esther (Esther Phillips) and Mel Walker with the Johnny Otis Orchestra released a 78 r.p.m. in 1950 with Savoy. "Just Can't Get Free" and "Cupid's Boogie," both written by Johnny Otis, were on the A and B sides, respectively.

[6] David Yaffe notes that "Help Me" is "Joni's only Top 10 single as a recording artist." He calls it "*Love, American Style* as only Joni could have written it" (Yaffe, *Reckless Daughter: A Portrait of Joni Mitchell* [New York: Farrar, Straus and Giroux, 2017], 178).

[7] Morgan McKoy called my attention to the relevance of these two Billie Holiday songs.

[8] See Anne Carson, *Eros the Bittersweet* (Princeton: Princeton University Press, 1986).

[9] Anon., "Love Me Little, Love Me Long," *Norton Anthology of Poetry*, 4th ed., 117.

[10] Joni Mitchell, *The Complete Poems and Lyrics* (New York: Three Rivers, 1998), 113-14.

[11] John Freccero, "The Fig Tree and the Laurel: Petrarch's Poetics," *Diacritics* 5 (1975), 38-39. Freccero understands the blazon as an allegory concerning poetic autonomy, resistance to reference altogether.

[12] Nancy J. Vickers, "Diana Described: Scattered Woman and Scattered Rhyme," *Critical Inquiry*, VIII, 2 (winter 1981), 266-67.

[13] For an excellent analysis of the blazon, in particular as display or exposure, see Patricia Parker, *Literary Fat Ladies* (London: Methuen, 1987), ch. 7, esp. pp. 126-30. Parker analyzes the work of various critics on the figure of the blazon, and she, like Vickers, directs attention to the aggressiveness of the figure indicated by the sense of publicizing, emblazoning, intimate knowledge of the beloved.

[14] *Proensa: An Anthology of Troubadour Poetry,* ed. George Economou; trans. Paul Blackburn (Berkeley: University of California Press, 1978), 154.

[15] Bertran de Born, "Domna, puois de me no us chal" [Lady, since you do not care for me], in *Lyrics of the Troubadours and Trouvères*, trans. Frederick Goldin (1973; Gloucester MA: Peter Smith, 1983), 234-37.

[16] Vendler, *The Art of Shakespeare's Sonnets*, 170-171.

[17] See Barbara Correll, "'Terms of Indearment': Lyric and General Economy in Shakespeare and Donne," *ELH* 75 (2008), esp. 255-56. On the turning-point of potlatch as heightened intensity, see Georges Bataille, *Visions of Excess*, trans. Allan Stoekl (Minneapolis: University of Minnesota Press, 1985), 119.

[18] Jule Styne and Sammy Cahn wrote "I Fall in Love Too Easily" in 1944. Johnny Hartman's 1956 version is on his *Songs from the Heart* for Bethlehem. Joni Mitchell did not record the song, though it lies behind "Help Me."

[19] Charis Charalampous, "Thinking (of) Feelings in Donne's Poetry: The Signifying Rift and 'The Evidence of Things Not Seen,'" *Religion and Literature*, 47, 1 (Spring 2015), 75.

[20] John Donne, *Poetical Works*, ed. Sir Herbert Grierson (London: Oxford University Press, 1933), 21.

[21] Judith Scherer Herz, "Resisting Mutuality," *John Donne Journal* 9, 1 (1990), 27.

[22] Augustine, *The Confessions*, trans. Philip Burton (New York: Knopf, 2001), 235.

[23] "Change Partners" was written by Irving Berlin for the film *Carefree* (1938) in which Fred Astaire introduced the song.

NOTES TO CHAPTER 7

[1] In 1988 Joe Williams and Shirley Horn recorded Valerie Parks Brown's "Love without Money" for their Verve album *In Good Company* (1989).

[2] "Money, Honey," written by Jesse Stone, was recorded by Clyde McPhatter and the Drifters in 1953 on the Atlantic label.

[3] C. P. Cavafy, *The Canon*, trans. Stratis Haviaras (Cambridge, MA: Center for Hellenic Studies, 2007), 345-47.

[4] It is difficult to determine accurately the magnitude of prostitution, because research is often motivated by a wish to regulate the sex trade. In the US 16% of men are said to pay for sex with women; this is thought to be a conservative estimate. There is evidence that among those who use the services of female prostitutes, many form relationships with the same prostitute. One study indicates that "more than two thirds of devotees used the services of a particular prostitute more than 50 times." Nikolas Westerhoff, "Why Do Men Buy Sex," *Scientific American*, (1 October 2012).

[5] Kenneth Rexroth and Ling Chung, trans. *Women Poets of China* (1972; New York: New Directions, 1982), 17.

[6] Cole Porter, *The Complete Lyrics*, ed. Robert Kimball (New York: Da Capo, n.d.), 145. "Love for Sale" was composed for *The New Yorkers* (1930), a Broadway musical about high and low life. The tune was performed by a white female singer in a street-corner setting. After the premiere, that had to be changed to a Harlem setting, and the role given to a black singer. For years the song could not be broadcast on U.S. radio.

[7] Langston Hughes' fine "Listen Here Blues" is an example of such a moralizing poem.

> Sweet girls, sweet girls,
> Listen here to me.
> All you sweet girls,
> Listen here to me:
> Gin an' whiskey
> Kin make you lose yo' ginity.
> I used to be a good chile,
> Lawd, in Sunday School.
> Used to be a good chile,—

Always in Sunday School,
Till these licker-headed rounders
Made me everybody's fool.

Good girls, good girls,
Listen here to me.
Oh, you good girls,
Better listen to me:
Don't you fool wid no men cause
They'll bring you misery. (Langston Hughes, *Collected Poems*, eds.
Arnold Rampersad and David Roessel [New York: Knopf, 1994], 69.) This
is an example of the sub-genre of advice from older to younger women.
The basic counsel here too is prudence and self-defense, though this one
warns girls off of sexual activity altogether. No explicit mention is made of
money, but to be made everybody's fool suggests that alcohol has led her
to the accessibility of a prostitute.

[8] Charles Baudelaire, *Les Fleurs du Mal*, trans. Richard Howard (Boston:
Godine, 1982), 100-01.

[9] T. S. Eliot, "Baudelaire," in *Selected Essays* (New York: Harcourt, Brace
& World, 1960), 380.

[10] "To the tune 'I Paint My Lips Red,'" translated by Kenneth Rexroth and
Ling Chung, *Women Poets*, 43.

[11] The famous song of this title was written by Jerry Leiber and Matt Stoller
in 1967. Peggy Lee had a hit with it two years later.

[12] "Gentleman Friend" was written in 1947 by Richard Lewine (music)
and Andrew B. Horwitt (words) for the Broadway musical *Make Mine
Manhattan* (1948). Sarah Vaughan was the first to record it (1948).

[13] C. P. Cavafy, *Collected Poems*, trans. Evangelos Sachperoglou (Oxford:
Oxford University Press, 2007), 187.

[14] Joni Mitchell, *Complete Poems and Lyrics*, 126-27; she wrote "Raised on
Robbery" and released it on *Court and Spark* in 1974.

NOTES TO CHAPTER 8

[1] Alain Badiou, *In Praise of Love*, trans. Peter Bush (London: Serpent's Tail, 2012), 81- 82.

[2] Jimmy Van Heusen wrote the music, and Sammy Cahn the lyrics of "The Second Time Around," which Bing Crosby sang for the film *High Time* (1960). Frank Sinatra is identified with the song for his 1960 and 1963 recordings of it.

[3] Badiou, 33.

[4] Sir Walter Ralegh, "Walsingham," *Norton Anthology of English Literature*, eds. M. H. Abrams, et al., 4th edition (New York: Norton, 1979) I, 984-85.

[5] [trans. Vladimir Nabokov] in Jon Stallworthy, ed., *A Book of Love Poetry* (New York: Oxford University Press, 1973), 183-84.

[6] Stanley Kunitz, *Passing Through* (New York: Norton, 1995), 158-9.

[7] The last song George Gershwin wrote before his sudden death in 1937 was "Love Is Here to Stay," to which his brother Ira later wrote lyrics. The song was commissioned for the film *The Goldwyn Follies* (1938). It became especially popular when Gene Kelly sang it in the film *An American in Paris* (1951). Ella Fitzgerald recorded it for her *Ella Fitzgerald Sings the George and Ira Gershwin Songbook* (1959).

[8] Robert Hass, *Praise* (New York: Ecco, 1979), 11.

[9] Robert Duncan, looking fit and handsome, read at Stanford in early 1979. He had just turned 60, he said, and was looking forward to writing poems of old age. He was unembarrassed about his ambition, but it seemed incongruous, because he wanted to write as though he were aged and feeble. Yeats was the apt predecessor.

[10] Yeats, *Collected Poems*, 40-41.

[11] See Irvin Ehrenpreis, *Swift, The Man, His Works, and the Age* (Cambridge MA: Harvard University Press, 1983), III, 405; and, on Swift's mockery of passionate romance, 418.

[12] Swift, "Stella's Birthday," in *Norton Anthology of Poetry*, 3rd edition, 394-96.

[13] Wyatt, *Complete Poems*, 76-7.

[14] J. V. Cunningham, *The Poems*, ed. Timothy Steele (Athens OH: Swallow/

Ohio University Press, 1997), 69.

¹⁵ Charles Olson, *The Maximus Poems* (New York: Jargon/Corinth, 1960), 5.

¹⁶ Edwin Muir, *Collected Poems* (New York: Oxford University Press, 1965), 159-60.

¹⁷ Roland Barthes, *Mythologies*, trans. Annette Lavers (New York: Hill and Wang, 1972), 11.

¹⁸ Stendhal, *On Love*, trans. Sophie Lewis (London: Hesperus, 2009), 13-14.

¹⁹ Stephen Booth, *Shakespeare's Sonnets* (New Haven: Yale University Press, 1977), 119.

²⁰ David West notes that "No one swears that they are true unless doubts have been raised." (*Shakespeare's Sonnets*, ed. David West [London: Duckworth, 2007], 422.)

²¹ Helen Vendler, *The Art of Shakespeare's Sonnets* (Cambridge MA: Belknap, 1997), 586.

²² Booth, 477.

²³ Don Paterson, *Reading Shakespeare's Sonnets* (London: Faber, 2010), 421; David West, op. cit., 425.

NOTE TO CONCLUSION

¹ William Empson, *Argufying*, ed. John Haffenden (Iowa City: University of Iowa Press, 1987).

Index

CPSIA information can be obtained
at www.ICGtesting.com
Printed in the USA
JSHW080733170223
37883JS00003B/5